Universal Methods of Ethical Design

100 Ways to Become More Ethically Aware,
Responsible, and Active in Your Design Work

Sai Shruthi Chivukula PhD
Colin M. Gray PhD

ROCKPORT

Quarto.com

© 2025 Quarto Publishing Group USA Inc.

Text © 2025 Sai Shruthi Chivukula and Colin M. Gray

First published in 2025 by Rockport Publishers, an imprint of The Quarto Group,
100 Cummings Center, Suite 265-D, Beverly, MA 01915, USA.
T (978) 282-9590 F (978) 283-2742

Rockport Publishers titles are also available at discount for retail, wholesale, promotional, and bulk purchase. For details, contact the Special Sales Manager by email at specialsales@quarto.com or by mail at The Quarto Group, Attn: Special Sales Manager, 100 Cummings Center, Suite 265-D, Beverly, MA 01915, USA.

10 9 8 7 6 5 4 3 2 1

ISBN: 978-0-7603-9308-6

Digital edition published in 2025
eISBN: 978-0-7603-9309-3

Library of Congress Cataloging-in-Publication Data
Names: Chivukula, Sai Shruthi, author. | Gray, Colin Michael, author.
Title: Universal methods of ethical design : 100 ways to become more
   ethically aware, responsible, and active in your design work / Sai
   Shruthi Chivukula, Colin M. Gray.
Description: First edition. | Beverly, MA : Rockport Publishers, 2025. |
   Includes index.
Identifiers: LCCN 2024041030 (print) | LCCN 2024041031 (ebook) | ISBN
   9780760393086 (hardcover) | ISBN 9780760393093 (ebook)
Subjects: LCSH: Design--Human factors. | Design--Moral and ethical aspects.
Classification: LCC NK1520 .C49 2025 (print) | LCC NK1520 (ebook) | DDC
   745--dc23/eng/20240918
LC record available at https://lccn.loc.gov/2024041030
LC ebook record available at https://lccn.loc.gov/2024041031

Cover Design: Burge Agency and Sai Shruthi Chivukula
Page Design and Layout: Colin M. Gray

Printed in China

The art and infographics throughout this book have retained typos and style and grammatical errors from original outside sources in order to maintain source integrity.

Dedication

We dedicate this book to:

Members and collaborators from the UXP^2 (UX Pedagogy and Practice) lab and Translate research group who sustain our work through their collective care for social responsibility, design ethics, and design character.

The many technology and design practitioners who have trusted us with their stories and inspired us throughout our research projects over the past decade.

Dedicated method designers and researchers who paved the way for us to build this collection.

Contents

& resource types M T C P

Resource Types   **M** Method   **C** Conceptual

T Theoretical   **P** Principle

Introduction

WHAT IS THIS BOOK ABOUT?

There is a growing interest in socially responsible design, evidenced by the efforts of practitioners and third-sector organizations alike in building awareness and support for ethically centered design practices like dark patterns, white UX design, and codes of ethical conduct. Through this book, our goal is to provide designers with a collection of resources to support their ethical awareness, action, and reflection—aiding them in advocating for and building socially responsible products and services. Ethics is often discussed by philosophers in complex language. However, our goals in this book are more practical. We intentionally build on many theories and paradigms of ethics, describing resources that can guide designers in enacting multiple ways of operationalizing ethics and values in their everyday work.

The presentation of the content in this book is empirically validated[1,2] to take into account the needs of designers, with the goal of making these resources relevant and accessible. We anticipate this book can support designers in many roles and contexts, including: design practitioners involved in designing digital systems that are concerned about social impact (e.g., UX designers, UX researchers, software engineers, product managers, CEOs/founders); design educators and students in technology and design disciplines that want to strengthen their ethical knowledge; and researchers in design-related fields that are addressing issues of social impact and responsibility.

RESOURCE TYPES

The resources in this book include a variety of forms encompassing methods, theoretical frameworks, conceptual frameworks, and principles. Each type of resource supports designers in creating ethical products, including considerations underlying ethical responsibility, conducting value-based evaluation of products, and supporting ethical decision-making in teams.

- **Methods** provide practical, step-by-step guidance for designers to activate ethics and apply values in everyday design work.

- **Theoretical Frameworks** align guidance about the designer's ethical commitments and attitudes in relation to a more abstract theoretical or philosophical framing.

- **Conceptual Frameworks** indicate expansive, action-oriented approaches that inspire designers to consider ethical issues in their work.

- **Principles** define different facets or considerations that might be relevant in assessing or implementing ethics or values into design processes.

1. Gray, C. M., Chivukula, S. S., Carlock, T. V., Li, Z., & Duane, J.-N. (2023). Scaffolding ethics-focused methods for practice resonance. *Proceedings of the 2023 ACM Designing Interactive Systems Conference*, 2375-2391. https://doi.org/10.1145/3563657.3596111

2. Chivukula, S. S., Gray, C., Li, Z., Pivonka, A. C., & Chen, J. (2024). Surveying a landscape of ethics-focused design methods. *ACM Journal of Responsible Computing, 1*(3), Article No. 22. https://doi.org/10.1145/3678988

ETHICAL FRAMEWORKS

We build upon four common ethical frameworks that engage the designer using different lenses:

- **Deontological** focuses on a designer's duty to consider ethics and values in their design process.

- **Consequentialist** prioritizes a designer's identification of consequences and potential impacts of their work.

- **Virtue** frames a designer's intentions toward ethical decision-making in a personal and moral sense.

- **Pragmatist** engages with a designer's work that is mediated through ecological, personal, disciplinary, and societal values.

What standards or codes should guide my (ethical) action?

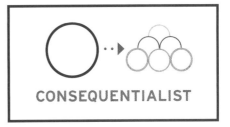

What kinds of harm or negative societal impact might result from my work?

What does it mean to be a "good" designer?

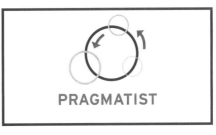

What do I do in ethically ambiguous or complex contexts?

How to Use This Book

We characterize each method, principles, approach, and framework in this book through the lens of designer intentions, which are indicated as **#hashtags**. Each intention identifies how you might incorporate ethical thinking into your design work. Across these intentions, you can support conversations around ethics and values, apply resources from the collection, use ethically ambiguous design spaces, and expand your ethical awareness when designing products.

#breakmydesign
envision how your product might fail

#evaluateoutcomes
evaluate the potential impact of a feature, product, or service

#newperspectives
consider the perspectives of users and stakeholders

#identifyvalues
identify appropriate values for your design context

#applyvalues
consider how you are incorporating values into a product

#alignmyteam
build consensus in your team about ethical goals, outcomes, and responsibilities

#designresponsibility
reflect on your ethical awareness toward a design's impact on user, stakeholder, and society

RESOURCE CHARACTERISTICS

Methods, principles, and frameworks are supportive tools that designers can use throughout their design process. Resources like these act as empty "vessels" that cannot magically give answers just based on the way they are prescribed but rather support your design thinking based on how you choose to activate them in your work. You choose how to perform the method! Resources are formulated based on what you need to bring to the resource, how you can interact with the resource, and what you can expect to get from the resource that will support ethical awareness and action in your design process.

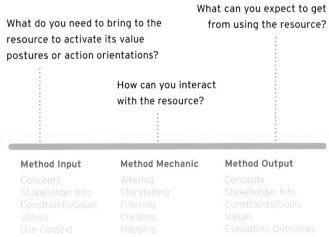

What do you need to bring to the resource to activate its value postures or action orientations?

What can you expect to get from using the resource?

How can you interact with the resource?

Method Input	Method Mechanic	Method Output
Concepts	Altering	Concepts
Stakeholder Info	Storytelling	Stakeholder Info
Constraints/Goals	Filtering	Constraints/Goals
Values	Creating	Values
Use Context	Mapping	Evaluation Outcomes

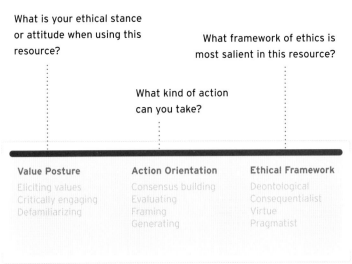

What is your ethical stance or attitude when using this resource?

What framework of ethics is most salient in this resource?

What kind of action can you take?

Value Posture	Action Orientation	Ethical Framework
Eliciting values	Consensus building	Deontological
Critically engaging	Evaluating	Consequentialist
Defamiliarizing	Framing	Virtue
	Generating	Pragmatist

BOOK SPREAD STRUCTURE

Methods, frameworks, and principles are organized alphabetically in this book for easy access. Each resource encompasses two pages. On the left side, you can find the type of support (method, framework, principle), its name, and a short description that demonstrates how you can use the resource. We also provide relevant intentions, an infographic with characteristics of the method, and additional reading material if you want to learn more. On the right side, readers can find visuals that activate the elements of the resource and its use and a list of other relevant resources from the collection.

AUTHORS' NOTE

Design is a value-laden and collaborative activity that has a potential for large impacts on society and our world. Ethics-focused and value-centered thinking should be an embedded and continuous facet of your design process rather than an afterthought or validation technique, hence we have not emphasized any particular design process stages throughout the book.

As you identify and adapt the resources to fit into your design process and work environment, consider how the resources are helping you become more capable in engaging in ethical decision-making, including deepening your awareness and potential for action.

01 360 Review

360 Review provides a system-based thinking approach to identify the impact of your product across a range of human, organizational, societal, and natural entities.[1]

#alignmyteam #identifyvalues

Designers and their products are part of an ecology—an interconnected and complex system consisting of employees who are part of the organization, other designers involved in creating the product, users/consumers interacting and affected directly by the product, stakeholders or shareholders who invest and engage with the product, communities (not particularly users/consumers), industries, and environments that are affected by the product. The interrelationships among these different entities in the system impacts ideation, production, shipping, scaling, and inadequacy of a product.[1]

360 Review builds on this system-based thinking approach, allowing you to evaluate, review, and map your product for its impact on, by, and toward all the relevant entities that are involved. The entities are visually connected with solid lines to indicate prominent impacts and dotted lines to indicate secondary impact, resulting in a 360° view of your product.

1. Zhou, K. (2021). 360 review. *Design Ethically* Toolkit. https://www.designethically.com/360-review

Further Reading

Zhou, K. (2023). *Design Ethically Toolkit.* https://www.designethically.com/toolkit

Value Posture	Action Orientation	Ethical Framework
Eliciting values	Consensus building	Deontological
Critically engaging	Evaluating	Consequentialist
Defamiliarizing	Framing	Virtue
	Generating	Pragmatist

Method Input	Method Mechanic	Method Output
Concepts	Altering	Concepts
Stakeholder Info	Storytelling	Stakeholder Info
Constraints/Goals	Filtering	Constraints/Goals
Values	Creating	Values
Use Context	Mapping	Evaluation Outcomes

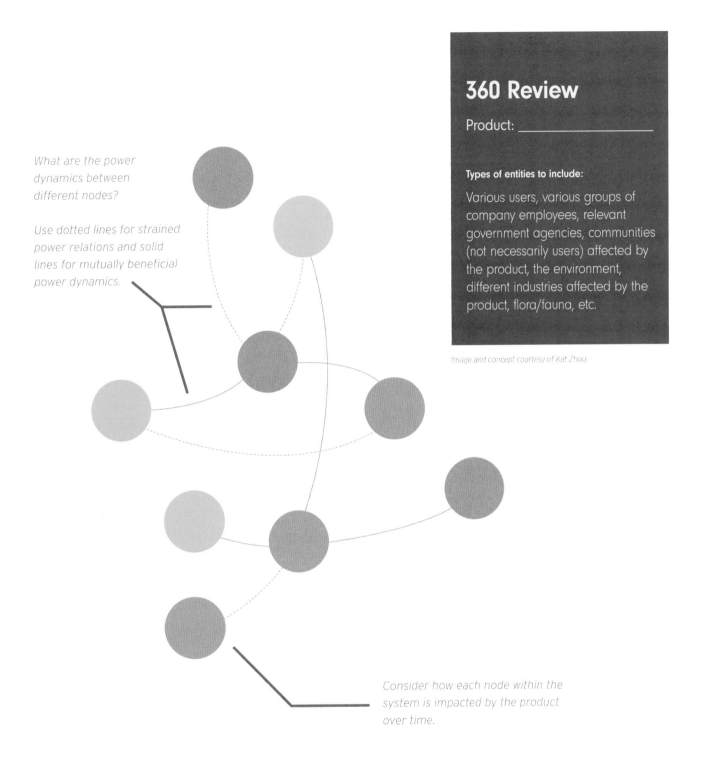

What are the power dynamics between different nodes?

Use dotted lines for strained power relations and solid lines for mutually beneficial power dynamics.

360 Review

Product: _____

Types of entities to include:

Various users, various groups of company employees, relevant government agencies, communities (not necessarily users) affected by the product, the environment, different industries affected by the product, flora/fauna, etc.

Image and concept courtesy of Kat Zhou.

Consider how each node within the system is impacted by the product over time.

See also *TRACING (ETHICAL) COMPLEXITY* • *STAKEHOLDER TOKENS*

02 Accessibility

Accessibility enables you to ensure that your design outcomes are usable for people across a range of input modalities and human capabilities.[1]

#evaluateoutcomes #breakmydesign #applyvalues

Accessibility is a value that helps designers consider how a wide range of people with disabilities can use technologies. Ensuring accessible products and features includes accommodations for blindness and low vision, deafness and hearing loss, limited movement, speech disabilities, photosensitivity, and combinations of these, and accommodation for learning disabilities and other cognitive limitations.[2]

The Web Content Accessibility Guidelines (WCAG) are a common set of standards that prescribe how to make digital content and interfaces more accessible at different levels of conformance that range from A (lowest) to AA (mid range) to AAA (highest). The WCAG standards are applied based on the following principles:[2]

- **Perceivable:** Information and user interface components must be presented to users in ways they can perceive. Accessibility factors include designing for better text alternatives, use of time-based media, and adaptable and distinguishable visuals.

- **Operable:** User interface components and navigation must be operable for all users, including those with disabilities. Accessibility factors include designing keyboard accessible interfaces, protecting against seizures and physical reactions, and providing usable navigation and input modalities for all users.

- **Understandable:** Information and the operation of the user interface must be understandable for all users, including those with cognitive and learning disabilities. Accessibility factors include designing readable, predictable, and input assistance solutions.

- **Robust:** Content must be robust enough that it can be interpreted by a wide variety of user agents, including assistive technologies. Accessibility factors include providing compatible designs and ensuring programmatic access to key functionality.

1. Web content accessibility guidelines (WCAG) 2.2. (n.d.). Retrieved July 21, 2024, from https://www.w3.org/TR/WCAG22/

2. Synthesized and quoted from the WCAG website.

Further Reading

Wobbrock, J. O., Kane, S. K., Gajos, K. Z., Harada, S., & Froehlich, J. (2011). Ability-based design: concept, principles and examples. *ACM Transactions on Accessible Computing, 3*(3), 1-27. https://doi.org/10.1145/1952383.1952384

Accessible color palette builder. (n.d.). Retrieved July 21, 2024, from https://toolness.github.io/accessible-color-matrix

Contrast. (n.d.). Figma. Retrieved July 21, 2024, from https://www.figma.com/community/plugin/748533339900865323/contrast

Value Posture	Action Orientation	Ethical Framework
Eliciting values	Consensus building	Deontological
Critically engaging	Evaluating	Consequentialist
Defamiliarizing	Framing	Virtue
	Generating	Pragmatist

Method Input	Method Mechanic	Method Output
Concepts	Altering	Concepts
Stakeholder Info	Storytelling	Stakeholder Info
Constraints/Goals	Filtering	Constraints/Goals
Values	Creating	Values
Use Context	Mapping	Evaluation Outcomes

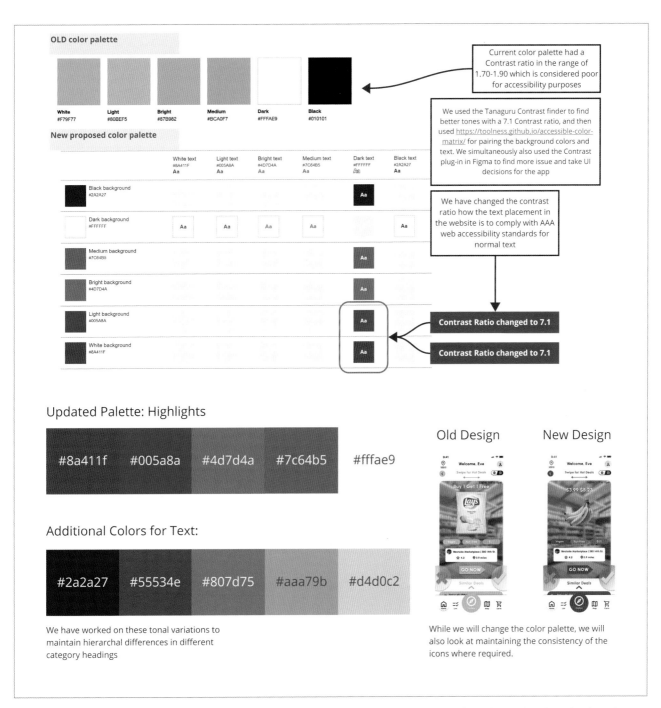

An example of designers auditing for AA or AAA accessibility conformance on a website, using a visual contrast scale of 4:1 or more to evaluate and redesign their mobile screen interfaces. The design team used existing browser tools to evaluate their existing color palette (top left) and used the results to create a new color palette (bottom left).

Image courtesy of Shikha Mehta, Evelyn Mukherjee, and Jiatong Gu.

See also SOCIAL ACCESSIBILITY CARDS • INCLUSIVE ACTIVITY CARDS

03 Adversarial Design

Adversarial Design encourages you to use tools and artifacts to express dissent, encourage debate, and recognize areas of contestation and conflicting hegemonies.[1]

#breakmydesign #newperspectives #identifyvalues

Designers actively participate in systems of power and politics, but these structural forces are often hidden and require further investigation to understand their impact. One way of identifying these structures is by leveraging *dissent* and *contestation* as mechanisms for people to build reflective awareness and identify issues they disagree with.

Adversarial Design is a process that focuses on using design as a means to engage with and challenge political issues. It draws on the principles of agonism, which include a "commitment to contestation and dissensus as integral, productive, and meaningful aspects of democratic society."[1] Adversarial design allows you to address, or "do the work of," agonism in design through the making of "contestational artifacts":[2]

- **Revealing hegemon(ies):** Identify and expose structures and systems of power that create influence or norms in society. Seek to find out what hidden norms or systems produce unjust or different outcomes for different people.

- **Prompting recognition of political issues and relations:** Create artifacts that manifest or represent some aspect of the political system, encouraging users to engage with these issues. Seek to amplify one or more issues in an accessible way that encourages additional questions to be asked about political relations.

- **Enabling contestational claims and arguments:** Provide spaces for users to "experientially encounter" and challenge current and potential outcomes. Consider ways to design for spaces that are participatory and focus on allowing dissenting views to be heard.

1. DiSalvo, C. (2012). *Adversarial design*. MIT Press

2. Adapted from DiSalvo (2012).

Further Reading

DiSalvo, C. (2010). Design, democracy and agonistic pluralism. *DRS Biennial Conference Series.* https://dl.designresearchsociety.org/drs-conference-papers/drs2010/researchpapers/31/

Value Posture	Action Orientation	Ethical Framework
Eliciting values	Consensus building	Deontological
Critically engaging	Evaluating	Consequentialist
Defamiliarizing	Framing	Virtue
	Generating	Pragmatist

Method Input	Method Mechanic	Method Output
Concepts	Altering	Concepts
Stakeholder Info	Storytelling	Stakeholder Info
Constraints/Goals	Filtering	Constraints/Goals
Values	Creating	Values
Use Context	Mapping	Evaluation Outcomes

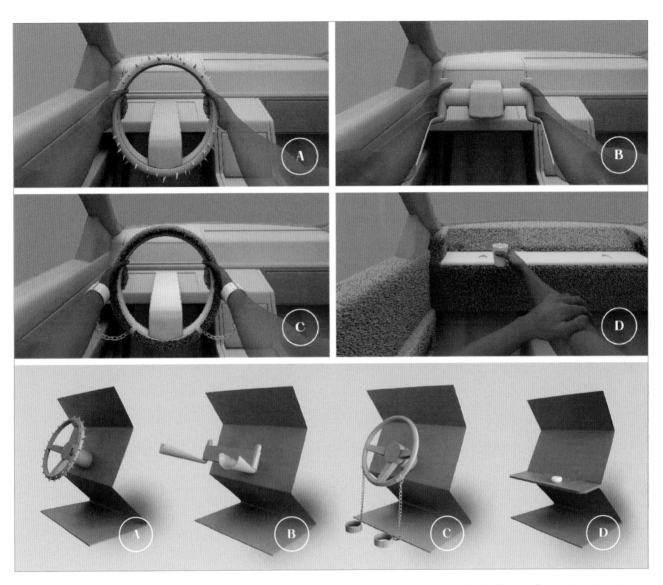

Examples of adversarial design concepts in the design of a steering wheel, which resulted in "a set of narrative tensions that can be used to question common beliefs surrounding automated driving futures."

Image courtesy of Maria Luce Lupetti. Reproduced by permission from Lupetti, M. L., Cavalcante Siebert, L., & Abbink, D. (2023, April 19). Steering stories: Confronting narratives of driving automation through contestational artifacts. Proceedings of the 2023 CHI Conference on Human Factors in Computing Systems. CHI '23: CHI Conference on Human Factors in Computing Systems. Hamburg, Germany. https://doi.org/10.1145/3544548.3581194.

See also QUEERING • CRITICAL DESIGN

04 Adversary Personas

Adversary Personas guide you to think from the perspective of people who create cybersecurity threats (i.e., adversaries), resulting in "anti"-personas that can help you identify digitally mediated threats.[1]

#newperspectives #identifyvalues

Cybersecurity experts seek to protect individuals and organizations from attacks by considering different kinds of threats that may be experienced in different digital contexts. For example, products that might put consumers at risk include applications for fintech, healthcare, and gaming. Products used within organizations might also include roles such as employees or stakeholders, and include services such as email, data servers, financial data, and copyrighted information.

In this method, you take on the attitude of a cybersecurity expert, considering threat models that help you better understand the vulnerabilities of systems, applications, or features. In doing so, you can better understand threats against vulnerable users and, in turn, identify new ways to protect these users through changes to your concepts. Adversary Personas is a role-playing game where you draw the personas of cyberattackers—a.k.a. adversaries. You can draw an adversary's persona by engaging with three different parts of the card deck[1].

- **Human impacts:** Identify what and who you are trying to protect in your design situation. It could be related to personal, physical, monetary, emotional, and ecological well-being.

- **Adversary motivations:** Identify related motivations for why an adversary would potentially plan their move. It could be related to personal scarcity, monetary benefits, political influence, and counterattack or revenge.

- **Adversary resources:** Identify what resources they might possess that you need to shield through your design. It could be related to human or monetary resources, influence, rights, and insider information.

1. Daylight security research lab. (2021). https://daylight.berkeley.edu/adversary-personas/

Value Posture	Action Orientation	Ethical Framework
Eliciting values	Consensus building	Deontological
Critically engaging	Evaluating	Consequentialist
Defamiliarizing	Framing	Virtue
	Generating	Pragmatist

Method Input	Method Mechanic	Method Output
Concepts	Altering	Concepts
Stakeholder Info	Storytelling	Stakeholder Info
Constraints/Goals	Filtering	Constraints/Goals
Values	Creating	Values
Use Context	Mapping	Evaluation Outcomes

Adversary motivations
They need to feed a desire, an obsession

Adversary motivations
They need to influence politics

Adversary resources
They are above the law, or beyond its reach

Human impacts
Financial wellbeing

Examples from the Adversary Personas card deck that relate to motivations (e.g., they need to influence politics), resources (e.g., beyond reach from the law), and human impacts (e.g., financial well-being).

Image courtesy of Nick Merrill.

05 A.E.I.O.YOU

A.E.I.O.YOU encourages you to address various dimensions of your design practice that shape ethical design complexity, including combinations of artifacts, actors, interactions, and ecologies.[1]

#newperspectives #identifyvalues

The complexity that designers experience in their practice is mediated by the personal beliefs and disciplinary orientations of individual practitioners, values and policies prescribed by organizations, and applied ethics.[2] A.E.O.I.YOU: Vowels of Ethics is a framework that provides varied perspectives to investigate, describe, de-structure, and evaluate technology practice holistically with an ethical lens. These vowels help you identify the different variables that enable you to shape your work context.

A.E.I.O.YOU vowels include:

· **Artifacts** are existing or new design products, methods, or tools to support ethical decision-making, and/or policies as used, referred, or learned within and beyond ecological boundaries.

· **Ecology** refers to the environment the designer is a part of, including an individual's professional team, multiple interdisciplinary teams they interact with, the industry or organization they work at, and the external organizations they collaborate or strategize with.

· **Interactions** refers to communication, collaboration, and association with other members during ethical decision-making.

· **Others** refers to members from the team, other disciplinary teams, and/or external stakeholders.

· **YOU** refers to you as a designer, including your personal values, professional responsibilities, and ethical awareness within and beyond ecological, role-focused, and disciplinary boundaries.

If you are a **design and ethics researcher,** you can use the framework as a reflective tool. If you are a **design practitioner,** you can use the framework as a support to expose the complexity in your everyday work. If you are an **educator,** you can use the framework to design pedagogical supports and mechanisms to scaffold the complexity of design practice in your classroom.

1. Chivukula, S. S. (2021). *Designing for co-creation to engage multiple perspectives on ethics in technology practice* [Unpublished doctoral dissertation]. Purdue University, West Lafayette, IN. https://doi.org/10.25394/PGS.15036321.v1

2. Gray, C. M., & Chivukula, S. S. (2019). Ethical mediation in UX practice. *Proceedings of the 2019 CHI Conference on Human Factors in Computing Systems*, Paper 178. https://doi.org/10.1145/3290605.3300408

Value Posture	Action Orientation	Ethical Framework		Method Input	Method Mechanic	Method Output
Eliciting values	Consensus building	Deontological		Concepts	Altering	Concepts
Critically engaging	Evaluating	Consequentialist		Stakeholder Info	Storytelling	Stakeholder Info
Defamiliarizing	Framing	Virtue		Constraints/Goals	Filtering	Constraints/Goals
	Generating	Pragmatist		Values	Creating	Values
				Use Context	Mapping	Evaluation Outcomes

ARTIFACTS A
- Methods
- Frameworks or practices
- Attitudes

ECOLOGICAL FACTORS E
- Industry standards
- Business goals
- External factors

INTERACTIONS I
- Collaborations with external clients
- Coordination with internal and external teams

OTHERS O
- Team members
- Stakeholders or clients
- Users

YOU YOU
- Practitioners
- Educators
- Students

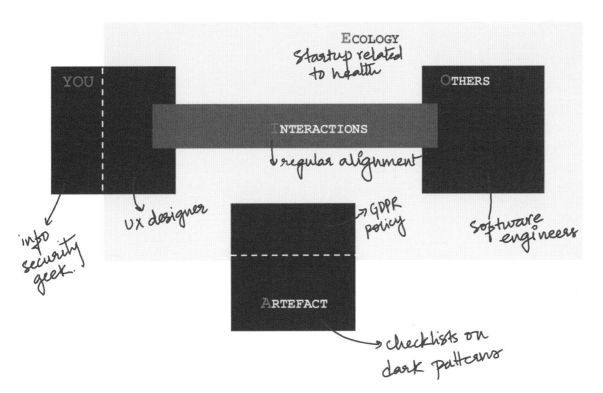

A UX designer using the A.E.I.O.YOU framework to plot their ethical complexity at work to make sense of their own position that shapes their ethical decision-making.

Image courtesy of Sai Shruthi Chivukula.

06 Afrofuturism

Afrofuturism encourages you to build speculative futures that center engagement with race, community, culture, and unexamined assumptions.[1]

#newperspectives #applyvalues #alignmyteam

Designing systems inherently involves assumptions about the cultural groups that will use them, including beliefs about potential use and the types of knowledge that are celebrated or suppressed. However, it can be complex to examine these cultural assumptions, including the ways that biases, privilege, and power intersect with current and future design realities.

Afrofuturism, a term coined by Mark Dery, is a speculative lens that can be used "when designing futures along racially minoritized groups,"[2] "explicitly plac[ing] the often disenfranchised black voice central in the design narrative, with an intent of universal betterment through and by technology."[1] Using an Afrofuturist approach, designers can "examine the implicit cultural assumptions of present design practices and broaden the scope of the design imagination in human centered design."[2] One way of using this approach in your design work can be realized through the Building Utopia deck, which contains five different types of cards:[3]

- **Forecasting:** Select the time period your design work will be situated within—ten or even one hundred years from now.

- **Hopes and concerns:** List topics that represent hopes for the future or concerns that the community will need to address.

- **Liberation prompts:** Use open-ended questions to describe how freedom or emancipation can be sustained or realized within a community.

- **Tools:** Identify resources you will need to design or consider potential community-focused futures.

- **Methods:** Employ collaborative techniques such as storytelling, radical future thinking, or storyboarding to design those futures.

1. Winchester, W. W., III. (2018). Afrofuturism, inclusion, and the design imagination. *Interactions*, 25(2), 41-45. https://doi.org/10.1145/3182655

2. Bray, K. E., Harrington, C., Parker, A. G., Diakhate, N., & Roberts, J. (2022, April 29). Radical futures: supporting community-led design engagements through an Afrofuturist speculative design toolkit. *CHI Conference on Human Factors in Computing Systems.* https://doi.org/10.1145/3491102.3501945

3. Klassen, S., Mendy, J. J. E., Buford, M., & Fiesler, C. (2024, July). Black to the future-the power of designing afrofuturist technology with black women, femmes, and non-binary people. *Designing Interactive Systems Conference.* https://doi.org/10.1145/3643834.3661605

Value Posture	Action Orientation	Ethical Framework	Method Input	Method Mechanic	Method Output
Eliciting values	Consensus building	Deontological	Concepts	Altering	Concepts
Critically engaging	Evaluating	Consequentialist	Stakeholder Info	Storytelling	Stakeholder Info
Defamiliarizing	Framing	Virtue	Constraints/Goals	Filtering	Constraints/Goals
	Generating	Pragmatist	Values	Creating	Values
			Use Context	Mapping	Evaluation Outcomes

10
Years
in the Future
COMMUNITY VALUES
Shared commitments
Having a set of goals to commit to can help set a vision for what must be done and what has already been achieved. Values can strengthen and unite a community by affirming what is important.
What is valued in your time? How are these values shown?
GENERATIONAL HEALING
Sometimes, negative cycles or historical pains can be passed down from generation to generation. Breaking down these cycles takes work.
How do people find generational healing in your time?
WHAT LIBERATION LOOKS LIKE FOR OUR COMMUNITY
How do you define liberation in your community?
Reimagining futures is a liberatory act. Considering new versions of our world requires us to define freedom and the ways we can achieve that. What are your visions of liberation and how can you actualize those visions?
COMMUNITY CONVERSATIONS
1
2
3
4
Time: 10-15 minutes
Pair up with someone in your group; if there is an odd number of group members a group of three is fine. Take turns asking the following questions about the topic:
Do you have any experience with this topic?
What does it mean to you?
Does it exist in the time we're thinking of?

MOMENTS SHARED WITH COMMUNITY
HOW I LIFT OTHERS UP

Examples of the *Building Utopia Toolkit* toolkit. This toolkit is grounded in Afrofuturist Speculative Design and "designed by organizers, strategists, and educators to imagine the future of our communities and consider the legacy we are leaving for those communities—whether that be in the technologies we use, the spaces we live in, or the systems that make up our world."[3]

The toolkit and cards include activities that enable you to engage through in-person workshop activities (right) with several different decks (top) to consider "what liberation looks like in this time period within your problem area," using methods to ideate new potential states.

Image courtesy of Christina Harrington, Jennifer Roberts, Kirsten Bray, and N'deye Diaknate. Toolkit available at https://www.buildingutopiadeck.com/.

See also *ORACLE FOR TRANSFEMINIST TECHNOLOGIES • CRITICAL RACE THEORY*

07 Another Lens

Another Lens challenges you to better understand your perspective, biases, and worldview to build thoughtful and inclusive designs.[1]

#breakmydesign #newperspectives #designresponsibility

Designers of a product or a service must consider and balance user needs, business objectives, and product life cycle, while also embedding their own values, beliefs, and worldviews into their work. It is part of the designer's responsibility to constantly check on and update one's personal values and beliefs to build inclusive and ethical design products. Another Lens provides three lenses and specific reflective questions for designers to challenge their current positionality in their design process with respect to users, organization, and society.[2]

- **Balance your bias.** Designers are encouraged to learn the different lenses they constantly use while designing and challenge to reduce bias. Designers can ask: *What details here are unfair? Unverified? Unused? Am I holding on to something that I need to let go of? What's here that I designed for me? What's here that I designed for other people?*

- **Consider the opposite.** Designers are suggested to advocate for pluralistic or "other" lenses that they have not already included in their design process. Designers can ask: *What would the world look like if my assumptions were wrong? Who's someone I'm nervous to talk to about this? What do I believe? Who might disagree with what I'm designing?*

- **Embrace a growth mindset.** Designers are supported to learn through their own process, mindset change, and expansion of their own worldviews. Designers can ask: *Is my audience open to change? If I could learn one thing to help me on this project, what would that one thing be? How does my approach to this problem today compare with how I might have approached this one year ago? How can I reframe a mistake in a way that helps me learn? Do I need to slow down?*

1. Another lens. (n.d.). *Airbnb Design.* https://airbnb.design/wp-content/themes/airbnbdesign/microsites/anotherlens/Another_Lens.pdf

2. Quoted from Another Lens.

Value Posture	Action Orientation	Ethical Framework		Method Input	Method Mechanic	Method Output
Eliciting values	Consensus building	Deontological		Concepts	Altering	Concepts
Critically engaging	Evaluating	Consequentialist		Stakeholder Info	Storytelling	Stakeholder Info
Defamiliarizing	Framing	Virtue		Constraints/Goals	Filtering	Constraints/Goals
	Generating	Pragmatist		Values	Creating	Values
				Use Context	Mapping	Evaluation Outcomes

Balance Your Bias

What are my lenses? Am I just confirming my assumptions, or am I challenging them? What details here are unfair? Unverified? Unused? Am I holding on to something that I need to let go of? What's here that I designed for me? What's here that I designed for other people?

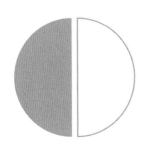

Consider the Opposite

Who might be impacted by what I'm designing? What would the world look like if my assumptions were wrong? Who's someone I'm nervous to talk to about this? What do I believe? Who might disagree with what I'm designing?

Embrace a Growth Mindset

What am I challenging as I create this? Is my audience open to change? If I could learn one thing to help me on this project, what would that one thing be? How does my approach to this problem today compare with how I might have approached this one year ago? How can I reframe a mistake in a way that helps me learn? Do I need to slow down?

Questions and lenses quoted from Another Lens research kit.

08 Anti-Heroes

Anti-Heroes cards expose a range of manipulative intentions that designers possess while creating solutions with anti-user values and counterparts of "Heroes" to help conceptualize and evaluate for ethical outcomes.[1]

#breakmydesign #evaluateoutcomes #newperspectives

Designers often have to balance user, shareholder, and business monetary values in their design process. The designer is the primary actor inscribing these values into their outcomes. In this balancing act, there are a range of designer intentions that can be surfaced, ranging from value-centered (supporting user values) to manipulative (deprioritizing user values).

Anti-Heroes is a card deck that clearly identifies these intentions in the form of designer roles. Inspired from Taylor Swift's "Anti-Hero" song lyrics that repeat "it must be too exhausting rooting for the anti-hero," this card deck encourages designer reflection by allowing designers to identify and respond to specific "Anti-Hero" or "Hero" moves. Anti-Hero | Hero combinations include Trap-Setter | Empowerer, Camouflager | Unveiler, Empathy Manipulator | Life Coach, and others.

Anti-Heroes focuses on designer reflection, dialogue, and concept generation, so it can be used in multiple stages of the design process:

- **Conceptualization,** where you can refer to Anti-Hero or Hero sides to develop solutions and then identify how can Hero moves be made if an Anti-Hero-focused solution is generated.

- **Reverse brainstorming,** where you refer to the Anti-Heroes to develop the worst-possible solutions that devalue user benefits and agency as a way of surfacing and countering potential side effects of unethical decision-making or anti-goals.

- **Evaluation,** where you critically evaluate your design work using Anti-Heroes and validate positive design attributes using Heroes, then use these outcomes to iterate toward ethical outcomes.

- **Ethical dialogue,** where you refer to Anti-Heroes or Heroes to discuss current technological design trends that might be problematic or show cards in your team meeting to respectfully tag a team member deflecting or supporting user values (like a football referee).

1. Mehta, S., Chivukula, S. S., Gray, C. M., & Gairola, R. (2024). Anti-heroes: an ethics-focused method for responsible designer intentions. In *arXiv [cs.HC]*. http://arxiv.org/abs/2405.03674

Further Reading

Gray, C. M., Chivukula, S. S., & Lee, A. (2020). What kind of work do "asshole designers" create? Describing properties of ethical concern on reddit. *Proceedings of the 2020 ACM Designing Interactive Systems Conference*, 61-73. https://doi.org/10.1145/3357236.3395486

Gray, C. M., Chivukula, S. S., Melkey, K., & Manocha, R. (2021). Understanding "dark" design roles in computing education. *Proceedings of the 17th ACM Conference on International Computing Education Research*, 225-238. https://doi.org/10.1145/3446871.3469754

Value Posture	Action Orientation	Ethical Framework
Eliciting values	Consensus building	Deontological
Critically engaging	Evaluating	Consequentialist
Defamiliarizing	Framing	Virtue
	Generating	Pragmatist

Method Input	Method Mechanic	Method Output
Concepts	Altering	Concepts
Stakeholder Info	Storytelling	Stakeholder Info
Constraints/Goals	Filtering	Constraints/Goals
Values	Creating	Values
Use Context	Mapping	Evaluation Outcomes

TRAP-SETTER

Designs a user task flow such that the user "can't get out of it," setting a trap for the user that enables the stakeholder's goal.

ANTI-HERO

EMPOWERER

Designs paths that enable users to make their own decisions in a task flow.

HERO

Example cards from the deck with the opposing anti-hero (left) and hero (right).

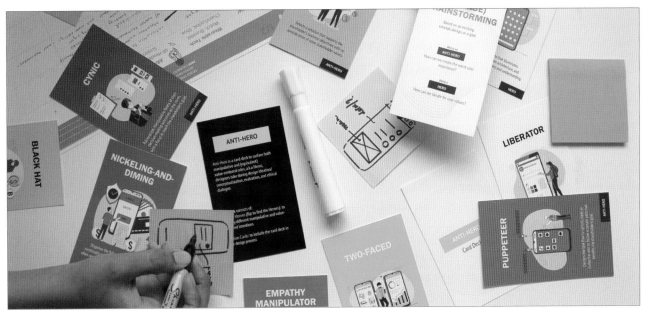

A team of designers interacting with Anti-Heroes card deck to identify ways in which their design solutions can be evaluated to identify how they devalue user agency currently (referring to the Anti-Hero side) and iterate on their ideas to promote user values (referring to the Hero side).

Image courtesy of Sai Shruthi Chivukula.

See also ADVERSARY PERSONAS • BLACK MIRROR BRAINSTORMING • REFUSAL

09 Bad Design Canvas

Bad Design Canvas enables you to evaluate your product or service based on potential or unintended "bad" consequences.[1]

#breakmydesign #evaluateoutcomes

Products and services have a range of impacts when released into real-use contexts and society. However, it is difficult to identify potentially "bad" impacts or unintended consequences.

Bad Design Canvas "is about uncovering the new problems our 'solutions' might generate; questioning our own perception of the problems we seek to solve in the first place."[1] Using the Bad Canvas Design, you can imagine your product or service in a range of contexts of use after launch, identifying potential unintended "bad" consequences such as:[2]

· **Cultural appropriation:** In what way(s) is the idea borrowed ("borrowed") from a culture you or your team are not representative of?

· **Band-Aid:** In what way(s) is the idea failing to recognize the root cause of the problem, instead serving as a temporary solution?

· **Unfair control:** In what way(s) is the idea leading to unfair control over the user/customer (i.e., privacy and data, restrictive ecosystems)?

· **Exploitation:** In what way(s) does the new idea inappropriately expose or objectify the community it aims to serve?

· **Inefficiency:** In what way(s) is the idea creating new inefficiencies, unnecessary complexity, confusion, or delay?

· **Environmental and societal impact:** In what way(s) is the idea using resources from finite sources or at risk of creating harsh conditions for workers?

· **Decreased safety:** In what way(s) is the idea creating, or contributing to, unsafe conditions?

· **Inequity:** In what way(s) is the idea contributing to inequity (not ensuring everyone has access, no matter their unique needs or circumstances)?

1. Less (bad) design: a toolkit for ethical ideation. (n.d.). *Gumroad.* https://reginald.gumroad.com/l/baddesign

2. Quoted from the Less (Bad) Design website.

Value Posture	Action Orientation	Ethical Framework
Eliciting values	Consensus building	Deontological
Critically engaging	Evaluating	Consequentialist
Defamiliarizing	Framing	Virtue
	Generating	Pragmatist

Method Input	Method Mechanic	Method Output
Concepts	Altering	Concepts
Stakeholder Info	Storytelling	Stakeholder Info
Constraints/Goals	Filtering	Constraints/Goals
Values	Creating	Values
Use Context	Mapping	Evaluation Outcomes

BAD DESIGN CANVAS

GUM.CO/BADDESIGN

CULTURAL APPROPRIATION	BAND-AID	UNFAIR CONTROL	EXPLOITATION
In what way(s) is the idea borrowed ("borrowed") from a culture you or your team are not representative of?	In what way(s) is the idea failing to recognize the root cause of the problem, instead serving as a temporary solution?	In what way(s) is the idea leading to unfair control over the user/customer? (i.e. privacy and data, restrictive ecosystems)	In what way(s) does the new idea inappropriately expose or objectify the community it aims to serve?

STAKEHOLDER ABANDONMENT	INEFFICIENCY	ENVIRONMENTAL & SOCIAL IMPACT	DISPLACEMENT
In what way(s) is the idea grounded in decisions made without considering the needs of all stakeholders?	In what way(s) is the idea creating new inefficiencies, unnecessary complexity, confusion, or delay?	In what way(s) is the idea utilizing resources from finite sources, or at-risk of creating harsh conditions for workers?	In what way(s) is the idea displacing communities or businesses in its effort to automate or streamline?

DECREASED SAFETY	INAPPROPRIATE	BORING	INEQUITY
In what way(s) is the idea creating, or contributing to, unsafe conditions?	In what way(s) is the idea generally offensive or inappropriate?	In what way(s) is the idea just plain boring?	In what way(s) is the idea contributing to inequity? (Not ensuring everyone has access, no matter their unique needs or circumstances)

Special thanks to @threecsevens, @uxthomas, @gotcatmaster, @virkadionakez, and @kevinbethune for the comments on Twitter, which contributed greatly to the creation of this canvas!

An example of the Bad Design Canvas, including multiple boxes that allow you to consider and identify different kinds of unintended or negative consequences.

Image courtesy of Matthew Manos, licensed under the Creative Commons CC-BY-ND license.

See also ETHICS CANVAS • JUDGMENT CALL

10 Black Mirror Brainstorming

Black Mirror Brainstorming encourages you to take on the role of a science fiction filmmaker, where you speculate on intentional or unintentional consequences through anti-goals.[1, 2]

#breakmydesign #evaluateoutcomes

Black Mirror Brainstorming is inspired by the *Black Mirror* Netflix series, which focuses on unease caused by the intentional or unintentional consequences of modern technology. Inspired by these Netflix series and drawing from techniques of brainstorming, Black Mirror Brainstorming is focused on considering the negative impacts and potential misuses of digital products in our society. The outcome from using Black Mirror Brainstorming is to define anti-goals of design in a team.[1]

Black Mirror Brainstorming can help you proactively explore *anti-goals*, rather than typical user goals. By identifying these anti-goals, you can use ideation practices to better understand and consider the potential implications of your design goals and concepts. Any kind of playful exploration of potentially negative future consequences is useful, but consider the following tasks:

- **Brainstorm** some ideas for what can go wrong within your design goal across areas of economic issues (*How could we enable bad faith actors to prey on vulnerable groups?*), politics (*How could a corrupt government use design information to identify and target dissidents?*), or social issues (*How could our product reinforce and amplify existing societal divides?*).

- **Explore by generating a plot with characters** as if you are narrating a Black Mirror episode with other members of your team. Consider typical elements of screenwriting, such as identifying relevant characters, the context or scene that allows the character(s) to interact with the original well-intended idea, the moment in the plot arc where the idea began to go "wrong," and the ultimate effect of the negative consequences on the characters or society at large.

- **Create a poster with a relevant quote** that uses elements of your team's plots and posters to visualize one or more "plot twists" that might elevate the Black Mirror qualities even further. Often, a memorable quote that might appear on a movie or TV show poster helps you distill the plot into its essence.

- **Derive anti-goals** from all your team's plots and posters that will help you act on the concerns you uncovered through additional ideation and evaluation.

1. Klassen, S., & Fiesler, C. (2022). "Run wild a little with your imagination": ethical speculation in computing education with black mirror. *Proceedings of the 53rd ACM Technical Symposium on Computer Science Education*, 836–842. https://doi.org/10.1145/3478431.3499308

2. Mauldin, J. (2018). *Black mirror brainstorms - a product design exercise.* https://uxdesign.cc/black-mirror-brainstorms-f919ccf5938c

Value Posture	Action Orientation	Ethical Framework
Eliciting values	Consensus building	Deontological
Critically engaging	Evaluating	Consequentialist
Defamiliarizing	Framing	Virtue
	Generating	Pragmatist

Method Input	Method Mechanic	Method Output
Concepts	Altering	Concepts
Stakeholder Info	Storytelling	Stakeholder Info
Constraints/Goals	Filtering	Constraints/Goals
Values	Creating	Values
Use Context	Mapping	Evaluation Outcomes

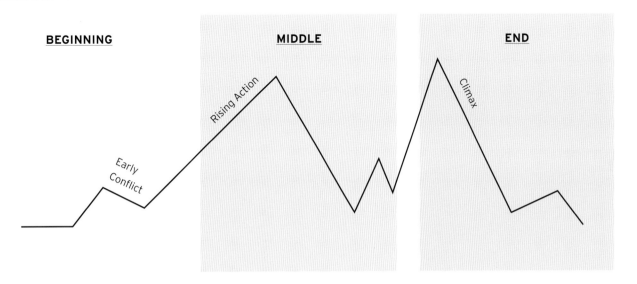

CHARACTERS
- Protagonist
- Antagonist
- Supporting Character(s)

+

CONTEXT(S) OR SCENE(S)
- Specific setting where characters interact
- Design concept or implications should fit within this context/scene

Sample elements of a character and plot sheet for your episode.

Adapted from a worksheet by Joshua Mauldin.

BEGINNING

MIDDLE

END

Early Conflict

Rising Action

Climax

Episode: LOST AND FOUND

"When your phone unlocks your life, it more than sucks when you lose it. No one knows this better than Thomas. He cannot open his car, get into his home, or enter his job. Stranded in his own city and isolated from his own life, Thomas turns to the digital outcasts of society in order to find his way back to it."

Example pitch quote from a student group's poster.

Text courtesy of Shamika Klassen and Ella Sarder.

See also *CRITICAL DESIGN • SPECULATIVE DESIGN • TIMELINES*

11 CIDER

CIDER helps you critically evaluate your assumptions about users identifying new ways for design outcomes to be more inclusive.[1]

#newperspectives #identifyvalues #designresponsibility

All designers have assumptions about the world that impact their ability to identify what kinds of design outcomes should exist, and whether those design outcomes are equitable and inclusive for a diverse user population. How can designers better understand their assumptions about users and their needs, designing in more inclusive ways that reject stereotyping? And in particular, how can designers come to the realization that functionality in systems can include or exclude users' access to particular types of functionality, but that designers can choose to actively work to mitigate decisions that limit access?

CIDER is an elicitation framework that enables designers to "identify the ways that [their] implicit or explicit assumptions about user ability, capacity, environment, or resources concretely manifest in and contribute to exclusionary interface designs."[1]

CIDER is made of up of five key stages:[2]

1. **Critique:** Designers critique the technology to identify implicit assumptions about users present in the design.

2. **Imagine:** Designers pick one assumption they identified and imagine how it could lead to exclusion.

3. **Design:** Designers (re)design the technology by brainstorming ways to change the design so that it doesn't rely on the chosen assumption.

4. **Expand:** Leaders collect and create a shared list of assumptions from stage 3, and designers use the list to expand their knowledge of design bias using team discussions and reviews.

5. **Repeat:** Designers repeat stages 1 and 4 using a new assumption from the shared list, growing their knowledge base for inclusive design.

1. Oleson, A., Solomon, M., Perdriau, C., & Ko, A. J. (2022). Teaching inclusive design skills with the CIDER assumption elicitation technique. *ACM Transactions on Computer-Human Interaction, 30*(1), Article No. 6. https://doi.org/10.1145/3549074

2. Quoted and adapted from Oleson, A. (2022, October 5). Beyond "average" users: building inclusive design skills with the CIDER technique. *Bits and Behavior.* https://medium.com/bits-and-behavior/beyond-average-users-building-inclusive-design-skills-with-the-cider-technique-413969544e6d

Value Posture	Action Orientation	Ethical Framework
Eliciting values	Consensus building	Deontological
Critically engaging	Evaluating	Consequentialist
Defamiliarizing	Framing	Virtue
	Generating	Pragmatist

Method Input	Method Mechanic	Method Output
Concepts	Altering	Concepts
Stakeholder Info	Storytelling	Stakeholder Info
Constraints/Goals	Filtering	Constraints/Goals
Values	Creating	Values
Use Context	Mapping	Evaluation Outcomes

Stages of the CIDER Assumption Elicitation Technique

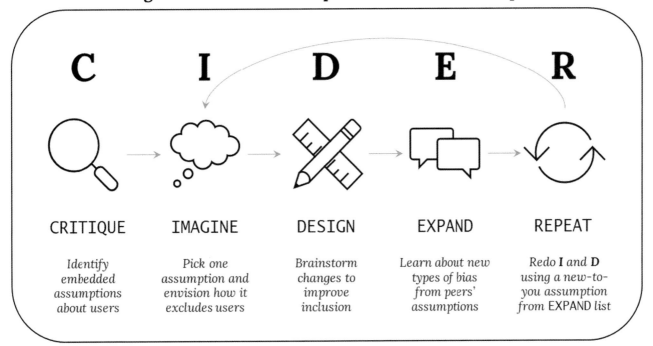

C I D E R

CRITIQUE	IMAGINE	DESIGN	EXPAND	REPEAT
Identify embedded assumptions about users	Pick one assumption and envision how it excludes users	Brainstorm changes to improve inclusion	Learn about new types of bias from peers' assumptions	Redo **I** and **D** using a new-to-you assumption from EXPAND list

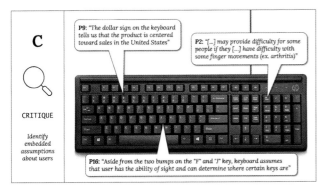

C

CRITIQUE

Identify embedded assumptions about users

P9: *"The dollar sign on the keyboard tells us that the product is centered toward sales in the United States"*

P2: *"[...] may provide difficulty for some people if they [...] have difficulty with some finger movements (ex. arthritis)"*

P16: *"Aside from the two bumps on the "F" and "J" key, keyboard assumes that user has the ability of sight and can determine where certain keys are"*

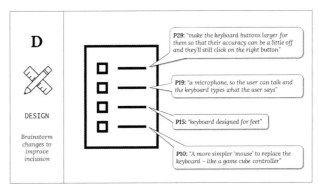

D

DESIGN

Brainstorm changes to improve inclusion

P29: *"make the keyboard buttons larger for them so that their accuracy can be a little off and they'll still click on the right button"*

P19: *"a microphone, so the user can talk and the keyboard types what the user says"*

P15: *"keyboard designed for feet"*

P10: *"A more simpler 'mouse' to replace the keyboard – like a game cube controller"*

An image summarizing the five stages of the CIDER elicitation technique (top) and an example of the Critique (bottom left) and Design (bottom right) stages of CIDER, where participants identified "embedded assumptions" that might limit access to a physical keyboard for certain users and designed alternatives that were more inclusive.

Image courtesy of Alannah Oleson, reproduced with permission from Oleson et al. (2022).

12 Critical Design

Critical Design encourages you to playfully reinterpret the role of design systems by building concepts that transgress, provoke, or disrupt our understanding of how society typically functions.

#newperspectives #breakmydesign #evaluateoutcomes

Critical Design is disruptive and transgressive, encouraging designers to provoke as a way of better understanding current norms and potential impacts of technology on society.[1] The designer can use multiple tactics to investigate and challenge these norms, often beginning by identifying social norm or "typical" configuration of a product feature or functionality, and then seeking to exploit, modify, or transgress the original or typical presentation of that norm. The practice of critical design is focused on "producing concept[s] that encourage complex and meaningful reflection on inhabitation of a ubiquitous, dematerializing, and intelligent environment: a form of social research to integrate critical aesthetic experience with everyday life."[2] These concepts are speculative and not meant to actually be produced, focusing on building awareness of one or more critical perspectives.

This approach is particularly helpful in understanding the social or technological norms of design systems or products, unpacking these norms in ways that are playful and aid the designer in considering consequences of design decisions or ultimate outcomes if certain norms are followed to their logical conclusion. There are many ways to incorporate critical perspectives, such as these four tactics or modes through which to consider critical perspectives (adapted from Ferri et al.[3]):

- **Thematic blending:** You can mix implications from different contexts that are potentially incompatible or unconventional (e.g., using a digital ticker to link prayers to an RSS news feed[4]).

- **Semantic shifts:** You can use a familiar framing or design element that is framed in an unexpected way (e.g., a vest that inflates to simulate a hug[5]).

- **Social transgression:** You can "stage social conflict" to transgress one or more social norms (e.g., a dress with porcupine spikes to discourage would-be sexual harassers[6]).

- **Body modification:** You can consider ways our bodies could be designed differently or how they could operate in unexpected ways (e.g., a tooth that transmits sound to the wearer through bone conduction[7]).

1. Bardzell, S., Bardzell, J., Forlizzi, J., Zimmerman, J., & Antanitis, J. (2012). Critical design and critical theory: the challenge of designing for provocation. *Proceedings of the Designing Interactive Systems Conference*, 288-297. https://doi.org/10.1145/2317956.2318001

2. Dunne, A. (2006). *Hertzian tales.* MIT Press. p. 147

3. Ferri, G., Bardzell, J., Bardzell, S., & Louraine, S. (2014). Analyzing critical designs: categories, distinctions, and canons of exemplars. *Proceedings of the 2014 Conference on Designing Interactive Systems*, 355-364. https://doi.org/10.1145/2598510.2598588

4. Gaver, W., Blythe, M., Boucher, A., Jarvis, N., Bowers, J., & Wright, P. (2010). The prayer companion: openness and specificity, materiality and spirituality. *Proceedings of the SIGCHI Conference on Human Factors in Computing Systems*, 2055-2064. https://doi.org/10.1145/1753326.1753640

5. Chow, M. K., Payne, A., & Seaton, P. (2011). *Like-a-hug.*

6. Gadani, A. (2010). *Porcupine dress.*

7. Auger, J., & Loizeau, J. (2001). *Audio tooth implant.*

Value Posture	Action Orientation	Ethical Framework		Method Input	Method Mechanic	Method Output
Eliciting values	Consensus building	Deontological		Concepts	Altering	Concepts
Critically engaging	Evaluating	Consequentialist		Stakeholder Info	Storytelling	Stakeholder Info
Defamiliarizing	Framing	Virtue		Constraints/Goals	Filtering	Constraints/Goals
	Generating	Pragmatist		Values	Creating	Values
				Use Context	Mapping	Evaluation Outcomes

The "Pee Timer" critical design project encourages designers to be more aware of workplace surveillance. The context chosen was workplace surveillance and productivity, and the social norm being addressed was the legitimacy of taking bathroom breaks throughout the workday. If the worker is away from their desk for what the system deems "too long," the vessel will be filled with yellow tinted water and eventually overflow, destroying the worker's computer.

Image courtesy of Shad Gross and Austin Toombs. Project available at https://www.instructables.com/The-Pee-Timer-Connecting-the-Arduino-the-intel-Per/.

The "Porcupine Dress" critical design has quills that stand up when the wearer leans over in a defensive posture, "brac[ing] themselves for the possibility of an attack while simultaneously decreasing the probability of an attack by the sudden and alarming display."[6]

Image and Model courtesy of Amisha Gadani. Project available at https://amishagadani.com/Work/porcupine/.

13 Critical Interviewing

Critical Interviewing guides you to deeply explore the "why" behind what your participants tell you, revealing underlying norms and situated forms of reasoning.[1]

#newperspectives #identifyvalues

Interviewing people can help designers increase empathy and aid in constructing design insights to guide design work. However, an interview participant cannot always give you straightforward answers to complex "why" questions that underlie their behaviors, beliefs, or worldview.

Critical Interviewing focuses your attention on the normative and evaluative judgments that people use to justify, motivate, or make sense of their perspective on the world. This approach to interviewing borrows some principles from conducting a semistructured interview, while using a different protocol format to highlight attention to specific "topic domains" of interest, using follow-up questions as a way to probe more deeply or understand a construct more closely.[1] To use this approach, create and leverage a protocol with the following components:[2]

· **Identify a topic domain of interest.** The topic should be related to a construct, concept, or point of focus that is relevant to your project.

· **Create lead-off and potential follow-up questions.** Start the conversation with a concrete lead-off question. List potential follow-up questions that allow you to explore the construct in many different ways. You may use many or virtually none of these questions in the actual interview, but this is the process of you doing your "homework" to prepare.

· **List covert categories.** These categories are ideas, perspectives, beliefs, or other elements you want to understand further but cannot ask without leading the conversation too much. Consider listing covert categories about both "things" and normative issues, such as oppression, power, or whether something is good or bad.

· **Follow up on normative-evaluative issues.** Use question-asking strategies that help you gain a full picture of both what your participants have done or believe and why they make sense of their world in that way. These can include underlying values, beliefs about why the world works in the way it does, or knowledge that guides or shapes their actions.

1. Carspecken, P. F. (1996). *Critical ethnography in educational research: a theoretical and practical guide.* Routledge.

2. Adapted from Carspecken (1996).

Value Posture	Action Orientation	Ethical Framework		Method Input	Method Mechanic	Method Output
Eliciting values	Consensus building	Deontological		Concepts	Altering	Concepts
Critically engaging	Evaluating	Consequentialist		Stakeholder Info	Storytelling	Stakeholder Info
Defamiliarizing	Framing	Virtue		Constraints/Goals	Filtering	Constraints/Goals
	Generating	Pragmatist		Values	Creating	Values
				Use Context	Mapping	Evaluation Outcomes

Topic 1: Individual practitioners personal values

Lead-off Question:

in the past

Tell me about a time when you made a project decision that made you feel uncomfortable.

Back-up Question:

Tell me about an instance where a project decision was made that you thought was ethically questionable.

'Data' → marketing campaign.

Emergency Question:

(If the participant narrates the experience as a user)-Have you ever faced similar situations when you were responsible for designing such technological artifacts or systems?

Remember this structure

(lead)
data modelling

Follow-up Questions: *lead data architect | protective.*

"device the solution".

Designer- Designer

- Why did the decision make you uncomfortable?
    a. Were there specific aspects of this decision that conflicted with your <personal beliefs>? [Note: **Use their terms to build on constructs such as values, ethics, personal beliefs. For example, if they say "immoral", build on asking, "why do you think this is immoral"?**]
- How did you tackle this situation?
- What did you feel like your role was in this situation?
    a. Was it appropriate or inappropriate?
    b. Were you seeking to advocate for users? Prevent poor outcomes?

Covert Categories
Individual:
- Perceived role of ethics in design (conflict/ support)
- Awareness of ethical role
- Drivers of ethical sensitivity/awareness
- Personal design values or philosophy

Example of a Critical Interviewing protocol with handwritten notes from an interview with a data architect, illustrating the use of topic domains, lead-off questions, follow-up questions, and covert categories to identify normative concerns in relation to ethics and values in design practice.

Image courtesy of Sai Shruthi Chivukula and protocol courtesy of Colin M. Gray and the UXP² research lab.

14 Critical Race Theory

Critical Race Theory supports you in deconstructing the socially constructed nature and impacts of racism on society.[1,2]

#evaluateoutcomes #newperspectives #applyvalues

The design of systems, policies, and tangible design outcomes can often produce harm to individuals and society. However, some forms of harm are more systemic and discriminatory, revealing the need for new frameworks to elucidate and disrupt these harms.

Critical Race Theory (CRT) is a legal framework created by US legal scholars in the 1970s to inspect and document the impacts of race on one's ability to live and thrive in society. CRT challenges the dominant discourse on race and racism, revealing the ordinary, pervasive, and systemic nature of racism. It provides tools to deconstruct how race impacts one's experience and how power and identity shape—and are shaped by—perceptions of race.

CRT offers a way to inspect and identify elements of the Black experience often left out of traditional design approaches to create more inclusive and equitable designs. Key themes of CRT to start your investigation include:[3]

- **Racism is ordinary, not aberrational.** Racism is embedded in institutions, practices, and systems, and is often propagated unknowingly by those in power to the detriment of others. Consider how your products or systems might encode racism into your product or service.

- **Race and racism are socially constructed.** Racial categories are human-made, not based on biological truths, and have historically been fluid. Consider how the role of race as an input or output of your product or service is considered or problematized.

- **Identity is intersectional.** Each person has overlapping identities (e.g., race, gender, age, sexuality) that in combination create unique contexts for experiencing racism. Consider how different people can or cannot use your system based on intersectional characteristics.

- **Liberalism can hinder anti-racist progress.** Aspiring to "color blindness" or equality without a change in systems can impede anti-racist efforts to right historical wrongs. Consider how your product and service can actively resist racism rather than upholding a neutral stance.

1. Ogbonnaya-Ogburu, I. F., Smith, A. D. R., To, A., & Toyama, K. (2020). Critical race theory for HCI. *Proceedings of the 2020 CHI Conference on Human Factors in Computing Systems*, 1-16. https://doi.org/10.1145/3313831.3376392

2. Delgado, R., & Stefancic, J. (2023). *Critical race theory, fourth edition: an introduction.* New York University Press

3. Synthesized and quoted from Ogbonnaya-Ogburu et al. (2020).

Value Posture	Action Orientation	Ethical Framework		Method Input	Method Mechanic	Method Output
Eliciting values	Consensus building	Deontological		Concepts	Altering	Concepts
Critically engaging	Evaluating	Consequentialist		Stakeholder Info	Storytelling	Stakeholder Info
Defamiliarizing	Framing	Virtue		Constraints/Goals	Filtering	Constraints/Goals
	Generating	Pragmatist		Values	Creating	Values
				Use Context	Mapping	Evaluation Outcomes

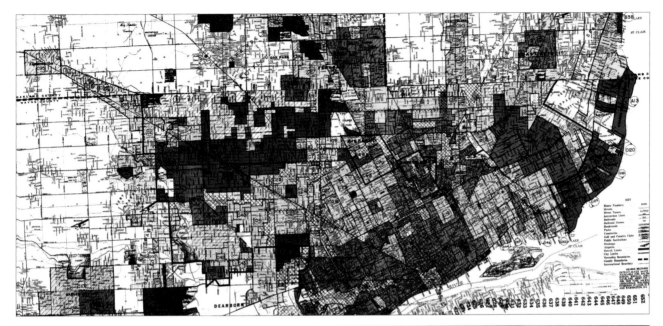

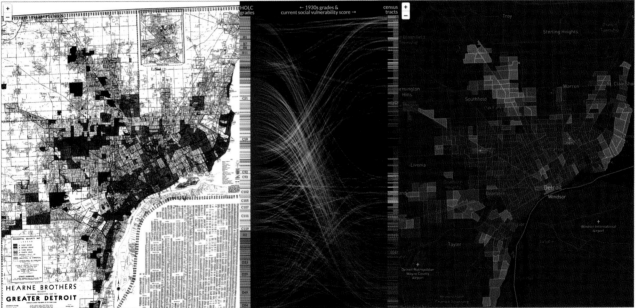

A visualization of a practice commonly known as "redlining." On the top, this map of Detroit in the 1930s shows grades assigned by the Home Owners' Loan Corporation (HOLC), which strongly correlated with race. "Neighborhoods of color received D or C grades with only white neighborhoods receiving A and B grades," revealing that "[r]acism was not subtext; it was text." The bottom image shows a comparison between these redlined districts in the 1930s and the Center for Disease Control and Prevention's Social Vulnerability Index (SVI) scores in these same areas, demonstrating the lasting impact of systemic racism.

See also INTERSECTIONALITY • SOCIAL JUSTICE STRATEGIES • AFROFUTURISM

METHOD

15 Culture Co-Creation Cards

Culture Co-Creation cards support you in navigating cultural barriers, identifying how values can be expressed in culturally appropriate ways.[1]

#newperspectives #identifyvalues #applyvalues

Designers consider a range of human values while designing products and services, including the cultural values experienced across geographic and cultural borders. Design outcomes are often localized, requiring the designer to understand the user's cultural values and expectations that might not be the same as the designer's values.

Culture Co-Creation cards help navigate the "cultural barrier limiting an effective discussion,"[1] especially with "group[s] for whom the articulation of values might be expected to be difficult."[2] These cards enable you to build a scenario as a way to understand a certain use of your product or service in a cultural context. To use these cards in user interviews or activities, you can:[3]

1. Identify a design feature or context you want to investigate and conduct user research. For instance: *"How might we support Saudi women's self-disclosure in the digital media (with minimum violation of their cultural values)?"*[1]

2. Pick one card each from the deck of Culture Co-Creation cards, each pertaining to a kind of user, media, or stakeholder. For instance, a random selection of cards could be a man, a newspaper, and a woman running.

3. Create a scenario using the three cards to further the conversation with your user about how they talk about implicit, individual, and cultural values, using the scenario as a starting point.

4. Translate these cultural values to build culturally appropriate features, products, and services beyond the particular design context you have identified in the first step. For instance: *How can we understand this [question in step 1] to design social media profile pages to preserve identity?*

1. Alshehri, T., Kirkham, R., & Olivier, P. (2020). Scenario co-creation cards: a culturally sensitive tool for eliciting values. *Proceedings of the 2020 CHI Conference on Human Factors in Computing Systems*, 1-14. https://doi.org/10.1145/3313831.3376608

2. Scenario co-creation cards: a tool for eliciting values. (n.d.). Retrieved July 22, 2024, from https://openlab.ncl.ac.uk/research/scenario-co-creation-cards-a-culturally-sensitive-tool-for-eliciting-values/

3. Adapted from Alshehri et al. (2020).

Value Posture	Action Orientation	Ethical Framework
Eliciting values	Consensus building	Deontological
Critically engaging	Evaluating	Consequentialist
Defamiliarizing	Framing	Virtue
	Generating	Pragmatist

Method Input	Method Mechanic	Method Output
Concepts	Altering	Concepts
Stakeholder Info	Storytelling	Stakeholder Info
Constraints/Goals	Filtering	Constraints/Goals
Values	Creating	Values
Use Context	Mapping	Evaluation Outcomes

38 Universal Methods of Ethical Design

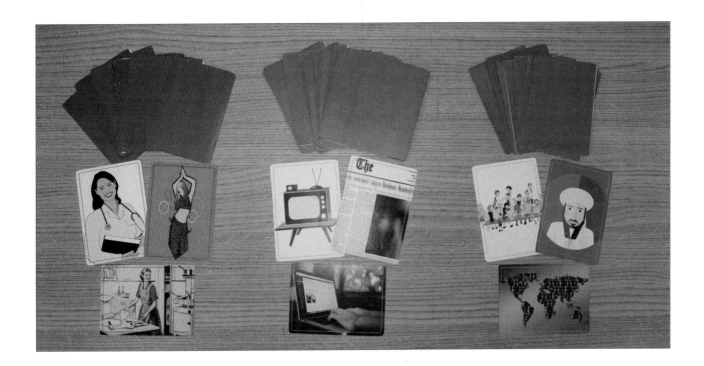

(top) The Culture Co-Creation card deck with green cards representing stakeholders, blue cards representing different types of media, and red cards that indicate the role the stakeholder could take on.

(right) An example of a set of cards (a bride and a groom, a newspaper, a woman in white coat, and a radio) that a participant used to discuss their ability to talk or be represented in different media types. The dialogue between the researcher and participant shows how the cards supported deeper reflection on the roles of different media types.

Researcher: *So, is it easier for you to talk in the newspaper about sensitive and personal topics than disclosing your photo and talking about mundane non-sensitive topics?*

Participant: *Yes, I don't know [why] maybe like I said I don't like to appear physically in the media, then if I appear I would appear with distinct writings, educational not trivial. The [social] image for me is important (laughter).*

Quoted from Alshehri et al. (2020).

See also HUVALUE • CRITICAL INTERVIEWING

16 DAH Cards

DAH (Design Against Humanity) Cards expose designers to problematic consequences and real-world impacts of existing products and services to become self-aware, humane, conscious, and responsible.[1]

#identifyvalues #designresponsibility

We are surrounded by digital and physical products that define how our world functions. These products are designed to be easily accessible, automated, quick, entertaining, and comfortable, but can also have adverse effects on humanity, environment, and society. DAH cards are designed to build a reflective space to be more conscious of these everyday objects and critically reflect about our beliefs and values. As designers, this reflective consciousness can lead toward being more responsible while creating products and services.

DAH (pronounced as DUHH) cards[1] provide a set of cards that present a range of features (e.g., unskippable ads), objects (e.g., gambling apps, driverless vehicles), mechanisms (e.g., autopayments), and services (e.g., two-day delivery). The two-sided cards reveal the product (black side) and description of the product and reports on problematic consequences of the product (white side). Designers can repeatedly filter the cards into ethical, unethical, and unsure categories; learn more about the products by flipping cards; and rearrange the cards across the three categories as a reflective practice asking "What changed?"

You can use the DAH cards to:

- Learn playfully about impacts of products on society

- Self-reflect to build your own ethical manifesto

- Draft a vision on what kinds of products you would like to design in the future

1. Design against humanity?. (2020). *Ziqq Rafit.* https://www.ziqq-rafit.com/design/against-humanity/2020

Value Posture	Action Orientation	Ethical Framework
Eliciting values	Consensus building	Deontological
Critically engaging	Evaluating	Consequentialist
Defamiliarizing	Framing	Virtue
	Generating	Pragmatist

Method Input	Method Mechanic	Method Output
Concepts	Altering	Concepts
Stakeholder Info	Storytelling	Stakeholder Info
Constraints/Goals	Filtering	Constraints/Goals
Values	Creating	Values
Use Context	Mapping	Evaluation Outcomes

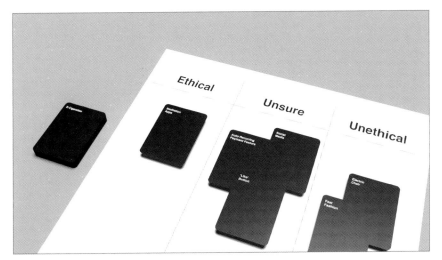

DAH cards sorted into Ethical, Unsure, and Unethical categories.

Image courtesy of Ziqq Rafit.

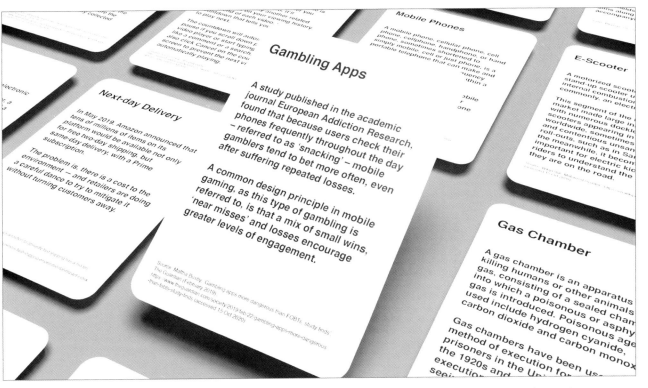

A set of DAH Cards (flip side) detailing a product and service with their problematic consequences and impacts.

Image courtesy of Ziqq Rafit.

17 Data Ethics Canvas

Data Ethics Canvas enables you to identify and manage ethical issues relating to your data practices through reflection and critical questioning across the project life cycle.[1]

#evaluateoutcomes #applyvalues #designresponsibility

Designers continuously need to address data as part of their design work—considering the collection, sharing, use, or disposal of data in relation to products or services. However, it can be difficult to identify what ethical considerations might be related to these data practices.

Data Ethics Canvas guides you in identifying and managing ethical issues at the start of a project and continuously throughout its duration. Using this method, you are prompted to ask critical questions about your data projects and reflect on the responses to ensure ethical integrity. Consider using this tool at various points in your project life cycle to:[2]

- **Identify ethical issues.** Consider the primary purpose of using data in your project and reflect on who could be negatively affected by the project and in what ways.

- **Ask important questions.** Identify the primary purpose of using data in your project and who could be negatively affected by the project or its outcomes.

- **Develop ethical guidance.** Develop ethical guidance tailored to your project's context, size, and scope, building upon both this tool and the *Ethics Canvas* framework, which support you in assessing the ethical implications of your project.

- **Act.** Complete questions in an area of the canvas and create actions to respond to the prompts using the online tool.[3] For each action identified, set a priority level (Low, Medium, High), assign responsibility, and involve relevant stakeholders to ensure accountability.

1. The data ethics canvas. (n.d.). *The ODI*. Retrieved July 25, 2024, from https://theodi.org/news-and-events/blog/data-ethics-canvas/

2. Adapted from the Data Ethics Canvas site.

3. Interactive data ethics canvas. (n.d.). *The ODI*. https://theodi.github.io/interactive-data-ethics-canvas/

Value Posture	Action Orientation	Ethical Framework
Eliciting values	Consensus building	Deontological
Critically engaging	Evaluating	Consequentialist
Defamiliarizing	Framing	Virtue
	Generating	Pragmatist

Method Input	Method Mechanic	Method Output
Concepts	Altering	Concepts
Stakeholder Info	Storytelling	Stakeholder Info
Constraints/Goals	Filtering	Constraints/Goals
Values	Creating	Values
Use Context	Mapping	Evaluation Outcomes

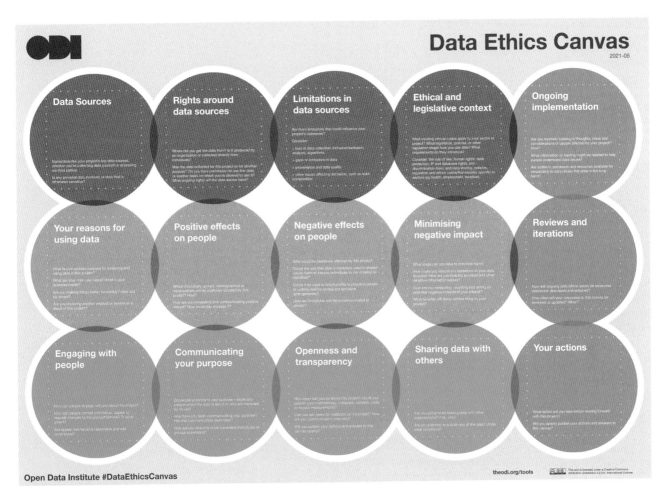

A portion of the data ethics canvas worksheet, which includes a set of considerations relating to data collection, use, impacts, and implementation. Each consideration includes a set of guiding questions.

Image courtesy of the Open Data Institute, licensed under a Creative Commons Attribution-ShareAlike 4.0 UK International License.

See also DATA GOVERNANCE WORKBOOK • PRIVACY BY DESIGN • DIGITAL ETHICS COMPASS

18 Data Feminism

Data Feminism encourages you to consider issues at the intersection of data science and data ethics, identifying power structures to achieve more inclusive and embodied data classifications.[1]

#newperspectives #identifyvalues #designresponsibility

The authors of *Data Feminism*, Catherine D'Ignazio and Lauren Klein, ask, "How can we use data to remake the world?"[1] Through this approach to data science, they argue that feminism—expansively defined—is a critical and important lens to understand how data enact and create power and hierarchy and must be challenged. By considering data science through an intersectional and feminist lens, designers are able to "name and challenge sexism and other forces of oppression, as well as those which seek to create more just, equitable, and livable futures."[1]

As designers, we continuously interact with data, including collecting data from users for research, gathering data for design inspiration, or embedding data and data structures into the digital systems we create. Data Feminism exposes the power structures within all these data-focused actions, spanning a set of "core principles" that include:[2]

- **Examine power.** Data Feminism begins by analyzing how power operates in the world.

- **Challenge power.** Data Feminism commits to challenging unequal power structures and working toward justice.

- **Rethink binaries and hierarchies.** Data Feminism requires us to challenge the gender binary, along with other systems of counting and classification that perpetuate oppression.

- **Embrace pluralism.** Data Feminism insists that the most complete knowledge comes from synthesizing multiple perspectives, with priority given to local, Indigenous, and experiential ways of knowing.

- **Make labor visible.** The work of data science, like all work in the world, is the work of many hands. Data Feminism makes this labor visible so that it can be recognized and valued.

1. D'Ignazio, C., & Klein, L. F. (2020). *Data feminism*. MIT Press

2. Quoted from D'Ignazio & Klein (2020).

Further Reading

Data feminism. (n.d.). https://data-feminism.mitpress.mit.edu/

Value Posture	Action Orientation	Ethical Framework
Eliciting values	Consensus building	Deontological
Critically engaging	Evaluating	Consequentialist
Defamiliarizing	Framing	Virtue
	Generating	Pragmatist

Method Input	Method Mechanic	Method Output
Concepts	Altering	Concepts
Stakeholder Info	Storytelling	Stakeholder Info
Constraints/Goals	Filtering	Constraints/Goals
Values	Creating	Values
Use Context	Mapping	Evaluation Outcomes

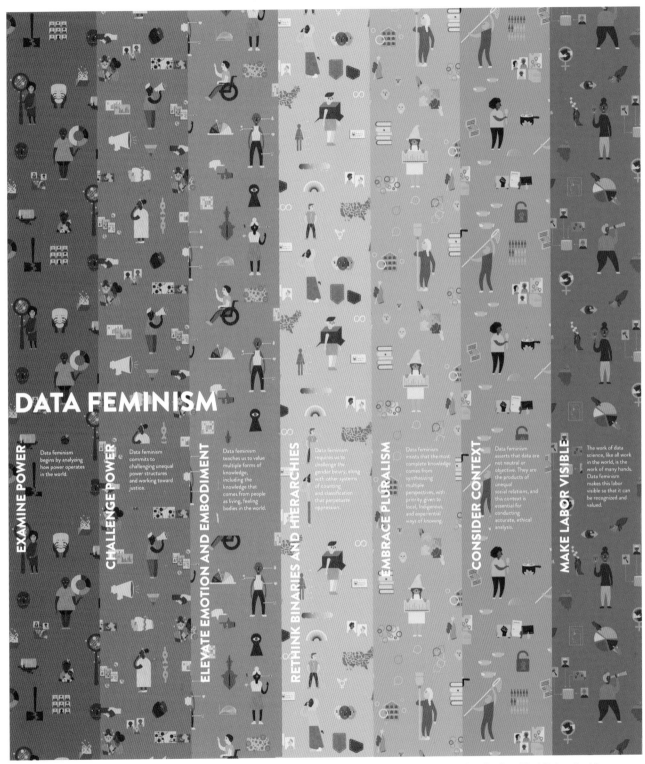

DATA FEMINISM

EXAMINE POWER
Data feminism begins by analyzing how power operates in the world.

CHALLENGE POWER
Data feminism commits to challenging unequal power structures and working toward justice.

ELEVATE EMOTION AND EMBODIMENT
Data feminism teaches us to value multiple forms of knowledge, including the knowledge that comes from people as living, feeling bodies in the world.

RETHINK BINARIES AND HIERARCHIES
Data feminism requires us to challenge the gender binary, along with other systems of counting and classification that perpetuate oppression.

EMBRACE PLURALISM
Data feminism insists that the most complete knowledge comes from synthesizing multiple perspectives, with priority given to local, Indigenous, and experiential ways of knowing.

CONSIDER CONTEXT
Data feminism asserts that data are not neutral or objective. They are the products of unequal social relations, and this context is essential for conducting accurate, ethical analysis.

MAKE LABOR VISIBLE
The work of data science, like all work in the world, is the work of many hands. Data feminism makes this labor visible so that it can be recognized and valued.

Data Feminism infographic courtesy of Catherine D'Ignazio, Lauren Klein, and Marcia Diaz, 2020, licensed under a Creative Commons Attribution-ShareAlike 4.0 International license.

See also FEMINIST INTERACTIONAL QUALITIES • KALEIDOSCOPE

19 Data Governance Workbook

The Data Governance Workbook guides you in planning and executing safe, ethical, and responsible data governance practices within your organization.[1]

#breakmydesign #identifyvalues #applyvalues

Digital products and services are built on and shaped by data collected from user interactions. However, it is important to safeguard user data across the product life cycle and ensure that the entire organization uses ethical and responsible data practices.

The Data Governance Workbook allows you to leverage a policy and data inventory that "promotes the availability, quality and security of an organization's data ... determin[ing] data owners, data security measures and intended uses for the data."[2] The Data Governance Workbook guides you to build and use these resources through three specific practices that build upon your organization's mission statement:[3]

- **Data mission:** Forecast data needs to achieve your organization's mission, identifying ways of gathering data, building partnerships or strategies to use that data to its full potential, tracking upcoming regulatory changes, and listing impacts of data changes on financial resources.

- **Digital data inventory:** Identify what data your organization manages, who is responsible for it, where it is located, what software is used to manage it, and what regulations or policies govern the collection, use, or removal of this data.

- **Organizational policy inventory:** Monitor the data inventory over time, identifying people responsible within the organization and additional resources that might be needed (e.g., training, new software, new contracts) for each entry in the Digital Data Inventory.

1. Fair, K. (2015, September 5). *Data governance toolkit*. Digital Impact. https://digitalimpact.io/toolkit/worksheets/

2. What is data governance? (2022, June 16). *IBM*. https://www.ibm.com/topics/data-governance

3. Adapted from the data governance workbook. https://digitalimpact.io/wp-content/uploads/2019/03/Data-Governance-Workbook.pdf

Value Posture	Action Orientation	Ethical Framework
Eliciting values	Consensus building	Deontological
Critically engaging	Evaluating	Consequentialist
Defamiliarizing	Framing	Virtue
	Generating	Pragmatist

Method Input	Method Mechanic	Method Output
Concepts	Altering	Concepts
Stakeholder Info	Storytelling	Stakeholder Info
Constraints/Goals	Filtering	Constraints/Goals
Values	Creating	Values
Use Context	Mapping	Evaluation Outcomes

Stanford PACS
Center on Philanthropy
and Civil Society
—
Digital Civil Society Lab

STEP ONE

STEP TWO

What data does your organization manage?	Thinking about your org chart, who is responsible for this data? (roles)	Where is it? (e.g. cloud, servers, individual laptops, staff phones, board laptops, etc.)	What software is used to manage it? (e.g. email program, database, grants mgmt., cloud, financial)	What regulation governs this data? (If you don't know, write "?")	What internal policy governs this data? (If you don't have one, write "N/A")

Example of a Data Governance Worksheet to create an inventory of data types and organizational or regulatory policies that govern this data.

Image courtesy of the Digital Civil Society Lab, licensed under a Creative Commons 4.0 International License.

See also **PRIVACY BY DESIGN** • *DATA FEMINISM*

20 De-scription

De-scription allows you to deconstruct the what, how, and why of your designs to make you more morally, ethically, and socially sensitive.[1]

#breakmydesign #identifyvalues #designerresponsibility

Design outcomes are not inevitable but rather result from the shaping influence of the designer. Designer intentions are often invisible in the final product, but can be inspected to better understand how particular designer values and motivations are embedded into a product or service. Intentionally decoding these different elements of a product or service makes designers more morally, ethically, and socially sensitive to the impacts of their design actions.

De-scription is not about just describing a product, but to "de-script" it—thereby learning more about the underlying intentions and potential impacts of a product. You can deconstruct your products and services using the following three sets of questions:[2]

- **WHAT** the product or service is, including its form, function, aesthetics, and interactions. Designers can answer questions like: *"What is it?"* or *"What does it look like?"*

- **HOW** an artifact prescribes or "scripts" its users' behavior. Explicitly write down the "script" of the product, which defines how to feel, react, and behave upon interaction with the product or service. Designers can answer questions like: *"How does a user use it?," "How is the interaction?,"* or *"How does it define one's behavior for now and for longer?"*

- **WHY** an artifact exists to learn the worldview of a designer and their intentions. Designers and their team can ask questions such as *"Why does it exist?," "Why was the designer intending to design this product?," "How does the designer view the world?,"* or *"What does the designer characterize as a 'good' life?"*

1. Gispen, J. (2017). De-scription. *Ethics for Designers.* https://www.ethicsfordesigners.com/description

2. Questions quoted from Gispen, 2017.

Further Reading

Gispen, J. (2017). Ethics for designers toolkit. *Ethics for Designers.* https://www.ethicsfordesigners.com/tools

Akrich, M. (1992). The de-scription of technical objects. In W. E. Bijker & J. Law (Eds.), *Shaping Technology/Building Society: Studies in Sociotechnical Change* (pp. 205-224). MIT Press.

Value Posture	Action Orientation	Ethical Framework
Eliciting values	Consensus building	Deontological
Critically engaging	Evaluating	Consequentialist
Defamiliarizing	Framing	Virtue
	Generating	Pragmatist

Method Input	Method Mechanic	Method Output
Concepts	Altering	Concepts
Stakeholder Info	Storytelling	Stakeholder Info
Constraints/Goals	Filtering	Constraints/Goals
Values	Creating	Values
Use Context	Mapping	Evaluation Outcomes

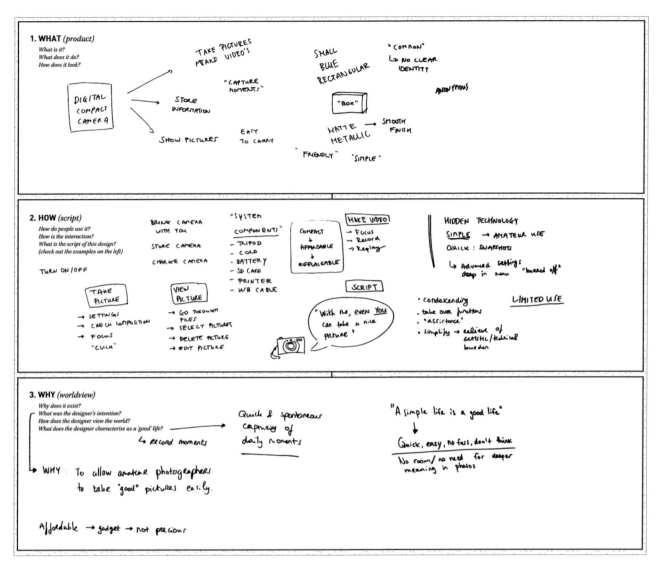

1. WHAT *(product)*

What is it?
What does it do?
How does it look?

DIGITAL COMPACT CAMERA

TAKE PICTURES
MAKE VIDEO'S

"CAPTURE MOMENTS"

STORE INFORMATION

SHOW PICTURES

EASY TO CARRY

SMALL
BLUE
RECTANGULAR

"Box"

MATTE METALLIC → SMOOTH FINISH

"COMMON"
↳ NO CLEAR IDENTITY

ANONYMOUS

"FRIENDLY"   "SIMPLE"

2. HOW *(script)*

How do people use it?
How is the interaction?
What is the script of this design?
(check out the examples on the left)

TURN ON/OFF

BRING CAMERA WITH YOU

STORE CAMERA

CHARGE CAMERA

TAKE PICTURE
→ SETTINGS
→ CHECK COMPOSITION
→ FOCUS
   "CLICK"

VIEW PICTURE
→ GO THROUGH FILES
→ SELECT PICTURES
→ DELETE PICTURE
→ EDIT PICTURE

"SYSTEM COMPONENTS"
- TRIPOD
- CORD
- BATTERY
- SD CARD
- PRINTER
- WB CABLE

COMPACT
↓
APPENDABLE
↓
REPLACEABLE

MAKE VIDEO
→ FOCUS
→ RECORD
→ REPLAY

SCRIPT

"With me, even YOU can take a nice picture"

HIDDEN TECHNOLOGY

SIMPLE → AMATEUR USE

QUICK : SNAPSHOTS

↳ Advanced settings deep in menu "buried off"

• condescending
• take over function
• "assistance"
• simplify → relieve of artistic/technical burden

LIMITED USE

3. WHY *(worldview)*

Why does it exist?
What was the designer's intention?
How does the designer view the world?
What does the designer characterise as a 'good' life?

Quick & spontaneous capturing of daily moments
↳ record moments

→ WHY : To allow amateur photographers to take "good" pictures easily.

Affordable → gadget → not precious

"A simple life is a good life"
↓
Quick, easy, no fuss, don't think
No room/ no need for deeper meaning in photos

An example of the De-Scription worksheet filled out to explore the use of a camera, including what it is as a product, how people use it as a script, and why it exists.

Image courtesy of Jet Gispen.

21 Design Ethicquette

The Design Ethicquette toolkit enables you to leverage philosophical ethical theories in a practical way to embed ethics into different stages of your design process.[1]

#breakmydesign #evaluateoutcomes #identifyvalues #applyvalues

Designers typically go through a design process starting with research and discovery about their design space, proceeding to ideation and development of solutions for their product or service, and ending with evaluation and refinement of the generated design outcomes. Designers embed ethical considerations and values throughout their design process with varying levels of awareness as they undertake activities such as framing, concept generation, and evaluation of their features, product, and/or service.

The Design Ethicquette toolkit provides a way to practically embed ethics as a part of every stage in your design process, drawing guidance from philosophical ethical theories of deontological, consequential, and virtue ethics. The Design Ethicquette toolkit includes three tools:[2]

- The **(A)lignment tool** is built on virtue ethics, encouraging the designer to consider different virtues of the society through research or synthesis at the start of the design process. Using this knowledge, designers can then build their product and/or service based on these virtues, building initial alignment that can support designers throughout the design process.

- The **(B)est Practice tool** is built on deontological ethical theory, encouraging the designer to adhere to principles of accessibility, inclusivity, and sustainability during the ideation stage of a design process. The designer can engage in brainstorming to filter out bad ideas that violate societal needs and industry standards.

- The **(C)onsequences tool** is built on consequentialist ethical theory, encouraging the designer to surface unintended negative consequences from the designed product and/or service at the evaluation and refinement stage. The designer can consider negative consequences through the lens of environmental, societal, and business impact.

1. Rafit, Z. (2021). Design ethicquette: toolkit. https://www.ziqq-rafit.com/design/designethicquette-toolkit/2021

2. Quoted from Rafit (2021).

Value Posture	Action Orientation	Ethical Framework
Eliciting values	Consensus building	Deontological
Critically engaging	Evaluating	Consequentialist
Defamiliarizing	Framing	Virtue
	Generating	Pragmatist

Method Input	Method Mechanic	Method Output
Concepts	Altering	Concepts
Stakeholder Info	Storytelling	Stakeholder Info
Constraints/Goals	Filtering	Constraints/Goals
Values	Creating	Values
Use Context	Mapping	Evaluation Outcomes

Design *Ethic*quette

Design *Ethic*quette is a toolkit for designers and design teams to consider ethics in their design process.

The toolkit is inspired by the three pillars of modern ethics: Virtue Ethics (Alignment), Duty Ethics (Best Practice), and Consequentialism (Consequences). Bridging the world of philosophy to the practical world of design, the three pillars of modern ethics is reintroduced as the **ABCs** of Design Ethics.

Bb – Best Practice

The 'Best Practice' tool is most effective during the ideation and development phase. Designers will refer to best of class examples and standards that are set by the industry to adhere, consider, and take inspiration from their successes and failures. The tool helps to filter our bad ideas and surfaces the best ones with prompts around accessibility, inclusivity, and sustainability. It also questions the behaviors and standards that the designs (product/service) will set for society and the industry.

Research & Discover
Alignment

Define & Synthesize

Ideate & Develop
Best Practice

Refine & Account
Consequences

Aa – Alignment

The 'Alignment' tool is best utilized at the start of the design process. As part of research and synthesis, designers look both inwards and outwards to better understand themselves and the people they are designing for. As ethics is contextual, this process of alignment helps designers to be aware of the virtues of the society and ensure that their designs (product/service) will respect these virtues. Though the tool is used at the start, aligning of virtues happens throughout the design process and acts as a guiding principle that can help influence ethical design decisions.

© Ziqq Rafit

Cc – Consequences

The 'Consequences' tool is the last line of defense, to be used right at the tail end of the design process. The tool is meant to surface unintended negative consequences through the lens of environmental, social, and business impact. It prompts for an action plan to how to address and mitigate the negatives and assigning accountability for the design's (product/service) impact.

Design Ethicquette toolkit overlapped on the Double-Diamond design process to guide designers through embedding ethics in their design process.

Image courtesy of Ziqq Rafit.

A group of designers aligning themselves using the worksheets as a part of the Design Ethicquette toolkit.

Image courtesy of Ziqq Rafit.

See also KALEIDOSCOPE • VALUE-SENSITIVE DESIGN

22 Design Fiction Memos

Design Fiction Memos enable you to critically interpret power relations and ethical considerations in everyday work practices.[1]

#identifyvalues #newperspectives

Ethical issues are implicated in the mundane, everyday activities of designers and design teams. Even routine tasks such as writing an email or using Slack to communicate within an organization include discussion of ethical considerations, even if the ethical dimension of these interactions is not made explicit.

Design Fiction Memos help designers create and interpret a related artifact and commentary in order to consider how values and ethical positions might occur in practical workplace scenarios. The use of text and images provides "an invitation to the reader to: follow the linkages between the data and the design fictions, consider their own interpretations of the designs and data, and imagine alternate designs."[1] While this method was originally designed to allow a researcher to find new insights in existing qualitative data about design practices, designers can also use this tool to speculate on potential scenarios in their workplace or interrogate specific artifacts that have actually been generated in their workplace.

To create a Design Fiction Memo:[2]

1. Determine the name and type of a fictional company, including a product or service they offer.

2. Choose a challenge the designer at the fictional company is facing and what resources they have generated (e.g., email, software, team discussions) to resolve or address them. These challenges can be generated based on the findings from an interview or ethnographic study.

3. Create a fictional artifact based on the resource you have chosen and write an accompanying fictional commentary to explore how the artifact embodies ethical considerations.

1. Wong, R. Y. (2021). Using design fiction memos to analyze UX professionals' values work practices: a case study bridging ethnographic and design futuring methods. *Proceedings of the 2021 CHI Conference on Human Factors in Computing Systems*. https://doi.org/10.1145/3411764.3445709

2. Adapted from Wong (2021).

3. Quoted from Wong (2021).

Value Posture	Action Orientation	Ethical Framework
Eliciting values	Consensus building	Deontological
Critically engaging	Evaluating	Consequentialist
Defamiliarizing	Framing	Virtue
	Generating	**Pragmatist**

Method Input	Method Mechanic	Method Output
Concepts	Altering	**Concepts**
Stakeholder Info	Storytelling	Stakeholder Info
Constraints/Goals	Filtering	Constraints/Goals
Values	**Creating**	**Values**
Use Context	Mapping	Evaluation Outcomes

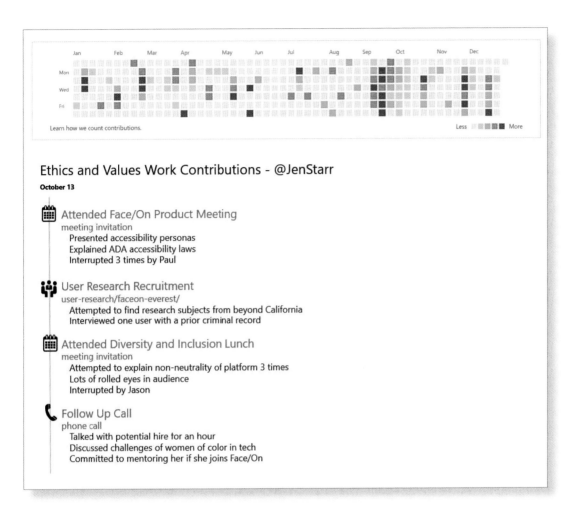

Ethics and Values Work Contributions - @JenStarr

October 13

📅 Attended Face/On Product Meeting
meeting invitation
 Presented accessibility personas
 Explained ADA accessibility laws
 Interrupted 3 times by Paul

👥 User Research Recruitment
user-research/faceon-everest/
 Attempted to find research subjects from beyond California
 Interviewed one user with a prior criminal record

📅 Attended Diversity and Inclusion Lunch
meeting invitation
 Attempted to explain non-neutrality of platform 3 times
 Lots of rolled eyes in audience
 Interrupted by Jason

📞 Follow Up Call
phone call
 Talked with potential hire for an hour
 Discussed challenges of women of color in tech
 Committed to mentoring her if she joins Face/On

This Design Fiction Memo takes the form of a screenshot of an imagined ethics work tracking tool. Someone can use this tool to track work tasks related to raising discussion of and addressing values at the workplace. In the heat map portion at the top of the screen, each square represents a day and darker squares indicate more "contributions" to ethics and values work.

The interface shows the details of (fictional) user researcher Jen Starr for one day. She tracks activities like attending a product meeting where she presented a set of user personas around accessibility, but she also had to explain ADA accessibility laws to coworkers. She notes that she got interrupted three times by Paul. Later she records tasks related to user research recruitment. Then she attends a diversity and inclusion lunch, where she tried to explain the non-neutrality of platforms multiple times, only to face rolled eyes and another interruption. At the end of the day she spends time talking to a woman of color who has been offered a job at Face/On but is undecided about joining a technology company. Jen shares her experiences and challenges, and offers to mentor the new worker if she chooses to work at Face/On.

Image courtesy of Richmond Wong and text quoted from Wong (2021).²

23 Design Justice Principles

Design Justice Principles encourage you to consider your work from the perspective of those typically marginalized by design work, using design as a tool for "collective liberation."[1]

#identifyvalues #designresponsibility

Design is a tool that can exploit individuals, devalue the knowledge of marginalized people, and disempower communities. As described by Sasha Costanza-Chock, "most design processes today reproduce inequalities structured by what Black feminist scholars call the matrix of domination."[1] However, to counter this tendency of design to take power away from communities and individuals, the designer can use a set of principles created by the Design Justice Network that focuses on "justice" as a key philosophical commitment of doing design work.

Design Justice Principles are informed by a range of critical perspectives toward design, drawing from participatory design, feminist human-computer interaction (HCI), and disability justice.[2] The resulting principles frame design work in relation to goals of empowerment and collective liberation, seeking specifically to reduce exploitation and oppression.

Examples of these principles that can aid the designer include[3]:

- We use design to **sustain, heal, and empower our communities,** as well as to seek liberation from exploitative and oppressive systems.

- We **center the voices** of those who are directly impacted by the outcomes of the design process.

- We prioritize design's **impact on the community** over the intentions of the designer.

- We work toward **non-exploitative solutions** that reconnect us to the earth and to each other.

- Before seeking new design solutions, we look for what is already **working at the community level.**

- We **honor and uplift traditional, indigenous, and local knowledge and practices.**

1. Costanza-Chock, S. (2018). Design justice: towards an intersectional feminist framework for design theory and practice. *DRS Biennial Conference Series.* https://doi.org/10.21606/drs.2018.679

2. Costanza-Chock, S. (2020). *Design justice: community-led practices to build the worlds we need.* MIT Press.

3. Principles quoted from Design Justice Network.

Further Reading

Design justice network (n.d.). https://designjustice.org

Value Posture	Action Orientation	Ethical Framework
Eliciting values	Consensus building	Deontological
Critically engaging	Evaluating	Consequentialist
Defamiliarizing	Framing	Virtue
	Generating	Pragmatist

Method Input	Method Mechanic	Method Output
Concepts	Altering	Concepts
Stakeholder Info	Storytelling	Stakeholder Info
Constraints/Goals	Filtering	Constraints/Goals
Values	Creating	Values
Use Context	Mapping	Evaluation Outcomes

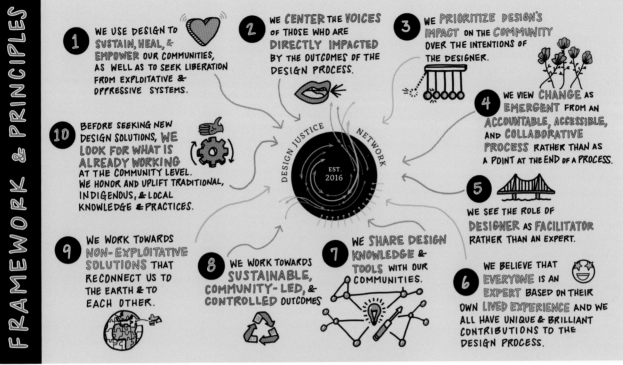

Sketch note of the Design Justice Network principles and framework.

Design Justice Principles infographic courtesy of Tamra Carnart.

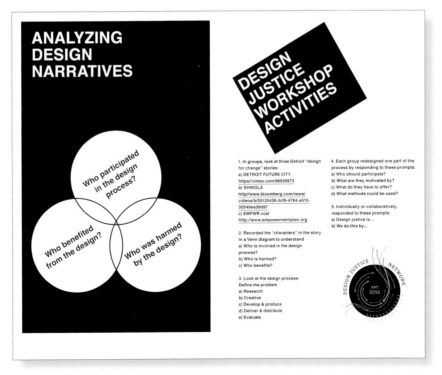

A workshop activity on "Analyzing Design Narratives" from the Zine "Principles for Design Justice."

Image courtesy of Zine editors Una Lee, Nontsikelelo Mutiti, Carlos Garcia, and Wes Taylor and designers Nontsikelelo Mutiti and Alexander Chamorro. Available at https://designjustice.org/zines.

See also DATA FEMINISM • WORKERS TAROT DECK

24 Design with Intent

Design with Intent facilitates an intentional exploration of human behavior across digital and physical spaces and objects, helping you consider how outcomes might encourage or shape behavior change.[1]

#applyvalues #evaluateoutcomes

As designers, our work has an impact on society and user behavior. As described by Dan Lockton, "All design influences our behavior, but as designers we don't always consciously consider the power this gives us to help people (and, sometimes, to manipulate them)."[2] The Design with Intent method helps designers better understand what kinds of impacts their concepts have on the behavior change of users, encouraging intentional and reflective design approaches.

The Design with Intent method provides eight "lenses" encompassing 101 cards that allow reflective considerations about impacting socially and environmentally beneficial behavior change. Examples of lenses and related cards include[1]:

- **Architectural lens** (e.g., converging or diverging, hiding things, material properties, roadblocks)

- **Ludic lens** (e.g., leave gaps to fill, make it a meme, playfulness, rewards)

- **Perceptual lens** (e.g., contrast, fake affordances, mood, prominence)

- **Cognitive lens** (e.g., assuaging guilt, emotional engagement, framing, personality)

Using the Design with Intent cards, you might consider:

- Laying out all of the cards, grouped by lens, and using each lens to identify whether the questions inspire any concepts for addressing your problem.

- Analyzing existing examples by using cards to draw out some behavior-influencing principles behind products, services, or environments you are familiar with.

- Picking two random cards and considering the possibilities of applying them to your problem, both individually and together.

1. Lockton, D., Harrison, D., & Stanton, N. A. (2010). The design with intent method: a design tool for influencing user behaviour. *Applied Ergonomics, 41*(3), 382-392. https://doi.org/10.1016/j.apergo.2009.09.001

2. Design with intent toolkit. (2018). *Imaginaries Lab.* http://imaginari.es/projects/downloadable-resources/

Value Posture	Action Orientation	Ethical Framework
Eliciting values	Consensus building	Deontological
Critically engaging	Evaluating	Consequentialist
Defamiliarizing	Framing	Virtue
	Generating	Pragmatist

Method Input	Method Mechanic	Method Output
Concepts	Altering	Concepts
Stakeholder Info	Storytelling	Stakeholder Info
Constraints/Goals	Filtering	Constraints/Goals
Values	Creating	Values
Use Context	Mapping	Evaluation Outcomes

Example of a lens card from the Design with Intent card deck.

Image courtesy of Dan Lockton.

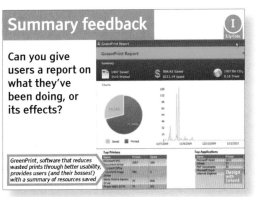

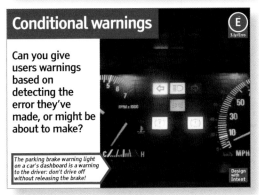

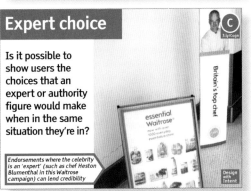

Examples of cards relating to four different lenses in the deck.

Image courtesy of Dan Lockton.

See also *INVERTED BEHAVIOR MODEL • DIGITAL ETHICS COMPASS*

25 Dichotomy Mapping

Dichotomy Mapping advances forecasting the beneficial and harmful impacts of your designs.[1]

#breakmydesign #evaluateoutcomes

Designs around us are often appropriated in ways that users see fit for their everyday needs. For example, a feature, product, and/or service can be used in multiple other ways than its intended purpose. Sometimes, these appropriated uses of technology can also lead to detrimental experiences for other users—creating a dichotomy in the impacts of designs on users, society, and environment.

Dichotomy Mapping helps designers take a micro-view into the impacts of their designs by forecasting both beneficial and harmful outcomes. The mapping is grounded in human needs by looking into the impacts on individual users as well as one or more groups of users when the design outcome is implemented to its "extreme."

Using Dichotomy Mapping, products or services are first deconstructed to a set of features. For each feature, impacts are placed on either side to identify "Beneficial" and "Harmful" results. Dichotomy Mapping will help you list contradictory outcomes based on each feature, which can be used to evaluate your designs based on human needs.

1. Zhou, K. (2021). Dichotomy mapping. *Design Ethically Toolkit.* https://www.designethically.com/dichotomy-mapping

Further Reading

Zhou, K. (2023). *Design Ethically Toolkit.* https://www.designethically.com/toolkit

Value Posture	Action Orientation	Ethical Framework
Eliciting values	Consensus building	Deontological
Critically engaging	Evaluating	Consequentialist
Defamiliarizing	Framing	Virtue
	Generating	Pragmatist

Method Input	Method Mechanic	Method Output
Concepts	Altering	Concepts
Stakeholder Info	Storytelling	Stakeholder Info
Constraints/Goals	Filtering	Constraints/Goals
Values	Creating	Values
Use Context	Mapping	Evaluation Outcomes

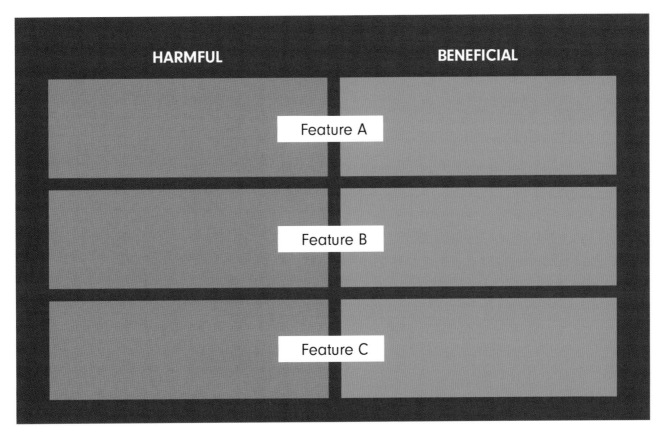

HARMFUL	BENEFICIAL
Feature A	
Feature B	
Feature C	

An example of the Dichotomy Mapping process, including identifying features as rows and listing harmful or beneficial qualities (top). You can also use this technique on a whiteboard, using sticky notes to indicate different qualities for each feature (right).

Images courtesy of Kat Zhou.

See also ETHICS ASSESSMENT • WORRYSTORMING

26 Digital Ethics Compass

Digital Ethics Compass guides you to reflect on your product and business development goals through heuristics relating to data, automation, and behavioral design.[1]

#breakmydesign #evaluateoutcomes

Big tech companies design solutions that rely on data and algorithmic intelligence to change users' behavior. Unfortunately, these companies often use data in unethical ways such as automating the user's choice or developing addictive behaviors through digital solutions.

Digital Ethics Compass acts as an ethical navigator for companies and design teams to consider evaluating and refining their products using a set of heuristics, ethical recommendations, and ethical/unethical case studies. The compass can be read from the center outward to evaluate a part of or a complete digital product or service. At the center of the wheel are ethical principles that ground the design team, such as "put the human at the center" and "avoid manipulating." Moving outward, the compass provides designers with reflective ethical questions in several categories:

- **Data:** Products and services can be customized based on user data for personalization, but this data utilization is unequal since it is "the company that reaps all the benefits while customers are left without knowledge of or control over their own data."[1] Example heuristics include kinds of data points, length of data storage, data anonymization, and informing users about data profiles.

- **Automation:** Products are built with AI or algorithmic automation to improve efficiency, but "machines also make mistakes that can be quite significant and have serious consequences for humans."[1] Example heuristics include level of risk due to automation, hacking potential of automated systems, algorithmic prejudice, and compliance with legislation and human rights.

- **Behavior change:** Products use behavioral design techniques to help people make informed decisions, but these same techniques can be used to manipulate users through nudging or toying with emotions. Example heuristics include forms of emotions being used (positive or negative), difficulty in finding information or functionality, and validating vs. challenging users.

1. The digital ethics compass. (2021). *Danish Design Center.* https://ddc.dk/tools/toolkit-the-digital-ethics-compass/

Value Posture	Action Orientation	Ethical Framework
Eliciting values	Consensus building	Deontological
Critically engaging	Evaluating	Consequentialist
Defamiliarizing	Framing	Virtue
	Generating	Pragmatist

Method Input	Method Mechanic	Method Output
Concepts	Altering	Concepts
Stakeholder Info	Storytelling	Stakeholder Info
Constraints/Goals	Filtering	Constraints/Goals
Values	Creating	Values
Use Context	Mapping	Evaluation Outcomes

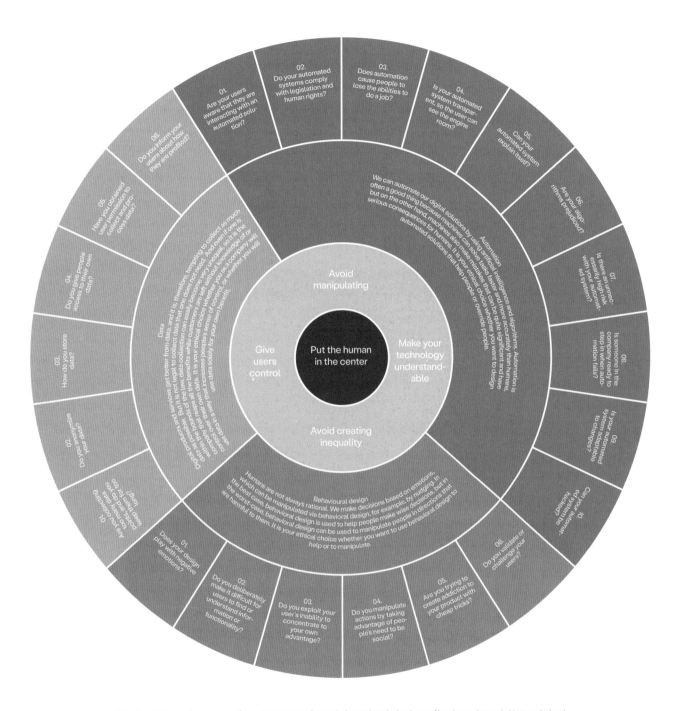

Put the human in the center

Avoid manipulating

Make your technology understandable

Avoid creating inequality

Give users control

Data

Digital products and services get better from data, and it is, therefore, tempting to collect as much as possible. But it is not legal to collect data that one does not need. And even if one is within the law, data collection can easily become very unequal, so it is the user who reaps all the benefits while customers are left without knowledge of or control over their own data. It is your ethical choice whether you as a company will use data in a way that increases people's sense of control, or whether you will use data solely for your own benefit.

01. Are you collecting too many data points and do you keep them too long?

02. Do you anonymize your data?

03. How do you store data?

04. Do you give people access to their own data?

05. Have you obtained user permission to collect and process data?

06. Do you inform your users about how they are profiled?

Automation

We can automate our digital solutions by using artificial intelligence and algorithms. Automation is often a good thing because machines can solve tasks faster and more accurately than humans, but on the other hand, machines also make mistakes that can be quite significant and have serious consequences for humans. It is your ethical choice whether you want to design automated solutions that help people or override people.

01. Are your users aware that they are interacting with an automated solution?

02. Do your automated systems comply with legislation and human rights?

03. Does automation cause people to lose the abilities to do a job?

04. Is your automated system transparent, so the user can see the engine room?

05. Can your automated system explain itself?

06. Are your algorithms prejudiced?

07. Is there an unnecessarily high risk with your automated system?

08. Is someone in the company ready to step in when automation fails?

09. Is your automated system adapted to changes?

10. Can your automated system be hacked?

Behavioural design

Humans are not always rational. We make decisions based on emotions, which can be manipulated via behavioral design, for example, by nudging. In the best case, behavioral design is used to help people make wise decisions, but in the worst case, behavioral design is used to manipulate people in directions that are harmful to them. It is your ethical choice whether you want to use behavioral design to help or to manipulate.

01. Does your design play with negative emotions?

02. Do you deliberately make it difficult for users to find or understand information or functionality?

03. Do you exploit your user's inability to concentrate to your own advantage?

04. Do you manipulate actions by taking advantage of people's need to be social?

05. Are you trying to create addiction to your product with cheap tricks?

06. Do you validate or challenge your users?

Digital Ethics Compass for designers to print and rotate to reflect on heuristics related to data, automation, and behavior change.

Image courtesy of the Danish Design Center (DDC).

See also DESIGN WITH INTENT • RESPONSIBLE AI PRACTICES

27 Dilemma Postcards

Dilemma Postcards provide a structure for you to express and share your stories of ethical dilemmas you face in your design work.[1]

#breakmydesign #alignmyteam #designresponsibility

Designers wrangle a wide range of issues through ethical decision-making and often express this process in the form of ethical dilemmas ("I am not sure if I should do something good or moral"), ethical tensions ("I need to see if I have to support my shareholder vs. user"), and/or ethical situations ("I went through this situation where I had to design...").[2]

Dilemma Postcards are tools to write, express, and share a designer's story relating to a dilemma they have faced. While writing a postcard, designers share a short story that engages clearly with the ethical dilemma faced in their design decision-making. The ethical dilemmas can be regarding one or a combination of products, people, interactions, and methods. The postcards then become the starting point for a bigger conversation about frequent ethical dilemmas designers face in a domain (health, finance), type of company (large, start-up), teams (internal, external, interdisciplinary), and/or line of decision-making (toward values, graphical design, trade-offs, evaluation).

Using the Dilemma Postcards, you can:

- Write to the CEO of your company, member of your team or other disciplinary team, manager, and interns—signing your name or anonymously—to share the regular ethical dilemmas you face in your design work.

- Post a card to "Whomsoever concerned" when you want to vent about an ethical dilemma that has been bothering your design work.

- Make it a regular team practice to position a Dilemma Post-Box and regularly share and resolve ethical dilemmas, tensions, or situations in your teams to create ethical products.

1. Chivukula, S. S. (2021). Dilemma postcards. *Shruthichivukula*. https://shruthichivukula.com/aeiou-toolkit/dilemmapostcards-ethicstool

2. Chivukula, S. S., Obi, I., Carlock, T. V., & Gray, C. M. (2023). Wrangling ethical design complexity: dilemmas, tensions, and situations. *Designing Interactive Systems Conference (DIS Companion '23)*. https://dl.acm.org/doi/abs/10.1145/3563703.3596632

Value Posture	Action Orientation	Ethical Framework
Eliciting values	Consensus building	Deontological
Critically engaging	Evaluating	Consequentialist
Defamiliarizing	Framing	Virtue
	Generating	Pragmatist

Method Input	Method Mechanic	Method Output
Concepts	Altering	Concepts
Stakeholder Info	Storytelling	Stakeholder Info
Constraints/Goals	Filtering	Constraints/Goals
Values	Creating	Values
Use Context	Mapping	Evaluation Outcomes

My contribution towards this system is the dilemma
I was working for a healthcare employer. Looking at the system in a
healthcare industry, made me think about the money flow in this system
and my contribution towards it, about how much I get paid, how much
the hospitals pay for the software, and how that impacts how patients
have to pay higher bills.

During this time, I was working as a designer to build a solution that
compares doctors based on how many deaths they've had over a certain
amount of time. Because you are servicing all this information, a
stakeholder in the system I am designing for might get fired. But, you
can't surface all of the information behind, like why that person
might have died. The context makes so much difference, but the interpretation is for someone
doing all you can to design, but the interpretation is for someone
else who manages that person. Although you are not an ultimate decision maker, surfacing what feels like the worse information about some
type of professionals was not the best feeling.

Danielle Guerrero's Story

Dilemma Postcard written by an
UX designer sharing a dilemma
related to industry standards.

Images courtesy of Sai Shruthi Chivukula.

EXAMPLE DILEMMA:

I was a designer at a company in the real estate industry. I was supposed to design a client profile for the agents to see their clients' browsing activity, so that the agents could have a better idea of what is interesting to the clients. It is well known in the industry that "buyers are liars," and that a client profile is a typical way to help the agents understand their clients. I was really uncomfortable with this direction, but I could not turn down what apparently is an industry standard that is technically legal, not to mention that the agents are only trying to make a living while sometimes clients do try to get a deal by not telling the full truth. Fortunately, after voicing my concerns to my boss, I was given the space to experiment with alternatives, and I came up with a much more ethical design that would allow for mutual exchange of information between an agent and a client. In short, my strategy was to replace the industry standard with something better.

See also ETHICAL TENSION CARDS • ETHICAL CONTRACT

28 Diverse Voices

Diverse Voices allows you to expand expert reviews of draft tech policy documents to include underrepresented "experiential experts."[1]

#evaluateoutcomes #newperspectives

The development and evaluation of technology policies often include practices of expert review, whereby different stakeholders and experts can provide input on the final form and potential impact of policy documents. However, these processes can often neglect the full range of stakeholders that are impacted, particularly those that come from underrepresented populations.

Diverse Voices encourages your team to discuss emerging technology issues and related policies with "experiential experts," using these expert perspectives to inform the further development of draft technology policy documents.[1] Types of experience can include lived experience, institutional or organizational experience, and forms of social support given to those in groups of interest.

Use the following steps to introduce experiential experts into your process:[2]

1. **Select a tech policy document.** Identify a document that is still in the draft or comment phase, where the authors are open to making improvements based on feedback.

2. **Surface relevant underrepresented groups.** Brainstorm groups that will use the technology, not use the technology, or be implicated or overlooked.

3. **Assemble a panel of experiential experts.** Introduce the experts and their connection to the relevant underrepresented group and solicit open-ended and directed feedback on the technology, document, and panel process.

4. **Synthesize panel feedback.** Construct and synthesize key themes based on review of panel transcripts.

5. **Provide panel feedback.** Follow up with technology policy document authors and panelists, sharing the revised document and related rationale.

1. Diverse voices: a how-to guide for creating more inclusive tech policy documents. (n.d.). *Tech Policy Lab.* Retrieved May 12, 2020, from https://techpolicylab.uw.edu/news/diverse-voices-guide/

2. Quoted and synthesized from Diverse Voices.

Value Posture	Action Orientation	Ethical Framework
Eliciting values	Consensus building	Deontological
Critically engaging	Evaluating	Consequentialist
Defamiliarizing	Framing	Virtue
	Generating	Pragmatist

Method Input	Method Mechanic	Method Output
Concepts	Altering	Concepts
Stakeholder Info	Storytelling	Stakeholder Info
Constraints/Goals	Filtering	Constraints/Goals
Values	Creating	Values
Use Context	Mapping	Evaluation Outcomes

DIVERSE VOICES

A HOW-TO GUIDE FOR FACILITATING INCLUSIVENESS IN TECH POLICY

TECH POLICY LAB | UNIVERSITY OF WASHINGTON

Overview

The importance of creating inclusive policy cannot be overstated. In response to this challenge, the UW Tech Policy Lab (TPL) developed the Diverse Voices method in 2015. The method uses short, targeted conversations about emerging technology with "experiential experts" from under-represented groups to provide feedback on draft tech policy documents. This process works to increase the likelihood that the language in the finalized tech policy document addresses the perspectives and circumstances of broader groups of people—ideally averting injustice and exclusion.

MAIN STEPS IN THE METHOD

- Select a tech policy document
- Surface relevant under-represented groups
- Assemble a panel of experiential experts who represent those groups to examine and respond to the tech policy document
- Synthesize panel feedback
- Provide panel feedback to tech policy document authors

▶ About this Guide

The TPL seeks to make this process available to any group wanting to improve a draft technology policy document. This Guide provides detailed instructions and materials for using the Diverse Voices method. The Guide is organized as follows: (1) overview of the method, (2) planning for panel discussions, (3) running panels, (4) analyzing panel conversations, and (5) providing feedback to authors. A Frequently Asked Questions section and glossary precede appendices, which include sample letters, forms, materials and checklists useful for implementing the Diverse Voices method.

diversevoices@techpolicylab.org

▶ Key Terms

Here we provide definitions for key terms. We acknowledge that some of these terms may be contested, in part, due to the way in which language may reflect power relations and implicit assumptions.

Tech Policy Document
An informative, authoritative report designed to familiarize lawmakers with a technology and its policy implications. For example, a white paper or policy strategy.

Mainstream
We use the term *mainstream* to describe the segments of the population represented in conventional approaches to technology policy research, development, and writing.

Under-represented Group
We use the term *under-represented group* to refer to a segment of the population that is often insufficiently consulted in the policymaking process due to factors such as structural inequality across racial, socio-economic, and other lines.

Tech Policy Document Author
A person(s) who writes a tech policy document.

Experiential Expert
People who have either lived experience as a member of a particular group or those closely associated with someone with this experience (such as family members or institutional advocates).

Expert Panel
A group of experiential experts assembled to comment on a tech policy document.

Facilitator
A person who moderates the expert panels, synthesizes the panel discussion, and provides the resulting feedback to the tech policy document author(s).

Reference sheet for Diverse Voices, including key terms and steps to complete the method.

See also *MORAL AND LEGAL DECKS • PARTICIPATORY DESIGN*

29 Empathic Walk-Through

Empathic Walk-Through supports you in creating new design ideas that arise through empathizing deeply with the end user and their context of use.[1]

#breakmydesign #evaluateoutcomes #newperspectives

Designers often need to evaluate whether their solutions take a user's needs, perspective, and goals into account. However, linking insights from user research to design decisions can sometimes be challenging.

The Empathic Walk-Through, building on the common cognitive walk-through method, supports design teams in identifying and activating user needs. Through role-play, designers identify critical information that comes from performing key action sequences to intentionally iterate on existing solutions. Using this approach, designers can generate new solutions, which are more likely to resonate with the lived experience of the people who will use the final product or service.

The Empathic Walk-Through can be conducted with two or more designers:[1]

1. **Use a story to activate the action needed for each task.** A designer uses their knowledge of the target user population to tell a story about an existing design concept, taking into consideration how a user might conduct some interactions that might include multiple steps over different points in times and/or locations.

2. **Record critical information.** During the user story, another designer identifies parts of the concept that were confusing or strange, that somehow seemed inappropriate to the user, or that didn't work correctly.

3. **Group concerns.** After the user story and listing of concerns is complete, the designers work together to group the concerns into five categories: form, function, temporal, use/user, and system.

4. **Generate targeted ideas.** Using the concerns grouped by categories as a point of departure, the participant(s) generate new ideas within each category. Design Heuristics prompts[2] or other ideation heuristics can be used as a set of strategies to create additional concepts.

1. Gray, C., Yilmaz, S., Daly, S., Seifert, C., & Gonzalez, R. (2015). Idea generation through empathy: reimagining the 'cognitive walkthrough.' *2015 ASEE Annual Conference and Exposition Proceedings*, 122nd ASEE, 26.871.1-26.871.29. https://doi.org/10.18260/p.24208

2. Yilmaz, S., Daly, S. R., Seifert, C. M., & Gonzalez, R. (2016). Evidence-based design heuristics for idea generation. *Design Studies, 46*, 95-124. https://doi.org/10.1016/j.destud.2016.05.001

Value Posture	Action Orientation	Ethical Framework
Eliciting values	Consensus building	Deontological
Critically engaging	Evaluating	Consequentialist
Defamiliarizing	Framing	Virtue
	Generating	Pragmatist

Method Input	Method Mechanic	Method Output
Concepts	Altering	Concepts
Stakeholder Info	Storytelling	Stakeholder Info
Constraints/Goals	Filtering	Constraints/Goals
Values	Creating	Values
Use Context	Mapping	Evaluation Outcomes

WALK THROUGH THE USER STORY → **LIST & GROUP INFORMATION** → **TARGETED IDEA GENERATION**

PERSONA + TASK / TASK

Form
Function
Use/User
Temporal
System

FLATTEN 35
CREATE SERVICE 28

Steps to complete the Empathic Walk-Through, including telling a user story with a persona, listing and grouping critical information that emerges through the story, and then using that information to guide targeted idea generation through the use of Design Heuristics or another ideation support tool.

Image courtesy of Colin M. Gray and reproduced with permission from Gray et al. (2015).

Dimension	Dimension Definition	Example Design Heuristics[2]
Form	Form of the product	#32: Expand or collapse #38: Impose hierarchy on functions #55: Repurpose packaging
Function	Functions embedded in the product	#5: Adjust function through movement #16: Bend #50: Provide sensory feedback
Temporal	Use/function of the product over time or relation to sociocultural environment	#13: Apply existing mechanism in new way #21: Change product lifetime #46: Mimic natural mechanisms
Use/User	Situated use of the product or user interactions with the product	#9: Allow user to customize #10: Allow user to rearrange #40: Incorporate user input
System	Context in which the product is used or systems/services the product relies on	#24: Contextualize #28: Create service #29: Create system

Descriptions of the five dimensions that critical information can be grouped into with examples of Design Heuristics cards aligned with each dimension.

Table reproduced from Gray et al. (2015).

See also MOTIVATION MATRIX • WORRYSTORMING • MORAL AGENT

30 Envisioning Cards

Envisioning Cards help you imagine the future impacts of your product or service by considering stakeholders, values, time, multi-lifespan, and pervasiveness.[1]

#newperspectives #identifyvalues

Products and services are not static and continue to evolve over time. Engaging with the product life cycle in a generative way can allow you to envision the potential impacts of a product or service before, during, and after its launch into the surrounding community and larger society.[2]

Envisioning Cards guide and support your identification and consideration of potential impacts your product or services might produce in a multifaceted manner, using four lenses to guide your evaluation:[3]

- **Stakeholders** include a range of direct stakeholders (who come in contact with the product or service) and indirect stakeholders (who are affected by interactions with or by the product or service). Ask questions such as *What ways can we build our product to anticipate how children or new mothers might use our product?*

- **Values** emphasize the impact of the product or service on human values. For instance, if you consider the value of environmental sustainability, you might ask question such as *How could our product have unintended negative effects on the environment (e.g., pollution and waste created in the production of electronics)?*

- **Time** guides you to consider longer temporal effects of the product or service upon integration or later appropriation by society. Ask questions such as *How might a person's deliberate non-use of our system affect their daily life (e.g., employability, relationships, civic participation)?*

- **Pervasiveness** incorporates a range of policies, norms, customs, or infrastructure that impacts the use of your product or service as a user cross geographic or cultural boundaries. Ask questions such as *What challenges might a user encounter when using your system in another country?*

- **Multi-lifespan** forecasts the impact and considerations of temporal longevity and cycles of use of your product or service. Ask questions such as *What would happen to the product in the next fifty years?*

1. Friedman, B., & Hendry, D. (2012). The envisioning cards: a toolkit for catalyzing humanistic and technical imaginations. *Proceedings of the SIGCHI Conference on Human Factors in Computing Systems*, 1145–1148. https://doi.org/10.1145/2207676.2208562

2. Friedman, B., Nathan, L., Kane, S., Lin, J., Yoo, D., Logler, N., Ballard, S., and Hendry, D. G. (2024). *Envisioning cards: a value sensitive design toolkit* (2nd Ed.). University of Washington. https://vsdesign.org/toolkits/envisioningcards/

3. Adapted from Friedman & Hendry (2012).

Further Reading

VSD lab. (n.d.). https://vsdesign.org/toolkits/

Value Posture	Action Orientation	Ethical Framework
Eliciting values	Consensus building	Deontological
Critically engaging	Evaluating	Consequentialist
Defamiliarizing	Framing	Virtue
	Generating	Pragmatist

Method Input	Method Mechanic	Method Output
Concepts	Altering	Concepts
Stakeholder Info	Storytelling	Stakeholder Info
Constraints/Goals	Filtering	Constraints/Goals
Values	Creating	Values
Use Context	Mapping	Evaluation Outcomes

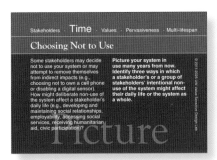

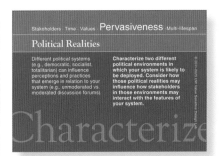

Examples of the Envisioning Cards, illustrating the differences in envisioning criteria, themes, and suggested design activities.

Image courtesy of the University of Washington Value Sensitive Design Lab licensed under a Creative Commons, Attribution-NonCommercial-NoDerivatives 4.0 International License.

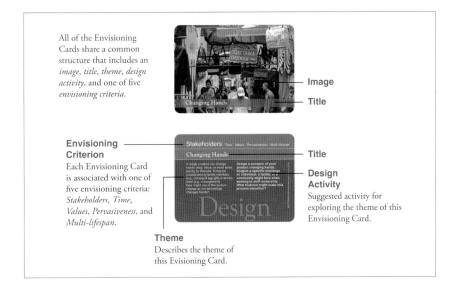

All of the Envisioning Cards share a common structure that includes an *image, title, theme, design activity,* and one of five *envisioning criteria.*

Image

Title

Envisioning Criterion
Each Envisioning Card is associated with one of five envisioning criteria: *Stakeholders, Time, Values, Pervasiveness,* and *Multi-lifespan.*

Title

Design Activity
Suggested activity for exploring the theme of this Envisioning Card.

Theme
Describes the theme of this Evisioning Card.

31 Ethical Blueprint

Ethical Blueprint enables you to visualize and reconstruct your task flows and information architecture elements, elevating user agency by incorporating Fair Patterns.[1]

#breakmydesign #applyvalues #alignmyteam

Task flows and the information architecture (IA) of digital product interfaces can promote user agency and fairness or create restrictions through forced action or obstruction that reduce user choice.[2] When ideating on potential design alternative, the designer needs to consider the multiple pathways and IA elements to enable a user to choose their actions across a range of interface types (e.g., apps, services with a voice UI, IoT device).

Ethical Blueprint incorporates specific actions that support user values when creating task flows, information architecture, and interaction flows, enabling designers to incorporate ethical considerations in their design systems. To create an Ethical Blueprint for a product or service:[3]

1. Identify the values you want to use to assess your task flows and information architecture, for instance, by leveraging values in existing methods such as HuValue or Fair Patterns.

2. Sketch elements of the information architecture for specific user tasks (e.g., onboarding, authentication, shopping, profile).

3. Evaluate how those elements are connected to each other in the architecture.

4. Use the selected value(s) and Fair Patterns to consider how the elements and/or connections between elements celebrate or obstruct the chosen value(s).

5. Reconstruct the information architecture using insights you derive to create a structure that celebrates user agency.

1. Falbe, T., Frederiksen, M. M., & Andersen, K. (2020). *Ethical Design Handbook*. https://ethicaldesignhandbook.com/

2. Deceptive patterns (aka dark patterns). (n.d.). https://www.deceptive.design/

3. Adapted from Falbe et al. (2020).

Value Posture	Action Orientation	Ethical Framework
Eliciting values	Consensus building	Deontological
Critically engaging	Evaluating	Consequentialist
Defamiliarizing	Framing	Virtue
	Generating	Pragmatist

Method Input	Method Mechanic	Method Output
Concepts	Altering	Concepts
Stakeholder Info	Storytelling	Stakeholder Info
Constraints/Goals	Filtering	Constraints/Goals
Values	Creating	Values
Use Context	Mapping	Evaluation Outcomes

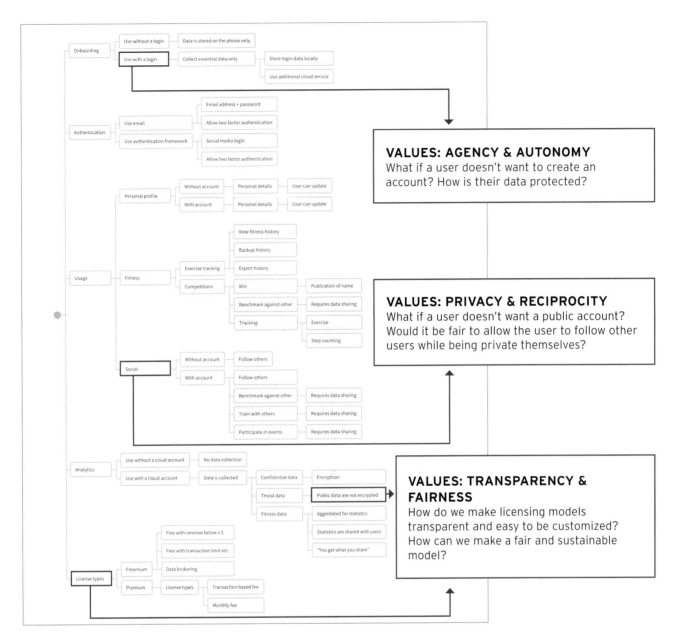

An example of an Ethical Blueprint for a fitness app that focuses attention on human values during Onboarding, Authentication, Usage, Analytics, and Licensing. Each part of the blueprint can be inspected and annotated based on values that the design team selects and uses to interpret the blueprint. More examples of Ethical Blueprints to adapt are available on the book website.[1]

Image courtesy of Trine Falbe, reproduced with permission from the Ethical Design Handbook.[1]

32 Ethical Contract

Ethical Contract enables your team to negotiate, share, and sign ethical objectives for your product with all stakeholders.[1]

#identifyvalues #alignmyteam

Design is a collaborative activity that involves a range of stakeholders, including designers, software developers, business stakeholders, product managers, and CEOs/founders. Every stakeholder has their own set of values that they negotiate as part of the product, and a lack of consensus can lead to value trade-offs within the design product. To balance or avoid value trade-offs, all stakeholders must be aligned and find a shared ethical foundation to shape the features of the product or service.

Ethical Contract[1] enables stakeholders involved in a product's development to make their ethical responsibility a contractual procedure as a part of that alignment process, indicating that ethical action is a shared responsibility. Creating an Ethical Contract requires all of the stakeholders involved in product development to discuss unethical situations that might potentially arise, collectively deriving and defining a set of ethical themes and objectives that they will follow throughout the product development process. The contract includes ways to divide and clearly state ethical responsibilities among different stakeholders, writing a design goal based on the ethical objectives, and placing a signature for each stakeholder as a gesture of commitment to shared ethical responsibility.

The Ethical Contract can be used to:

- Document shared ethical responsibility of your design team with other disciplinary teams.

- List and divide individual responsibilities for designing based on values in your design team.

- Create and share an ethical manifesto of design action among current and new members of your team.

1. Gispen, J. (2017). Ethical contract. *Ethics for Designers.* https://www.ethicsfordesigners.com/ethical-contract

Further Reading

Gispen, J. (2017). Ethics for designers toolkit. *Ethics for Designers.* https://www.ethicsfordesigners.com/tools

Value Posture	Action Orientation	Ethical Framework
Eliciting values	Consensus building	Deontological
Critically engaging	Evaluating	Consequentialist
Defamiliarizing	Framing	Virtue
	Generating	Pragmatist

Method Input	Method Mechanic	Method Output
Concepts	Altering	Concepts
Stakeholder Info	Storytelling	Stakeholder Info
Constraints/Goals	Filtering	Constraints/Goals
Values	Creating	Values
Use Context	Mapping	Evaluation Outcomes

Ethical contract

Designing is never a solitary act. Therefore it is important that everyone is on the same page. This technique guides you in a value negotiation with all stakeholders involved in order to find common ethical ground.

PROCESS

1 Explain your disclaimer to all involved stakeholders.

2 Go through the unethical situations and collect important ethical themes. Collectively define these themes for this project.

3 Discuss who is responsible for each situation. Write everyone's responsibilities down.

4 Formulate three main ethical objectives everyone agrees on. Make sure everyone knows what they mean.

5 Write down (an updated version of) the design goal as agreed upon by all stakeholders.

6 Place your signatures to commit to the design goal and ethical objectives.

SPECS

Suggested Time
30 - 45 minutes

Materials needed
An ethical disclaimer, this template, pens

Participants
Design team, stakeholders

Process phase
Framing, validating

for more tools check out:
www.ethicsfordesigners.com

1. EXPLAIN YOUR ETHICAL DISCLAIMER TO THE STAKEHOLDERS

2. DEFINE IMPORTANT ETHICAL THEMES:

THEME
DEFINITION

3. DIVIDE THE RESPONSIBILITIES:

NAME | RESPONSIBILITIES

4. OUR MAIN ETHICAL OBJECTIVES ARE...

1

2

3

5. OUR DESIGN GOAL IS...

6. PLACE SIGNATURES:

Toolkit Ethics for Designers

Ethical Contract template, including instructions to explain the ethical disclaimer, define important ethical themes, divide the responsibilities by team member, outline shared ethical objectives, and identify the ultimate design goal with signatures from all team members.

Image courtesy of Jet Gispen.

See also ETHICAL DISCLAIMER · PLEDGE WORKS

33 Ethical Design Scorecards

Ethical Design Scorecards allow you to assess and investigate the ethical implications of your products and services by choosing and weighting relevant assessment criteria.[1]

#evaluateoutcomes #applyvalues #alignmyteam

When working with multiple stakeholders to evaluate whether a product is ethically grounded, objective criteria can be useful in aligning perspectives to ensure that all stakeholders share the same standards of assessment. These standards of assessment can then be shared and weighted in relation to their relative ethical impact within a specific design organization, team, or product type.

The Ethical Design Scorecard is an assessment technique that is part of "a systematic approach to assessing the ethical level of products, businesses, and practices."[1] This method helps designers and teams investigate the ethical implications of their products and services. The method employs a weighted assessment to determine the ethical implications of different criteria (e.g., "users are not encouraged to submit information about other users"; "it is easy for users to see if information is stored on their own device or on a server"[1]) and provides information on areas that require improvement and those that are going well.

To complete an Ethical Design Scorecard, complete the following steps:[2]

1. Download the sample Excel sheet from the website or create your own tracking sheet with columns for the evaluation score (from 1 to 5), the weight (from 0 to 100), and the total criterion score (evaluation x weight).

2. Select the domain for evaluation within the Excel sheet (e.g., Data Science, UX).

3. Conduct your assessment by choosing a score for each assessment criterion.

4. Reflect on the resulting scores and determine ways for your team to respond or improve the product or service.

1. Falbe, T., Frederiksen, M. M., & Andersen, K. (2020). *Ethical Design Handbook*. https://ethicaldesignhandbook.com/

2. Adapted from https://ethicaldesignhandbook.com.

Value Posture	Action Orientation	Ethical Framework
Eliciting values	Consensus building	Deontological
Critically engaging	Evaluating	Consequentialist
Defamiliarizing	Framing	Virtue
	Generating	Pragmatist

Method Input	Method Mechanic	Method Output
Concepts	Altering	Concepts
Stakeholder Info	Storytelling	Stakeholder Info
Constraints/Goals	Filtering	Constraints/Goals
Values	Creating	Values
Use Context	Mapping	Evaluation Outcomes

Data storage

	1-5 Evaluation	0-100 Weighting	E x W Score
Data is stored in a secure location	1	100	100
Backups are encrypted	1	100	100
Access to stored data is limited to a minimum of staff	1	80	80
There are strong requirements for decryption of backups	1	90	90
In case of a security compromise, data in the database is hashed	1	90	90
There is a process for testing the security of the server and the network (penetration test)	1	100	100
In the case of multiple profiles on one account, user profiles are uniquely identifiable	1	50	50
When a user deletes their data via the front end, the data is also deleted from all backup files	1	100	100
No third parties (such as a cloud service) have access to our users' data. Admin rights to the database are never placed at the cloud service.	1	100	100
There is a test process to verify correct data storage	1	100	100
Actual score (highest possible score: 4150)			830
Test result quotient			**20**

An example of an Ethical Design Scorecard, including criteria for evaluating ethical components of your project related to data collection. Each criterion is evaluated on a scale from 1 to 5 and weighted based on their "impact on ethics."[1]

Image courtesy of Trine Falbe.

See also ETHICS ASSESSMENT • HUMANE DESIGN GUIDE • TAO FRAMEWORK

34 Ethical Disclaimer

Ethical Disclaimer allows you to identify potentially unethical outcomes earlier in the design process and identify what situations you will take responsibility for as designer.[1]

#breakmydesign #identifyvalues #alignmyteam

Products and services have intended or unintended impacts depending on the kinds of relevant stakeholders, types of users, and diversity of contexts and purposes. Designers often wonder how, or to what extent, they should identify their role in these impacts, particularly relating to unforeseen impacts through the products or services they designed.

Ethical Disclaimer is a living document that helps a designer evaluate and document their intentions, potential unethical situations, responsibilities, and nonresponsibilities through the design of a product or service:[1]

- To begin drafting an Ethical Disclaimer, designers need to clearly define their current design situation, their design intentions in relation to users, context and purpose, and direct and indirect stakeholders who might and can interact with the design product and service.

- Based on these drafted details, the designer can imagine and identify unethical situations that might result from the design product for stakeholders, contexts, and purposes that are different from what they originally envisioned. By asking the question *"How will they use/contribute to/gain from/be harmed by your design?,"*[2] identify what situations you take responsibility for and what unethical situations you do not take responsibility for based on your intentions.

- Ethical Disclaimer can be constantly used, updated, and expanded as the design outcomes become more concrete and the potential unethical situations become more evident.

1. Gispen, J. (2017). Ethical disclaimer. *Ethics for Designers.* https://www.ethicsfordesigners.com/ethical-disclaimer

2. Quoted from Gispen, 2017.

Further Reading

Gispen, J. (2017). Ethics for designers toolkit. *Ethics for Designers.* https://www.ethicsfordesigners.com/tools

Value Posture	Action Orientation	Ethical Framework
Eliciting values	Consensus building	Deontological
Critically engaging	Evaluating	Consequentialist
Defamiliarizing	Framing	Virtue
	Generating	Pragmatist

Method Input	Method Mechanic	Method Output
Concepts	Altering	Concepts
Stakeholder Info	Storytelling	Stakeholder Info
Constraints/Goals	Filtering	Constraints/Goals
Values	Creating	Values
Use Context	Mapping	Evaluation Outcomes

Ethical disclaimer

This tool helps you set the ethical terms at the start of your project. Use your imagination to think of unethical situations and discuss what you'll take responsibility for as designers.

PROCESS

1 Describe the current situation of your design context.

2 List all the people/companies/ institutions that have an interest in, or are affected by your design. Both direct stakeholders such as users and your client and indirect such as maintenance.

3 Write down your intentions. Be specific in terms of users, context and purpose. The more explicit, the easier you can discuss them with stakeholders throughout the project.

4 Imagine the context with your design in it. (If you don't know yet what you're designing, think of ways to change the current situation.) Think of situations with your design which might be unethical. Think from the perspective of the different stakeholders. How will they use/contribute to/gain from/be harmed by your design? Use post-its to speed things up.

5 Discuss for which of the unethical situations you will take responsibility by moving them down to the left or right section of the template. Substantiate your choices.

Note: the ethical disclaimer is a living document. As the design develops and becomes more concrete, so will the potential unethical situations. Therefore it is important to update the disclaimer at project milestones and discuss changes with all stakeholders.

SPECS

Suggested Time
45 - 60 minutes
Materials needed
This template, post-its, pens
Participants
Design team, stakeholders if possible
Process phase
Framing, envisioning, validating

for more tools check out:
www.ethicsfordesigners.com

---

1. THE CURRENT SITUATION IS...

2. THE STAKEHOLDERS ARE...

3. OUR DESIGN INTENTIONS ARE...
What do you want to change in the current situation? Why?

4. UNETHICAL SITUATIONS WITH OUR DESIGN...
What dark, wrong or weird situations can you come up with? What would be really wrong?
What happens when it is used over a longer period of time?
What if it is used by the 'wrong' people? Or shared by different people?
What if it is used in a different context? Or for a different purpose? Or combined with other technology?
Who can access it? What happens if people hack it?

5. WE TAKE RESPONSIBILITY FOR...
Which situations fall within the ethical scope of the project? Why?

5. WE DO NOT TAKE RESPONSIBILITY FOR...
Which situations are outside the ethical scope of the project? Why?
Which might be someone else's responsibility?

Toolkit Ethics for Designers

Ethical Disclaimer template, including instructions to explain the current situation, outline stakeholders and design intentions, indicate potentially unethical situations, and outline which situations the team does and does not take responsibility for.

Image courtesy of Jet Gispen.

See also ETHICAL CONTRACT • ETHICS CANVAS

35 Ethical Explorer

Ethical Explorer asks you to consider eight Tech Risk Zones such as algorithmic bias, bad actors, and disinformation in order to avoid potential risks to the company or society.[1]

#breakmydesign #evaluateoutcomes

Technology development results in not only positive developments for society but also issues such as privacy breaches, surveillance capitalism, AI bias and discrimination, and automated system failures. Designers need to continuously explore and question the potential downsides and risks associated with technological development in order to minimize or avoid these issues.

Ethical Explorer helps you facilitate conversations about these risks, "scout[ing] early warning signs, and build[ing] support for risk management."[1] The Explorer Pack includes a field guide for ethical navigators to explore their ethical responsibility. An example of some of the eight Tech Risk Zones are summarized below:[2]

- **Disinformation** results in intentionally deceiving users with bots pretending to be humans, deep fakes, and political campaign ads. Navigate this risk by asking: *How will we promote truth?*

- **Exclusion** highlights the risk of benefiting only the wealthy and literate, resulting in decreased access to digital literacy and representational bias. Mitigate this risk by asking: *How will we promote equity and include historically marginalized populations?*

- **Algorithmic bias** creates biases in AI systems, racial misrepresentation, and social inequality. Change this by asking: *How will we promote fairness?* at all stages of your development.

- **Addiction** manifests in tangible societal harms, including being unable to resist digital interactions and unhealthy consumer retention practices. Address this risk by asking: *How will we promote healthier behaviors?*

- **Outsized power** is the result of powerful industries abusing power, suppliers squeezing in unfavorable terms, and prioritizing market dominance. Keep this risk in check by asking: *How will we promote choice?*

1. The ethical explorer pack. (2020, June 18). *Artefact.* https://www.artefactgroup.com/case-studies/ethical-explorer-pack/

2. Quoted from The Ethical Explorer Pack (2020).

Value Posture	Action Orientation	Ethical Framework
Eliciting values	Consensus building	Deontological
Critically engaging	Evaluating	Consequentialist
Defamiliarizing	Framing	Virtue
	Generating	Pragmatist

Method Input	Method Mechanic	Method Output
Concepts	Altering	Concepts
Stakeholder Info	Storytelling	Stakeholder Info
Constraints/Goals	Filtering	Constraints/Goals
Values	Creating	Values
Use Context	Mapping	Evaluation Outcomes

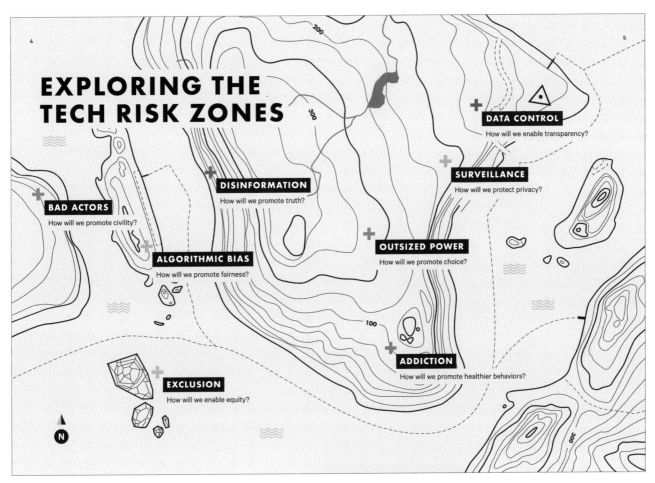

EXPLORING THE TECH RISK ZONES

BAD ACTORS
How will we promote civility?

DISINFORMATION
How will we promote truth?

DATA CONTROL
How will we enable transparency?

SURVEILLANCE
How will we protect privacy?

ALGORITHMIC BIAS
How will we promote fairness?

OUTSIZED POWER
How will we promote choice?

ADDICTION
How will we promote healthier behaviors?

EXCLUSION
How will we enable equity?

Eight Tech Risk Zones defined in the
Ethical Explorer Pack.

Image courtesy of Omidyar Network and Artefact Group.

EXCLUSION
LEFT OUT

EXCLUSION

Technology products and services touch many
aspects of our society, yet only a limited few influence
and create them.

Technology's benefits are increasingly a privilege
for the wealthy and digitally literate. Meanwhile,
historically marginalized populations suffer higher
consequences from a lack of data privacy and literacy,
like overrepresentation in the criminal justice system
and decreased access to tools that impact social
or financial mobility.

When technology is designed for a group of people,
and not *with* them, inequities inevitably emerge.

**How will we
enable equity?**

An example of one of the cards focusing on the
Exclusion Tech Risk Zone.

Image courtesy of Omidyar Network and Artefact Group.

See also RESPONSIBLE AI PRACTICES • BAD DESIGN CANVAS

36 Ethical Tension Cards

Ethical Tension Cards allow you to reflect on your present or past ethical tensions in design work, during team discussions, and within organizational structures.[1]

#alignmyteam #designresponsibility

Practitioners face a range of ethical tensions and dilemmas during their everyday design work due to the interplay of disciplinary values, personal values, design actions, organizational policies, and potential impacts. Ethical tensions can include felt conflicts, ethical dilemmas, or hypothetical conflicts or quandaries[2] that might lead to future ethically complex challenges in one's everyday decision-making.

Ethical Tension Cards provide a set of ethical tensions that practitioners face, focusing on:

- **Reflecting** about their present ethical tensions to surface moments that need more support or tools ("*I am facing this tension. How can I solve?*").

- **Considering** past ethical tensions to realize scaffolds for resolution ("*I have faced this tension before and this is how I solved it*").

- **Discussing** frequently experienced ethical tensions that can be proactively addressed through relevant tools ("*I was aware of a few tensions that might occur. What can I look out for?*").

- **Identifying** unfaced ethical tensions that are relevant to particular disciplines and reflect a solution ("*I have never faced these tensions. How would I handle it when I have to face it?*").

In a team setting, you can use Ethical Tension Cards to evaluate your current work practices and see which tensions you can change, reduce, or remove.

1. Chivukula, S. S. (2023). Ethical dilemmas/tension cards. *shruthichivukula*. https://shruthichivukula.com/aeiou-toolkit/dilemma-cards-elicitation-ethicstool

2. Chivukula, S. S., Obi, I., Carlock, T. V., & Gray, C. M. (2023). Wrangling ethical design complexity: dilemmas, tensions, and situations. *Designing Interactive Systems Conference (DIS Companion '23)*. https://dl.acm.org/doi/abs/10.1145/3563703.3596632

Value Posture	Action Orientation	Ethical Framework
Eliciting values	Consensus building	Deontological
Critically engaging	Evaluating	Consequentialist
Defamiliarizing	Framing	Virtue
	Generating	Pragmatist

Method Input	Method Mechanic	Method Output
Concepts	Altering	Concepts
Stakeholder Info	Storytelling	Stakeholder Info
Constraints/Goals	Filtering	Constraints/Goals
Values	Creating	Values
Use Context	Mapping	Evaluation Outcomes

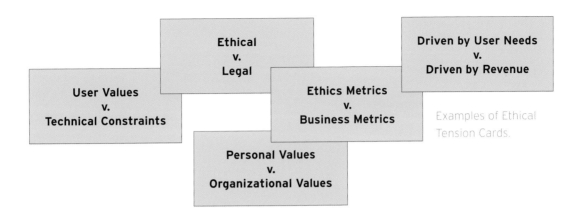

Examples of Ethical Tension Cards.

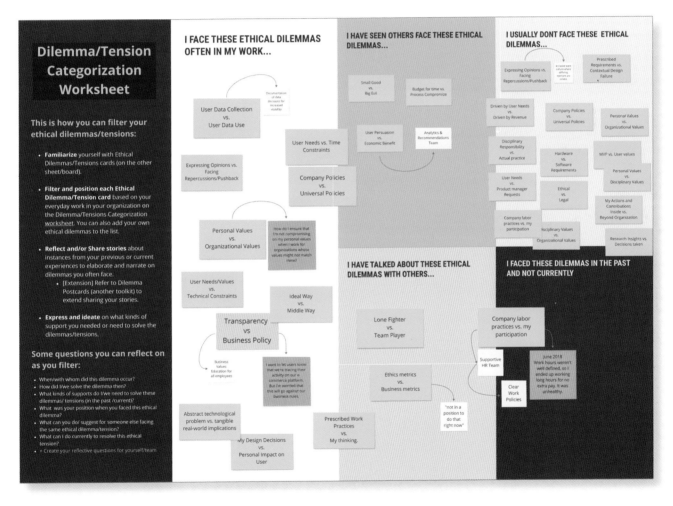

Ethical Tension Cards filtered in a Categorization Worksheet using a set of Tension Cards (in green) and personalized Tensions (in yellow) alongside stories and potential ways to resolve them (in orange).

Image courtesy of Sai Shruthi Chivukula.

See also ETHICS PATHWAYS • DILEMMA CARDS • LAKE OF ETHICAL TENSIONS

37 Ethicography

Ethicography enables design researchers to describe the ethical nuances of collaborative design decisions by linking value-centered and manipulative intentions.[1]

#breakmydesign #identifyvalues

Design activity is often a product of collaborative decision-making, whereby designers inscribe their own values and expectations into design outcomes. Throughout this process, designers consider different ideas and intentions, interacting with these components by extending, discarding, or modifying them either on their own or with other designers in the team. In this exchange, value-centered or manipulative intentions are temporally dispersed as part of the co-evolution of problem and solution.[2] Design researchers have used the Linkography method[3] to trace the evolution of ideas and links within a conversation. Ethicography is an ethically focused extension of this method, facilitating analysis of the value relationships that are implicitly and explicitly present in designers' decisions.

Ethicography starts with identifying each speech act of a designer as either value-centered (in blue) or manipulative (in orange), and related to a problem or a solution. Each speech act is then represented as a node on the ethicograph. As the conversation progresses, each node is connected with other related nodes that relate to the same problem or solution. The ethicograph provides an account of the evolution and extension of value-centered or manipulative moves by the designers, revealing what human values were considered, what manipulative intentions lie behind the considered human values, how quickly ethical decisions were taken, and how the links relate to or result in ethical outcomes.

In evaluating an ethicograph, links can reveal ethical complexity relating to design decisions:

- Links that are deep and densely interwoven can expose temporally dispersed decision-making, including how certain decisions were explicitly or implicitly considered.

- Links between two or more value-centered or manipulative speech acts describe how the designer's intentions are being extended based on human values or business values.

- Links between a value-centered and manipulative speech act describe moments when the designers switched from supporting human values to business values (or vice versa).

1. Chivukula, S. S., Gray, C. M., & Brier, J. A. (2019). Analyzing value discovery in design decisions through ethicography. *Proceedings of the 2019 CHI Conference on Human Factors in Computing Systems*, Article Paper 77. https://doi.org/10.1145/3290605.3300307

2. Chivukula, S. S., & Gray, C. M. (2020). Co-evolving towards evil design outcomes: mapping problem and solution process moves. *DRS Biennial Conference Series*. https://doi.org/10.21606/drs.2020.107

3. Goldschmidt, G. (2014). *Linkography: unfolding the design process*. MIT Press.

Further Reading

Ahuja, S., & Kumar, J. (2024). Understanding ethical thinking in design education: a linkographic study. *Proceedings of the 6th Annual Symposium on HCI Education*, 1–11. https://doi.org/10.1145/3658619.3658620

Chivukula, S. S., & Gray, C. M. (2024). Quant-ethico: an approach to quantifying and interpreting ethical decision making. In Gray, C. M., Ciliotta Chehade, E., Hekkert, P., Forlano, L., Ciuccarelli, P., Lloyd, P. (Ed.), *Proceedings of DRS. Design Research Society*. https://doi.org/10.21606/drs.2024.223

Value Posture	Action Orientation	Ethical Framework
Eliciting values	Consensus building	Deontological
Critically engaging	Evaluating	Consequentialist
Defamiliarizing	Framing	Virtue
	Generating	Pragmatist

Method Input	Method Mechanic	Method Output
Concepts	Altering	Concepts
Stakeholder Info	Storytelling	Stakeholder Info
Constraints/Goals	Filtering	Constraints/Goals
Values	Creating	Values
Use Context	Mapping	Evaluation Outcomes

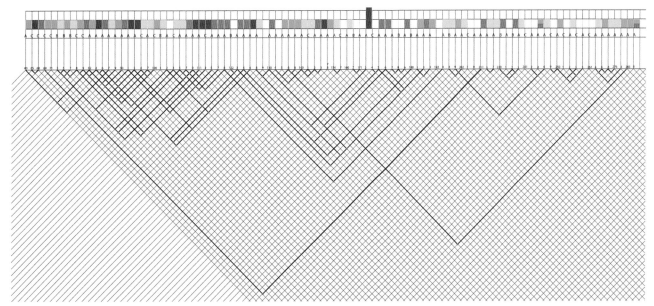

A sample Ethicograph with links indicated on the bottom two-thirds and ethical valence indicated in color on the top.

Image courtesy of Sai Shruthi Chivukula and Colin M. Gray.

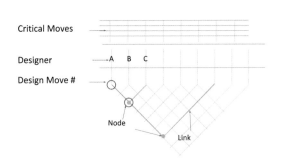

Ethicograph components, showing how critical moves, participants, and design moves are indicated diagrammatically with interconnected nodes and links.

Image courtesy of Sai Shruthi Chivukula and Colin M. Gray.

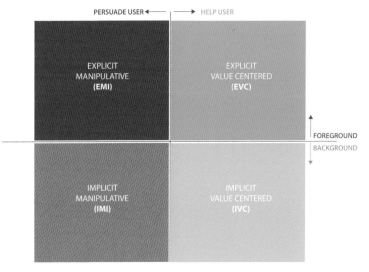

A matrix to code the ethical valence of each speech act based on the degree to which it is explicit or implicit, and whether the act is focused on persuading or manipulating a user or helping the user in a value-centered way.

Image courtesy of Sai Shruthi Chivukula and Colin M. Gray.

See also ETHICAL DESIGN SCORECARDS • DICHOTOMY MAPPING

38 Ethics Assessment

Ethics Assessment worksheet by Spotify allows you to evaluate effects your product might cause and identify and address potential physical, emotional, and social harms.[1]

#breakmydesign #evaluateoutcomes

Design products and services can cause intended or unintended harm to users. Often these harms can be anticipated but are not identified in a timely manner due to a lack of proper assessment protocols in place during the design process.

The Ethics Assessment worksheet provides a matrix to evaluate and prioritize addressing potential harms from your design product or service. The worksheet provides a range of negative impacts in categories that include physical harm, emotional harm, and societal harm. Use the Ethics Assessment worksheet to assess each harm across three columns:[1]

- **Examples of how your product might encourage or cause this effect:** List examples of potential effects your product or service could encourage or cause beyond primary users.

- **Chance of effect:** Assess each effect on a scale from Highly Probable (you have research that documents this effect) to Highly Improbable (you have research that documents no effect). The middle scores are based on anecdotal or weak evidence. You can choose to focus on the most highly probable effects.

- **Level of concern:** Assess the level of concern the team has about the particular harmful effect from Greatest Concern to Least Concern. Use this score in combination with the chance of effect score to prioritize which effects to focus on.

1. Investigating consequences with our ethics assessment. (2020, September). *Spotify Design*. https://spotify.design/article/investigating-consequences-with-our-ethics-assessment

Value Posture	Action Orientation	Ethical Framework
Eliciting values	Consensus building	Deontological
Critically engaging	Evaluating	Consequentialist
Defamiliarizing	Framing	Virtue
	Generating	Pragmatist

Method Input	Method Mechanic	Method Output
Concepts	Altering	Concepts
Stakeholder Info	Storytelling	Stakeholder Info
Constraints/Goals	Filtering	Constraints/Goals
Values	Creating	Values
Use Context	Mapping	Evaluation Outcomes

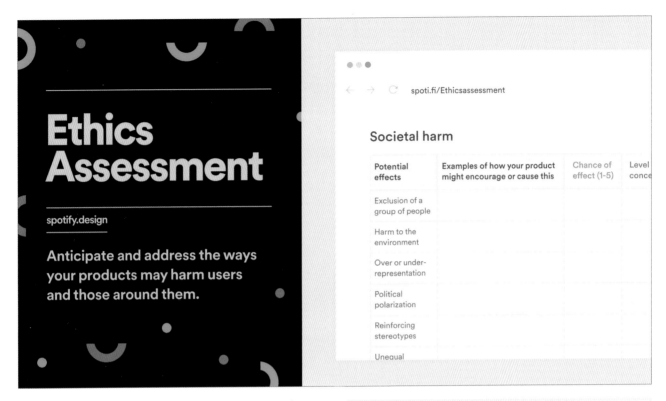

Ethics Assessment worksheet with columns that capture potential effects, examples of how your product or service might result in these effects, a chance of the effect (1 to 5), and the level of concern (1 to 5).

Image courtesy of Lu Han/Spotify Design.

PHYSICAL HARM
(e.g., death, exploitation, exposure, inactivity)

EMOTIONAL HARM
(e.g., addiction, anxiety, exclusion, abuse)

SOCIETAL HARM
(e.g., harm to environment, political polarization)

See also ETHICAL DESIGN SCORECARDS • DICHOTOMY MAPPING

39 Ethics Canvas

Ethics Canvas provides a space for you to collaboratively reflect on your product's or service's impacts, failures, and problematic use of resources.[1]

#breakmydesign #evaluateoutcomes #alignmyteam

Ethical decision-making during product development can include a range of considerations, including impacts on users, conflicts arising due to a product, effects on worldviews and judgments, product failures, and resource depletion from the design process.

Ethics Canvas provides a space to bring all of the product stakeholders into an ethical discussion, investigating and collaboratively considering a range of these ethical dimensions of your everyday work. Ethics Canvas enables you to collaboratively consider the following aspects of your work:[2]

- **Individuals/groups affected:** Identify the types or categories of individuals and kinds of groups, communities, or organizations affected by the product or service, using dimensions such as gender, user/nonuser, age category, and more.

- **Behavior and relations:** Discuss problematic changes and differences to individual behavior that may be prompted by the product or service.

- **Worldviews:** Discuss how the general perception of someone's role in society may be affected by the product or service.

- **Product or service failure:** Discuss the potential negative impact of your product or service failing to operate as intended.

- **Problematic use of resources:** Discuss possible negative impacts of the consumption of resources of building and developing the product or service.

- **What can we do?** Select the four most important ethical impacts and identify ways of solving these impacts by changing your product or service design. Also, provide recommendations for its use or spelling out more clearly to users the values driving the design.

1. The ethics canvas. (n.d.). Retrieved July 23, 2024, from https://www.ethicscanvas.org/

2. Quoted from https://www.ethicscanvas.org/canvas/index.php.

Value Posture	Action Orientation	Ethical Framework
Eliciting values	Consensus building	Deontological
Critically engaging	Evaluating	Consequentialist
Defamiliarizing	Framing	Virtue
	Generating	Pragmatist

Method Input	Method Mechanic	Method Output
Concepts	Altering	Concepts
Stakeholder Info	Storytelling	Stakeholder Info
Constraints/Goals	Filtering	Constraints/Goals
Values	Creating	Values
Use Context	Mapping	Evaluation Outcomes

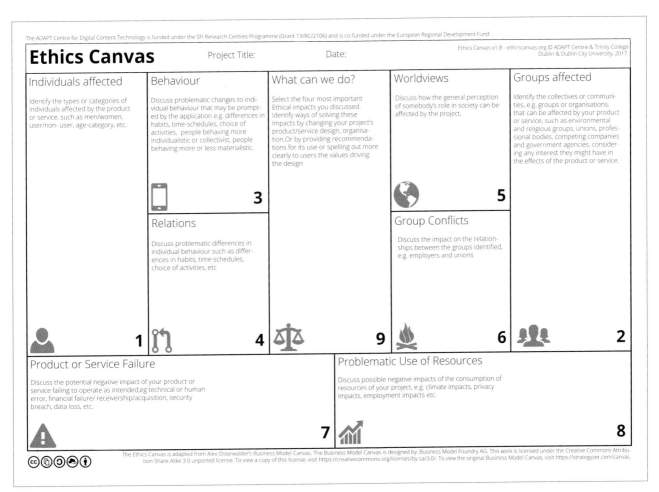

Ethics Canvas

Project Title: Date:

Individuals affected

Identify the types or categories of individuals affected by the product or service, such as men/women, user/non- user, age-category, etc.

1

Behaviour

Discuss problematic changes to individual behaviour that may be prompted by the application e.g. differences in habits, time-schedules, choice of activities, people behaving more individualistic or collectivist, people behaving more or less materialistic.

3

Relations

Discuss problematic differences in individual behaviour such as differences in habits, time-schedules, choice of activities, etc

4

What can we do?

Select the four most important Ethical impacts you discussed. Identify ways of solving these Impacts by changing your project's product/service design, organisation.Or by providing recommendations for its use or spelling out more clearly to users the values driving the design

9

Worldviews

Discuss how the general perception of somebody's role in society can be affected by the project.

5

Group Conflicts

Discuss the impact on the relationships between the groups identified, e.g. employers and unions

6

Groups affected

Identify the collectives or communities, e.g. groups or organisations, that can be affected by your product or service, such as environmental and religious groups, unions, professional bodies, competing companies and government agencies, considering any interest they might have in the effects of the product or service.

2

Product or Service Failure

Discuss the potential negative impact of your product or service failing to operate as intended,eg technical or human error, financial failure/ receivership/acquisition, security breach, data loss, etc.

7

Problematic Use of Resources

Discuss possible negative impacts of the consumption of resources of your project, e.g. climate impacts, privacy impacts, employment impacts etc.

8

An example of the Ethics Canvas worksheet, including a range of different tiles that represent different kinds of ethical impacts and relations.

Image courtesy of the ADAPT Centre for Digital Content Technology, licensed under the Creative Commons Attribution-Share Alike 3.0 unported license.

See also DATA ETHICS CANVAS • BAD DESIGN CANVAS • STAKEHOLDER TOKENS

40 Ethics Pathways

Ethics Pathways encourage you to visualize pathways that enable, serve as alternatives, or block your ethical engagement and decision-making.[1]

#breakmydesign #designresponsibility

Designers continuously bring their ethical awareness and point of view into the design situation, shaping their ethical decision-making as they develop a product and engage with other designers or stakeholders. Ethics Pathways provides an avenue for designers to reflect back on various "pathways" they have taken, could have taken, or instances where they faced barriers in identifying supports for their future ethical engagement.

Ethics Pathways help you construct a physical representation of your ethical engagement through four main steps:[2]

1. **Incident description:** Designers recall and explore the origin of an ethical issue faced in their everyday design work, product development, team, and/or organization.

2. **Character design:** Designers recount the roles they took and relevant stakeholders by describing them as characters in their ethics narrative, which can be identified using any form of physical "pucks."

3. **Path design and action notes:** Designers represent their chosen paths, possible alternative actions, and barriers to action related to their ethics engagement using "pathway blocks" such as straight roads, intersections, U-turns, or winding roads. Then they annotate the pathways created using "action notes."

4. **Reflection and emotion walk-through:** Designers revisit their representation of the narrative from steps 1 to 3, describing their emotions, resources, and lessons learned in the ethical decision-making journey.

1. Cha, I., Pillai, A. G., & Wong, R. Y. (2024). Ethics pathways: a design activity for reflecting on ethics engagement in HCI research. *Designing Interactive Systems Conference*, 3515-3533. https://doi.org/10.1145/3643834.3660714

2. Adopted and synthesized from Cha, Pillai, & Wong (2024).

Value Posture	Action Orientation	Ethical Framework
Eliciting values	Consensus building	Deontological
Critically engaging	Evaluating	Consequentialist
Defamiliarizing	Framing	Virtue
	Generating	Pragmatist

Method Input	Method Mechanic	Method Output
Concepts	Altering	Concepts
Stakeholder Info	Storytelling	Stakeholder Info
Constraints/Goals	Filtering	Constraints/Goals
Values	Creating	Values
Use Context	Mapping	Evaluation Outcomes

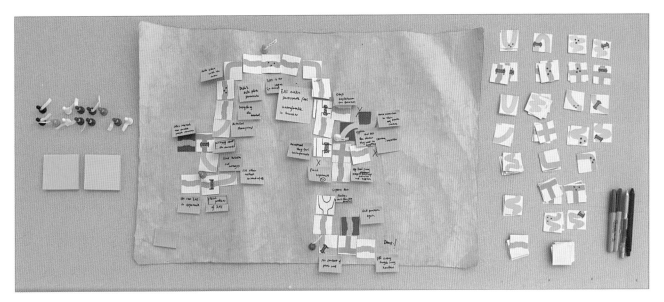

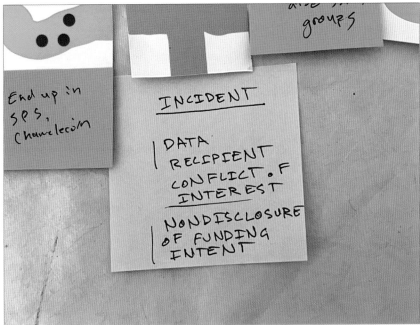

An example of the Ethics Pathway play materials, including the character pucks (left), the visualized pathways with action notes (center), and potential path design options (right).

Images courtesy of Inha Cha, Ajit Pillai, and Richmond Wong.

An example incident description about a data recipient conflict of interest that drove the pathways development process.

Images courtesy of Inha Cha, Ajit Pillai, and Richmond Wong.

41 Fair Patterns

Fair Patterns enable you to identify and correct instances of dark or deceptive patterns in digital products or services by employing fair countermeasures that positively impact users' agency.[1]

#evaluateoutcomes #applyvalues

Dark patterns, sometimes referred to as deceptive patterns, are instances where "user value is supplanted in favor of shareholder value."[2] These unethical design practices impact users' experiences by taking away their autonomy, impacting their decision-making or free choice, or coercing them into doing things they would otherwise not do. Dark patterns are ubiquitous in digital systems, impacting the majority of apps and websites—leading to the question: *What do we as designers do when we encounter dark patterns in the products we create?*

Fair Patterns "shift from a problem-oriented to a problem-solving perspective,"[1] using dark patterns as a prompt for designers to consider alternatives that respect users and their autonomy. The consultancy Amurabi has identified seven initial fair pattern types identified include:[1,3]

- **Protective default:** Using neutral or protective defaults instead of those against user interests.

- **Adequate information:** Providing sufficient information to support user goals instead of misleading users through selective disclosure.

- **Seamless path:** Addressing users needs when designing task flows instead of obstructing user's from reaching their goals through complex journeys.

- **Nonintrusive information:** Rejecting the use of triggers (e.g., emotion, time, social) that induce or push a particular behavior.

- **Plain and empowering language:** Using clear language that a user can understand instead of language that is confusing, manipulative, or impedes the user's goal.

- **Free action:** Allowing users to choose their own path and goals instead of making them do more or share more than they intend.

- **Fair UX:** Rejecting visual interface choices that trap users.

1. Potel-Saville, M., & Da Rocha, M. (2023). From dark patterns to fair patterns? Usable taxonomy to contribute solving the issue with countermeasures. *Annual Privacy Forum*, 145–165. https://doi.org/10.1007/978-3-031-61089-9_7

2. Gray, C. M., Kou, Y., Battles, B., Hoggatt, J., & Toombs, A. L. (2018). The dark (patterns) side of UX design. *Proceedings of the 2018 CHI Conference on Human Factors in Computing Systems*, 534:1-534:14. https://doi.org/10.1145/3173574.3174108

3. Fair patterns library. (2024). *Amurabi*. https://www.fairpatterns.com/resources/library

Further Reading

Gray, C. M., Santos, C. T., Bielova, N., & Mildner, T. (2024). An ontology of dark patterns knowledge: foundations, definitions, and a pathway for shared knowledge-building. *Proceedings of the CHI Conference on Human Factors in Computing Systems*, 1-22. https://doi.org/10.1145/3613904.3642436

Value Posture	Action Orientation	Ethical Framework
Eliciting values	Consensus building	Deontological
Critically engaging	Evaluating	Consequentialist
Defamiliarizing	Framing	Virtue
	Generating	Pragmatist

Method Input	Method Mechanic	Method Output
Concepts	Altering	Concepts
Stakeholder Info	Storytelling	Stakeholder Info
Constraints/Goals	Filtering	Constraints/Goals
Values	Creating	Values
Use Context	Mapping	Evaluation Outcomes

A mapping of countermeasures (columns) to the Gray et al. (2024) ontology[4] of dark patterns (rows) to demonstrate where fair patterns can be used to correct dark patterns in products.

Image courtesy of Amurabi.

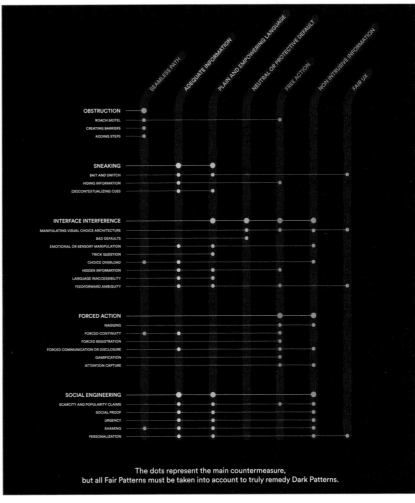

An example of a fair pattern that combats the dark pattern of "harmful default"—shifting from a bad default to a neutral or protective default.

Image courtesy of Amurabi

42 Feminist Design Qualities

Feminist Design Qualities allow designers to consider alternate perspectives, roles, and values by leveraging decades of feminist thought.[1]

#identifyvalues #applyvalues

Feminist scholars have worked for over half a century to identify how social systems and structures oppress women. Starting with the "third wave" of feminism that became popular in the 1990s, feminism became less about gender and more expansively framed in relation to how intersectional characteristics such as gender, class, and race impact one's ability to flourish and be seen as legitimate and empowered in the face of dominant social structures.

The designer can leverage feminist theory by using its value orientations as an "action-based design agenda,"[1] considering ways that feminism might impact the methodologies we use, the ways in which we frame research engagement, and the values that drive our evaluation of design outcomes. These interactions include questioning and redesigning against fundamental assumptions, designing for critical alternatives, and reflecting a sense of responsibility toward society through design.[2]

The interaction design qualities proposed by Shaowen Bardzell include:[3]

· **Pluralism:** Resisting any single, totalizing, or universal point of view.

· **Participation:** Valuing participatory processes that guide prototype creation and evaluation.

· **Advocacy:** Seeking to bring about political emancipation, encouraging the designer to question their position regarding what an "improved society" is and how best to achieve it.

· **Ecology:** Integrating an awareness of the effect of design artifacts through design reasoning, decision-making, and evaluation.

· **Embodiment:** Addressing commonalities and differences relating to gender identity, human sexuality, pleasure, and emotion.

· **Self-disclosure:** Calling attention to how systems currently define the user and create new opportunities for users to define themselves.

1. Bardzell, S. (2010). Feminist HCI: taking stock and outlining an agenda for design. *Proceedings of the SIGCHI Conference on Human Factors in Computing Systems*, 1301-1310. https://doi.org/10.1145/1753326.1753521

2. Chivukula, S. S. (2020). Feminisms through design: a practical guide to implement and extend feminism: position. *Interactions, 27*(6), 36-39. https://doi.org/10.1145/3427338

3. Bardzell (2010), pp. 1305-1307.

Value Posture	Action Orientation	Ethical Framework		Method Input	Method Mechanic	Method Output
Eliciting values	Consensus building	Deontological		Concepts	Altering	Concepts
Critically engaging	Evaluating	Consequentialist		Stakeholder Info	Storytelling	Stakeholder Info
Defamiliarizing	Framing	Virtue		Constraints/Goals	Filtering	Constraints/Goals
	Generating	Pragmatist		Values	Creating	Values
				Use Context	Mapping	Evaluation Outcomes

FtD Angles	As Educators... Based on these feminist angles, what do you want to incorporate or practice as an educator?	Towards Students... Based on these feminist values, what do you want your students to take on in future design education / practice?
Knowledge questioning and expanding fundamental assumptions		
Methodology curating antidisciplinary forms of knowledge		
Self/Community empowering and creating self-awareness		
Artifact giving it a form in design(s) action		

Feminisms through Design worksheet, mapping feminist values and interaction design qualities to knowledge, methodology, self/community, and artifact.

Worksheet courtesy of Sai Shruthi Chivukula.

KNOWLEDGE
Encouraging designers to engage with pluralistic views and assumptions and disclose any bias and privileges.

METHODOLOGY
Leveraging participatory design methods as an emancipatory opportunity for a range of stakeholders.

SELF/COMMUNITY
Advocating for collaboration in moments of cross-cultural opportunity, being aware of the ecological impact of design artifacts.

ARTIFACT
Building designs based on critical alternatives and affective dimensions and embodying "other ways" through problem frames.

See also SOCIAL JUSTICE STRATEGIES • REFUSAL • QUEERING

43 Futures Cone

Futures Cone aids you in visualizing how design decisions might impact alternative futures that range from potential to probable to preposterous.[1]

#breakmydesign #evaluateoutcomes #newperspectives

While designers cannot predict the future, they can engage in future-oriented speculation that can guide risk assessment, aid in generating creative ideas, and consider different ways of framing wicked problems.

The Futures Cone is a way of visualizing and reflecting upon different alternative futures, considering time and "classes" of the future as dimensions for reflection that may guide design decisions in a direct way or lead to other methods of evaluation to consider potential impacts on society. The Futures Cone categorizes potential futures into the following types (although there are many variations):[2]

- **Potential:** Everything beyond the present moment is a potential future, based on an assumption that the future is undetermined and open.

- **Preposterous:** Futures judged as ridiculous or impossible, highlighting the importance of considering even seemingly absurd ideas.

- **Possible:** Futures that might happen based on knowledge we do not yet possess but may acquire someday (e.g., warp drive for transportation).

- **Plausible:** Futures that could happen based on our current understanding of how the world works (e.g., physical laws, social processes).

- **Probable:** Futures that are likely to happen, usually based on current trends.

- **Preferable:** Futures that should or ought to happen, based on normative value judgments. This includes both preferred and unpreferred (undesirable) futures.

- **Projected:** The default, business-as-usual future, considered the most probable of the probable futures.

1. Voros, J. (2017). Big history and anticipation. In *Handbook of Anticipation* (pp. 1–40). Springer International Publishing. https://doi.org/10.1007/978-3-319-31737-3_95-1

2. Synthesized and quoted from Voros (2017).

3. Baxter, M. (2021, April 22). Model: futures cone. *Goal Atlas*. https://goalatlas.com/futures-cone/

Further Reading

Dunne, A., & Raby, F. (2013). *Speculative everything: design, fiction, and social dreaming*. MIT Press.

Value Posture	Action Orientation	Ethical Framework		Method Input	Method Mechanic	Method Output
Eliciting values	Consensus building	Deontological		Concepts	Altering	Concepts
Critically engaging	Evaluating	Consequentialist		Stakeholder Info	Storytelling	Stakeholder Info
Defamiliarizing	Framing	Virtue		Constraints/Goals	Filtering	Constraints/Goals
	Generating	Pragmatist		Values	Creating	Values
				Use Context	Mapping	Evaluation Outcomes

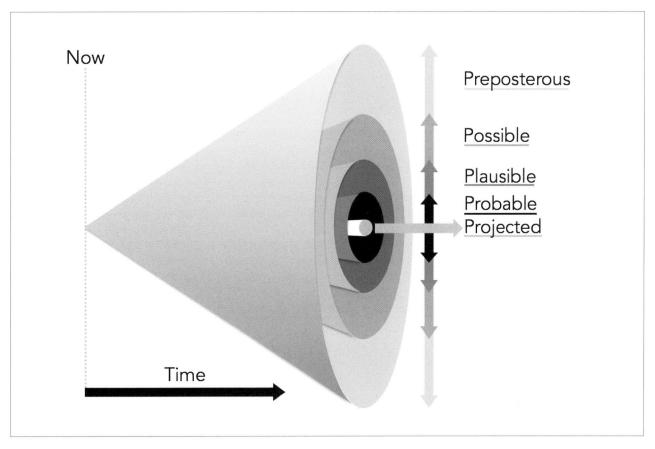

One version of the Futures Cone, containing different potential future states, including projected, plausible, probable, possible, and preposterous.

Image courtesy of Goal Atlas 2021,² licensed under Creative Commons Attribution 4.0 International License.

44 GenderMag

GenderMag enables designers to find gender-inclusivity "bugs" in their software, and then fix the bugs they find.[1]

#evaluateoutcomes #newperspectives

In order to realize more inclusive approaches to design, designers need generative evaluative tools to better understand how gender is represented or supported in the digital systems they create. GenderMag supports designers in finding and fixing gender-inclusivity "bugs" in their software. This method leverages a core of problem-solving "facets" that reflect a variety of user approaches to interaction that represent different aspects and presentations of gender in a nondeterministic way.[2]

Depending on the kinds of support the designer needs, they may focus on generative use through GenderMag-faceted personas, evaluative use through a GenderMag-faceted cognitive walk-through, or through more flexible use of the facets on their own.[3] The facets themselves are derived from gender research, encompassing Information Processing Styles, Computer Self-Efficacy, Attitudes Toward Risk, and Learning New Technologies. These facets are then activated through foundational yet customizable personas and an adapted cognitive walk-through approach.

To get started with GenderMag:

- Select and customize your persona.

- Identify your use case, including what your persona wants to accomplish.

- Set specific subgoals that relate to the use case.

- Evaluate the success of specific subgoals and use the action report to identify how (and if) the persona would take action within the system.

1. *GenderMag*. (n.d.). https://gendermag.org/index.php

2. Burnett, M., Stumpf, S., Macbeth, J., Makri, S., Beckwith, L., Kwan, I., Peters, A., & Jernigan, W. (2016). GenderMag: a method for evaluating software's gender inclusiveness. *Interacting with Computers, 28*(6), 760-787. https://doi.org/10.1093/iwc/iwv046

3. Burnett, M., Counts, R., Lawrence, R., & Hanson, H. (2017). Gender HCI and Microsoft: highlights from a longitudinal study. *2017 IEEE Symposium on Visual Languages and Human-Centric Computing (VL/HCC)*, 139-143. https://doi.org/10.1109/VLHCC.2017.8103461

Value Posture	Action Orientation	Ethical Framework
Eliciting values	Consensus building	Deontological
Critically engaging	Evaluating	Consequentialist
Defamiliarizing	Framing	Virtue
	Generating	Pragmatist

Method Input	Method Mechanic	Method Output
Concepts	Altering	Concepts
Stakeholder Info	Storytelling	Stakeholder Info
Constraints/Goals	Filtering	Constraints/Goals
Values	Creating	Values
Use Context	Mapping	Evaluation Outcomes

Abi (Abigail/Abishek)	Pat (Patricia/Patrick)	Tim (Timara/Timothy)
	 	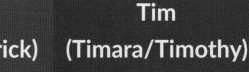
Motivation: Uses technology to accomplish their tasks.	**Motivation:** Learns new technologies when they need to.	**Motivation:** Likes learning all the available functionality on all their devices
Computer Self-Efficacy: Lower self-confidence than their peers about doing unfamiliar computing tasks. Blames themselves for problems.	**Computer Self-Efficacy:** Medium confidence doing unfamiliar computing tasks. If a problem can't be fixed, they will keep trying.	**Computer Self-Efficacy:** High confidence in technical abilities. If a problem can't be fixed, blame goes to software vendor.
Attitude Toward Risk: Risk-averse about using unfamiliar technologies that might require a lot of time.	**Attitude Toward Risk:** Risk-averse and doesn't want to expend time when they might not receive benefits.	**Attitude Toward Risk:** Doesn't mind taking risk using features of technology.
Information Processing Style: Comprehensive.	**Information Processing Style:** Comprehensive.	**Information Processing Style:** Selective information processing
Learning by Process vs. Tinkering: Process-orientated learning.	**Learning by Process vs. Tinkering:** Likes to explore and purposefully tinker.	**Learning by Process vs. Tinkering:** Likes tinkering and exploring.
Abi represents users with motivations/attitudes and information/learning styles similar to them. For data on people similar to and different from Abi, see http://gendermag.org/foundations.php	Pat represents users with motivations/attitudes and information/learning styles similar to them. For data on people similar to and different from Pat, see http://gendermag.org/foundations.php	Tim represents users with motivations/attitudes and information/learning styles similar to them. For data on people similar to and different from Tim, see http://gendermag.org/foundations.php

Examples of the components of the three core personas in GenderMag. Each persona is customizable and can include people of different ages and cultures that use different sets of pronouns.

Image courtesy of Margaret Burnett.

See also ADVERSARY PERSONAS • INCLUSIVE ACTIVITY CARDS

45 Hippocratic Oath

Hippocratic Oath encourages you to reflect on your responsibility as a designer and concretize the values you wish to live out in your design work.[1]

#alignmyteam #applyvalues #designresponsibility

Medical doctors take the Hippocratic Oath when they complete their training, promising to "do no harm" and "abstain from whatever is deleterious and mischievous"[1] on behalf of their patients. What might such an oath look like for designers—who arguably have even broader social impact through the work they produce?

Hippocratic Oath allows you to consider the core values you and your team wish to focus on in your design and make them relevant to specific aspects of your design work. You can write one or more oath statements as your "qualitative North Star" and then revisit the oath as needed to remind yourself and your team about the commitments you have made. Follow these steps to write your first Hippocratic Oath:[2]

1. Identify three to five core values (e.g., autonomy, safety, transparency, agency) that are relevant to your design work.

2. List three to five entities or stakeholders that you wish to support, better understand, or protect (e.g., underrepresented users, society, environment).

3. Create multiple combinations of the core values and entities that you have identified, pairing each combination with two or three action statements that indicate how you might operationalize the value in a specific, product-driven way.

1. Zhou, K. (2023). Hippocratic oath. *Design Ethically Toolkit*. Retrieved July 23, 2024, from https://www.designethically.com/hippocratic-oath

2. Adapted from Zhou (2023).

Further Reading

Zhou, K. (2023). *Design Ethically Toolkit*. https://www.designethically.com/toolkit

Value Posture	Action Orientation	Ethical Framework
Eliciting values	Consensus building	Deontological
Critically engaging	Evaluating	Consequentialist
Defamiliarizing	Framing	Virtue
	Generating	Pragmatist

Method Input	Method Mechanic	Method Output
Concepts	Altering	Concepts
Stakeholder Info	Storytelling	Stakeholder Info
Constraints/Goals	Filtering	Constraints/Goals
Values	Creating	Values
Use Context	Mapping	Evaluation Outcomes

Structure

In order to uphold the [insert value] **of** [insert entity], **I will** [insert action]

Example

In order to uphold the safety **of** ride-share passengers, **I will ensure that womxn riders have a way to request womxn drivers.**

Example of a completed Hippocratic Oath template, outlining specific values relating to gender and service provision for rideshare passengers.

Image courtesy of Kat Zhou.

See also PLEDGE WORKS • RESPONSIBLE DESIGN PRISM

46 Humane by Design

Humane by Design provides principles to enhance human abilities instead of exploiting vulnerabilities through your design outcomes.[1]

#identifyvalues #applyvalues #designresponsibility

Technology enables our modern society to exist. However, these same technologies too often minimize our humanity by "extracting our attention, monetizing our personal information, and exploiting our psychological vulnerabilities."[1] The Humane by Design Principles support designers to take responsibility to be "humane," enhancing precisely what makes us human when considering design outcomes:[2]

- **Resilient design** focuses on the well-being of the most vulnerable and anticipates the potential for abuse. Example practices include enabling content control and balancing data with research.

- **Empowering design** ensures products center on the value they provide to people over the revenue it can generate. Example practices include providing control over notification settings, message privacy and anonymity settings.

- **Finite design** maximizes the quality of time people spend by bounding the experience and prioritizing meaningful and relevant content. Example practices include feature indicating you are "all caught up," choice to turn on and off "autoplay."

- **Inclusive design** is a methodology that enables and draws on the full range of human diversity. Example practices include building diverse teams, designing for disabilities first.

- **Intentional design** uses friction to prevent abuse, protects privacy, steers people toward healthier digital habits, and considers long-term consequences over short-term gain. Example practices include using manual and algorithmic speed bumps to prevent error.

- **Respectful design** prioritizes people's time, attention and overall digital well-being. Example practices include personalization in notification settings, adapt to context.

- **Transparent design** is clear about intentions, honest in actions and free of dark patterns. Example practices include data transparency, supporting user's forgetfulness.

1. Yablonski, J. (n.d.). *Humane by Design*. Retrieved July 16, 2024, from https://humanebydesign.com/

2. Quoted and synthesized from Yablonski (n.d.).

Further Reading

Design Guide. (n.d.). Retrieved July 19, 2024, from https://www.humanetech.com/designguide

Value Posture	Action Orientation	Ethical Framework
Eliciting values	Consensus building	Deontological
Critically engaging	Evaluating	Consequentialist
Defamiliarizing	Framing	Virtue
	Generating	Pragmatist

Method Input	Method Mechanic	Method Output
Concepts	Altering	Concepts
Stakeholder Info	Storytelling	Stakeholder Info
Constraints/Goals	Filtering	Constraints/Goals
Values	Creating	Values
Use Context	Mapping	Evaluation Outcomes

Humane by Design

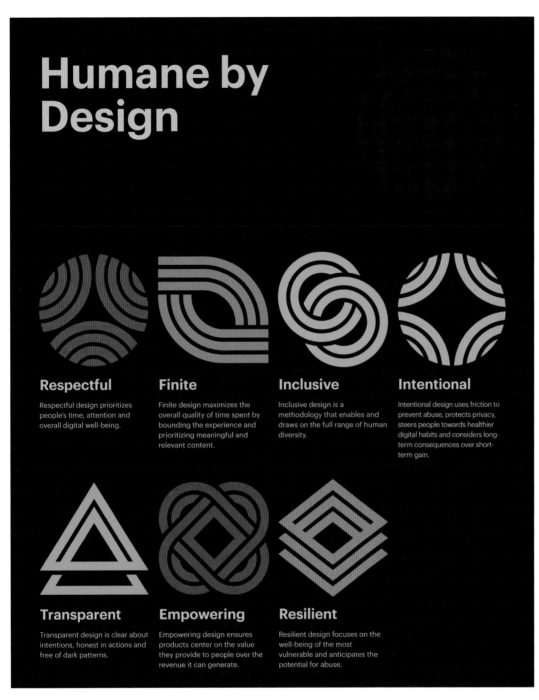

Respectful

Respectful design prioritizes people's time, attention and overall digital well-being.

Finite

Finite design maximizes the overall quality of time spent by bounding the experience and prioritizing meaningful and relevant content.

Inclusive

Inclusive design is a methodology that enables and draws on the full range of human diversity.

Intentional

Intentional design uses friction to prevent abuse, protects privacy, steers people towards healthier digital habits and considers long-term consequences over short-term gain.

Transparent

Transparent design is clear about intentions, honest in actions and free of dark patterns.

Empowering

Empowering design ensures products center on the value they provide to people over the revenue it can generate.

Resilient

Resilient design focuses on the well-being of the most vulnerable and anticipates the potential for abuse.

A reference sheet including the Humane by Design Principles with definitions.

Image courtesy of Jon Yablonski.

See also *MORAL VALUE MAP • FAIR PATTERNS*

47 Humane Design Guide

Humane Design Guide directs you to consider more humane design alternatives in your product or service based on human sensitivities.[1]

#breakmydesign #evaluateoutcomes

Digital technologies can take advantage of a range of human vulnerabilities, manipulating people into doing things they would not otherwise choose. For instance, designers can leverage addiction, distraction, or sustaining harmful habits in the service of business instead of human goals. Humane technologies, on the other hand, prioritize human sensitivities as a key element of one's design philosophy.

The Humane Design Guide helps designers evaluate and prioritize human sensitivities that the product currently engages, supports, or elevates, and does not capture. Human Sensitivities include "instincts that [humans have that] are often vulnerable to new technologies."[2] The Humane Design Guide encourages designers to consider the following range of human sensitivities, questioning how designers could use these vulnerabilities in positive or negative ways:[2]

- **Emotional:** What we feel in our body and in our physical health, which can be exploited or supported when we lack sleep, are afraid, or are stressed.

- **Attention:** How and where we focus our attention, which can be exploited or supported when we are overwhelmed or feel fragmented.

- **Sensemaking:** How we integrate what we sense with what we know, which can be exploited or supported when we see information that is out of context or uses a fear-based framing.

- **Decision-making:** How we align our actions with our intentions, which can be exploited or supported when our intentions or agency are not requested or supported.

- **Social reasoning:** How we understand and navigate our personal relationships, which can be exploited or supported when our status or self-image are manipulated.

- **Group dynamics:** How we navigate larger groups, status, and shared understanding, which can be exploited or supported when we are excluded or divided using fear tactics.

1. Design guide. (n.d.). Retrieved July 24, 2024, from https://www.humanetech.com/designguide

2. Quoted and synthesized from the Design Guide worksheet.

Further Reading

Center for humane technology. (2022). https://www.humanetech.com/

Value Posture	Action Orientation	Ethical Framework
Eliciting values	Consensus building	Deontological
Critically engaging	Evaluating	Consequentialist
Defamiliarizing	Framing	Virtue
	Generating	Pragmatist

Method Input	Method Mechanic	Method Output
Concepts	Altering	Concepts
Stakeholder Info	Storytelling	Stakeholder Info
Constraints/Goals	Filtering	Constraints/Goals
Values	Creating	Values
Use Context	Mapping	Evaluation Outcomes

Humane Design Guide

Use this worksheet to identify opportunities for Humane Technology.

Product or feature:
Value proposition:
Measure of success:

What are Human Sensitivities?

Human Sensitivites are instincts that are often vulnerable to new technologies.

Human Sensitivity	We are inhibited when	What inhibits	We are supported when	Opportunity to improve
Emotional What we feel in our body and in our physical health.	We are stressed, low on sleep, afraid or emotionally exhausted.	• Artificial scarcity • Urgency signalling • Constant monitoring • Optimizing for screentime	Design engenders calm, balance, safety, pauses and supports circadian rhythms.	High Low
Attention How and where we focus our attention.	Attention is physiologically drawn, overwhelmed or fragmented.	• Constant context switching • Many undifferentiated choices • Fearful information • No stopping cues (e.g. infinite scroll) • Unnecessary movement	Enabled to bring more focus and mindfulness.	
Sensemaking How we integrate what we sense with what we know.	Information is fear-based, out of context, confusing, or manipulative.	• Facts out of context • Over-personalized filters • Equating virality with credibility • Deceptive authority (ads vs. content)	Enabled to consider, learn, express and feel grounded.	
Decisionmaking How we align our actions with our intentions.	Intentions and agency are not solicited nor supported.	• Avatars to convey authority • Stalking ads and messages • Push content models • Serving preference over intent	Enabled to gain agency, purpose, and mobilization of intent.	
Social Reasoning How we understand and navigate our personal relationships.	Status, relationships and self-image are manipulated.	• Quantified social status • Viral sharing • Implied obligation • Enabling impersonation	Enabled to connect more safely and authentically with others.	
Group Dynamics How we navigate larger groups, status, and shared understanding.	Excluded, divided and mobilized through fear.	• Suppressing views and nuance • Enabling ad hominem or hate speech • Enabling viral outrage • Lack of agreed-upon norms	Enabled to develop a sense of belonging and cooperation.	

[Center for Humane Technology] www.humanetech.com

Now rank the sensitivities 1-6 based on what you now see as the largest opportunities for Humane Design. Then use the second sheet to develop an action statement.

A worksheet that enables you to map different human sensitivities and triggers for your product or service, identifying opportunities to improve on each type of vulnerability.

Image courtesy of Center for Humane Technology.

See also MASLOW MIRRORED • WELL-BEING DESIGN CARDS

48 HuValue

HuValue enriches your design framing, conceptualization, and evaluation of design outcomes based on human values.[1]

#evaluateoutcomes #identifyvalues #applyvalues

Design is a value-laden activity where designers consider and embed personal, professional, organizational, societal, and business values as they design a digital product. Values are considered and activated in decision-making processes, providing a more manageable entrance to considering ethical perspectives. HuValue allows the designer to identify a range of human values—based on artifacts, users/personas, and situation/context—facilitating the designer in considering different aspects of their process from the perspective of values.

Values can be organized on a visual "wheel" based on different value groupings. These values can then be characterized and prioritized from "Extremely Important" to "Not Important." Value groups can include *basic beliefs* that humans possess such as meaningfulness or spirituality; qualities of *nature* that relate to the environment; aspects of *self* that focus on respect, professional development, or pleasure; and expectations of *society* that include respect for others, justice, or status. HuValue lists specific values within nine value groups resulting in 45 human values for designers of technological products to consider. The value wheel supports designers in:[2]

- **Deriving values:** Identify values based on different value groups based on personas or user contexts. These derived values can help you generate concepts or frame your design goal.

- **Generating and iterating designs:** Generate or iterate upon concepts based on a design goal, using identified values to help you sketch or prototype. You can use the values to build new functionality or evaluate violations of values to iterate upon your concept.

- **Aligning the ecosystem of products:** Start with a collection of design artifacts that you would like to align based on particular values, identifying values that different products either encourage or neglect. This process can encourage values to translate across products.

- **Reflective practice:** Place yourself at the center of the value wheel to visualize your proximity to specific value groupings. Through this reflective process, you can consider how and why you wish to incorporate certain values into your design processes.

1. Human values in design. (n.d.). *HuValue*. https://huvaluetools.com/

2. Adapted from the HuValue website.

Further Reading

Kheirandish, S. (2018). *HuValue: a tool to enrich design concepts with human values.* [PhD Thesis]. Technische Universiteit Eindhoven. https://research. tue.nl/files/105880318/20181011_Kheirandish.pdf

Kheirandish, S., Funk, M., Wensveen, S., Verkerk, M., & Rauterberg, M. (2020). HuValue: a tool to support design students in considering human values in their design. *International Journal of Technology and Design Education, 30*(5), 1015–1041. https://doi. org/10.1007/s10798-019-09527-3

Value Posture	Action Orientation	Ethical Framework	Method Input	Method Mechanic	Method Output
Eliciting values	Consensus building	Deontological	Concepts	Altering	Concepts
Critically engaging	Evaluating	Consequentialist	Stakeholder Info	Storytelling	Stakeholder Info
Defamiliarizing	Framing	Virtue	Constraints/Goals	Filtering	Constraints/Goals
	Generating	Pragmatist	Values	Creating	Values
			Use Context	Mapping	Evaluation Outcomes

An example of designers using the Value Wheel to identify particular values related to an electric car. These values can be used to evaluate the impact of electric cars, as a design artifact, and on nature, self, and society.

Image courtesy of Shadi Kheirandish.

See also MORAL VALUE MAP • MORAL AGENT

49 In-Action Ethics

In-Action Ethics encourages you to reflect on your shared responsibility as a design team for ethical outcomes, negotiating a culture where ethical discussions can be facilitated.[1]

#applyvalues #alignmyteam #designresponsibility

Designers must contend with a range of formal ethical systems in their work that constrain action and act primarily as evaluative lenses with which to judge design outcomes. These systems focus on "anticipatory ethics," which are primarily focused on dictating what is right or wrong, good or bad. However, many issues in design are more complex and situated than these formal ethical frameworks allow.

In-Action Ethics is an approach to ethical engagement that is inherently reflective, situated, and experienced by individuals in unique configurations that relate to project work and outcomes. At its core, this approach to ethics places a focus on a shared "project ethos" that encourages team members to engage in the "negotiation of and agreement on moral statements for which a project stands."[1] Consider a comparison between the kinds of issues and questions that can be considered through an anticipatory or in-action approach:[2]

- **Anticipatory ethics** are often formalized codes or ethical frameworks, forming outer boundaries for unethical behavior (e.g., codes, legislation, research ethics principles) that should not be crossed. In this approach to ethics, you might ask questions such as *"Did we follow the appropriate ethical guidelines?"*

- **In-action ethics** rely on a project ethos that is generative, emerging from interactions among the people working on a particular project. This ethos focuses on characteristics such as situatedness, embodiment, participation, and identification and application of values local to a project. This approach is self-regulatory, since it involves the shared commitment of all team members (and their underlying value systems) to particular kinds of design norms. In this approach to ethics, you might ask questions such as *"Was this the right thing to do at the time?"*

1. Frauenberger, C., Rauhala, M., & Fitzpatrick, G. (2017). In-action ethics. *Interacting with Computers, 29*(2), 220-236. https://doi.org/10.1093/iwc/iww024

2. Adapted and synthesized from Frauenberger et al. (2017).

Value Posture	Action Orientation	Ethical Framework
Eliciting values	Consensus building	Deontological
Critically engaging	Evaluating	Consequentialist
Defamiliarizing	Framing	Virtue
	Generating	Pragmatist

Method Input	Method Mechanic	Method Output
Concepts	Altering	Concepts
Stakeholder Info	Storytelling	Stakeholder Info
Constraints/Goals	Filtering	Constraints/Goals
Values	Creating	Values
Use Context	Mapping	Evaluation Outcomes

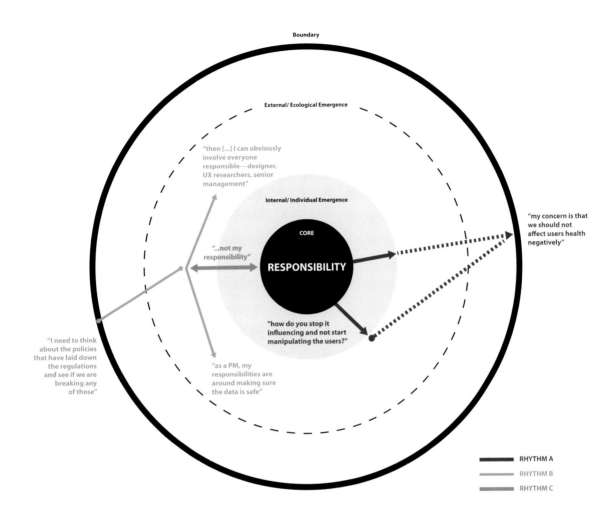

Boundary

External/ Ecological Emergence

Internal/ Individual Emergence

"then [...] I can obviously involve everyone responsible—designer, UX researchers, senior management"

"...not my responsibility"

CORE

RESPONSIBILITY

"my concern is that we should not affect users health negatively"

"how do you stop it influencing and not start manipulating the users?"

"I need to think about the policies that have laid down the regulations and see if we are breaking any of those"

"as a PM, my responsibilities are around making sure the data is safe"

RHYTHM A
RHYTHM B
RHYTHM C

A schema that visually describes an example of how ethics emerge and are mediated by the individual themself, instead of being defined by external codes. In contrast, the ethics are experienced in-action by the designer, relating to individual understanding of ethics in their workplace, the shaping influence of their organizational and professional ecology, and the ultimate boundaries they are unwilling to cross in particular situations or in general.

Image courtesy of Colin M. Gray and the UXP² research lab, reproduced with permission from Gray, C. M., Chivukula, S. S., Johns, J., Will, M., Obi, I., & Li, Z. (2024). Languaging ethics in technology practice. ACM J. Responsib. Comput., 1(2), 1-15. https://doi.org/10.1145/3656468.

See also VALUES LEVERS • A.E.I.O.YOU • (TACTICS OF) SOFT RESISTANCE

50 Inclusive Activity Cards

Inclusive Activity Cards encourage you to use inclusive design approaches across contexts, personas, technologies, and conditions.[1]

#breakmydesign #newperspectives #applyvalues

Inclusive design is focused on considering, understanding, and designing for a wide range of users. Inclusive Activity Cards allow you to get oriented, frame, ideate, iterate, and optimize your design outcomes across a wide range of inclusivity considerations. These cards are built on Microsoft Inclusive Design Principles,[1] which include *recognize exclusion* to acknowledge bias and recognize that exclusion occurs due to mismatches between people and experience; *learn from diversity* to center diverse perspectives for better insights; and *solve for one, extend to many* to design for people with permanent disabilities, thereby creating results that benefit everyone.

These principles can be put in action using a variety of lenses, such as:[2]

- **Contexts:** Different environments enable different capabilities, present different limitations, and have different rules and social norms. Contexts can be physical (home, car, library, wilderness) and social (alone, with coworkers, in a crowd, with friends and family).

- **Temporary/situational limits:** Disabilities can be temporary or situational, and include experiences such as unable to see, speak, touch, and/or hear.

- **Role of technology:** Technology can shape interactions by collecting and summarizing, translating, transporting, and listening.

- **Examples of mismatch:** Mismatched interactions can occur between other humans, humans and their environments, and humans and objects.

- **Conditions:** Environmental conditions can create or shape situational limitations and forms of interactions such as weather interruptions, temperature influences, and time of the day.

- **The persona spectrum:** Personas can incorporate different types of permanent, temporary, and situational disabilities across a spectrum (e.g., arm injury, distracted driver, deaf, and heavy accent).

1. Microsoft inclusive design. (n.d.). Retrieved July 18, 2024, from https://inclusive.microsoft.design/

2. Quoted or synthesized from the support cards in the Inclusive Activity Cards deck, available at https://inclusive.microsoft.design/tools-and-activities/InclusiveActivityCards.pdf.

Value Posture	Action Orientation	Ethical Framework		Method Input	Method Mechanic	Method Output
Eliciting values	Consensus building	Deontological		Concepts	Altering	Concepts
Critically engaging	Evaluating	Consequentialist		Stakeholder Info	Storytelling	Stakeholder Info
Defamiliarizing	Framing	Virtue		Constraints/Goals	Filtering	Constraints/Goals
	Generating	Pragmatist		Values	Creating	Values
				Use Context	Mapping	Evaluation Outcomes

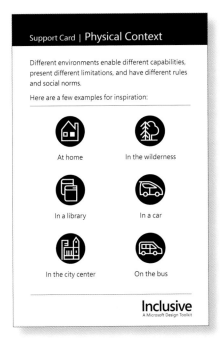

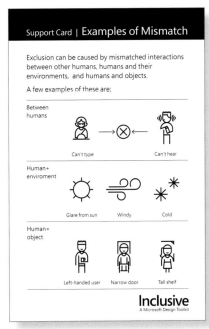

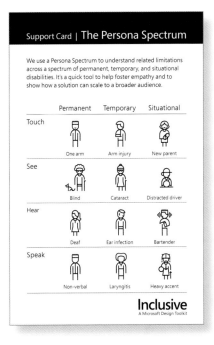

Examples of Inclusive Activity Cards, indicating different kinds of physical contexts, mismatches, and persona spectra to consider when incorporating inclusive design principles into your design work.

Images courtesy of Microsoft (2023), licensed under Creative Commons Attribution-NonCommercial-No Derivatives (CC BY-NC-ND).

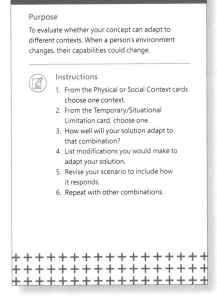

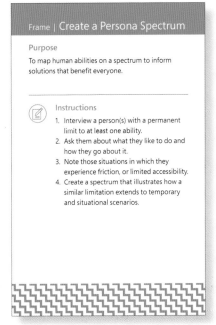

Examples of Inclusive Activity Cards that enable you to optimize or frame your project in more inclusive ways, including ensuring that context and capability match (left) and including a range of human abilities in your persona(s) (right).

Images courtesy of Microsoft (2023) licensed under Creative Commons Attribution-NonCommercial-No Derivatives (CC BY-NC-ND).

See also TAROT CARDS OF TECH • CIDER

51 Intersectionality

Intersectionality allows you to identify the many different identities that your users might take on, revealing instances of disempowerment, marginalization, or privilege.[1]

#evaluateoutcomes #newperspectives #identifyvalues

Humans are multifaceted beings and exist in many different social contexts with a range of identity characteristics. These characteristics, taken individually, can provide us with advantages or barriers—but it can be even more complicated when these characteristics overlap in a single individual. While human-centered methods can help designers empathize with some types of human characteristics, critical scholars argue that designers should actively contend with complex histories of discrimination and oppression when understanding the complexity of human behavior.

Intersectionality, a term coined by Kimberlé Crenshaw in the 1980s, "considers the various backgrounds and personal experiences that shape the lives and outcomes of marginalized populations, defined by factors including but not limited to race, gender, and class."[1] To account for this complex and overlapping set of identities, consider using these principles to begin to unpack and address issues of intersectional identity and privilege further in your design work:[2]

- **Understand and attend to context.** Go beyond demographic characteristics to consider which identities are present, how individuals have demonstrated resilience in the past, and what continuing challenges are faced by individuals within a particular context.

- **Self-reflect.** Use reflexive practices to acknowledge your own positionality and privilege in relation to the group(s) you are seeking to understand or empower, including gaps in your knowledge or biases you might bring with you to your design work.

- **Attend to and disclose dissent.** Identify the conflicts or tensions that occur when working with communities that have been historically marginalized, attuning yourself to "voices of dissent" that can explain why past efforts might have been unsuccessful.

1. Erete, S., Israni, A., & Dillahunt, T. (2018). An intersectional approach to designing in the margins. *Interactions, 25*(3), 66-69. https://doi.org/10.1145/3194349

2. Synthesized and adapted from Erete et al. (2018).

Further Reading

Jones, H., Schiebinger, L., Grimes, A., & Small, A. (2024). *Intersectional Design Cards*. https://intersectionaldesign.com/

Value Posture	Action Orientation	Ethical Framework
Eliciting values	Consensus building	Deontological
Critically engaging	Evaluating	Consequentialist
Defamiliarizing	Framing	Virtue
	Generating	Pragmatist

Method Input	Method Mechanic	Method Output
Concepts	Altering	Concepts
Stakeholder Info	Storytelling	Stakeholder Info
Constraints/Goals	Filtering	Constraints/Goals
Values	Creating	Values
Use Context	Mapping	Evaluation Outcomes

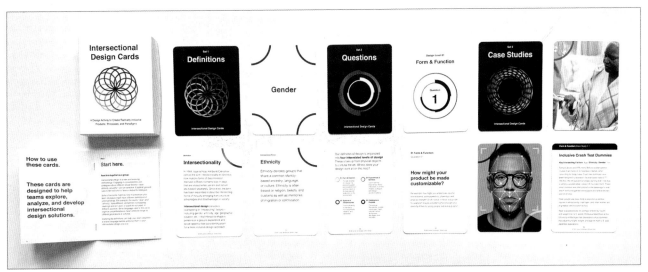

Intersectional Design Cards to help teams explore and develop intersectional design solutions.

Image courtesy of Jones, Schiebinger, Grimes, & Small (2024), licensed under a Creative Commons Attribution-NonCommercial-NoDerivatives 4.0 International License (CC BY-NC-ND 4.0).

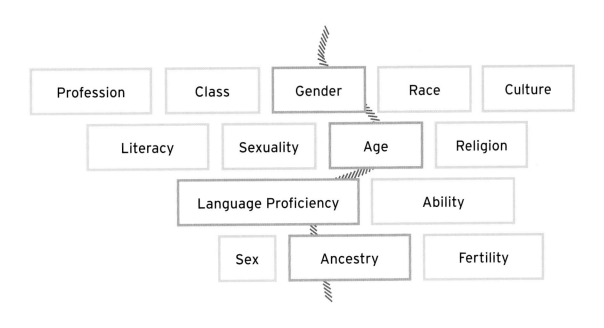

Different dimensions of intersectionality with a thread connecting a set of intersectional characteristics that may be a point of focus for the designer.

Image includes dimensions adapted from a diagram by Sheena Erete, which was previously adapted from Morgan, K. (2018). Describing the emperor's new clothes: Three myths of educational (in-)equity. The Gender Question in Education. https://doi.org/10.4324/9780429496530-11.

See also KALEIDOSCOPE • GENDERMAG

52 Inverted Behavior Model

Inverted Behavior Model supports you in identifying potential behaviors based on a forecast of what a feature or product motivates the user to do.[1]

#breakmydesign #evaluateoutcomes

Designers generate features, products, and services based on how intended users are likely to behave. These expectations are often grounded in knowledge of human psychology, or based on user research with the user populations that are likely to use a product or service.

B.J. Fogg proposed a model for behavior design that states: "Behavior (B) happens when Motivation (M), Ability (A), and a Prompt (P) come together at the same moment."[1] Using this behavior design approach, designers incorporate certain sets of motivations in the form of features (i.e., prompts) in relation to a user's ability to achieve a particular behavior change. By forecasting potential design outcomes, designers can start with those intended or unintended user behaviors to further ideate or evaluate features or product types in order to list what consequences those behaviors might trigger. Hence, the inversion of the behavior model is to start the ideation process with behaviors and not to focus on behaviors only as an inevitable outcome.

To use the Inverted Behavior Model:[2]

1. Deconstruct every product and service into features that are intended to act as "prompts" in behavior design.

2. For each feature, list motivating factors to use or apply that feature.

3. Based on these motivations, list intended or unintended behaviors to identify a range of outcomes that might result from that feature.

4. Across the collection of these behaviors, identify potential consequences that could positively or negatively impact users or society at large.

1. Fogg, B. J. (2009). *Behavior Model.* https://behaviormodel.org/

2. Quoted from Zhou, K. (2021). BJ Fogg's inverted behavior model. *Design Ethically Toolkit.* https://www.designethically.com/bj-fogg

Further Reading

Fogg, B. J. (2009). Creating persuasive technologies: an eight-step design process. *Proceedings of the 4th International Conference on Persuasive Technology,* 44. https://doi.org/10.1145/1541948.1542005

Value Posture	Action Orientation	Ethical Framework	Method Input	Method Mechanic	Method Output
Eliciting values	Consensus building	Deontological	Concepts	Altering	Concepts
Critically engaging	Evaluating	Consequentialist	Stakeholder Info	Storytelling	Stakeholder Info
Defamiliarizing	Framing	Virtue	Constraints/Goals	Filtering	Constraints/Goals
	Generating	Pragmatist	Values	Creating	Values
			Use Context	Mapping	Evaluation Outcomes

PROMPT (FEATURE)	MOTIVATION	BEHAVIOR	CONSEQUENCES

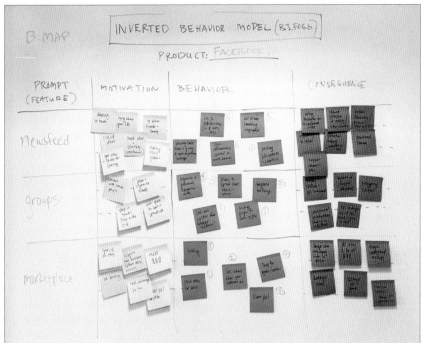

A worksheet to complete the Inverted Behavior Model, including columns for prompts, motivations, behaviors, and consequences (top). This technique can also be used to map the different elements on a whiteboard using sticky notes (left).

Images courtesy of Kat Zhou.

See also *MOTIVATION MATRIX • DESIGN WITH INTENT • DIGITAL ETHICS COMPASS*

53 Judgment Call

Judgment Call gamifies identifying the ethical implications of your design product across different stakeholder perspectives by writing fictional product reviews as a way of applying Microsoft's AI principles.[1]

#breakmydesign #evaluateoutcomes

Many technologies have uncertain or unclear ethical impacts on society, which demands that designers and technologies consider a range of stakeholders and scenarios and play an active role in considering the ethical implications for these stakeholders.

Judgment Call allows you to activate Microsoft's AI principles (including fairness, privacy and security, reliability and safety, transparency, inclusion, and accountability[2]) in relation to different stakeholder perspectives through a team-based game. The focus of the game is on "writ[ing] product reviews from the perspective of a particular stakeholder, describing what kind of impact and harms the technology could produce from their point of view."[3]

To play the game, follow these steps:

1. **Choose** a product or fictional scenario that is most representative or useful to your work context.

2. **Identify** the direct, indirect, and excluded stakeholders that are involved in this scenario.

3. **Draw** a rating card, stakeholder card, ethical principle card, and a new card based on the wild card you drew at the beginning of the game.

4. **Use** the cards you drew to write a review with the scenario in mind.

5. **Share** your reviews and discuss the results. Use common themes from the reviews to refine and generate design concepts.

1. Ballard, S., Chappell, K. M., & Kennedy, K. (2019). Judgment call the game: Using value sensitive design and design fiction to surface ethical concerns related to technology. *Proceedings of the 2019 on Designing Interactive Systems Conference*, 421–433. https://doi.org/10.1145/3322276.3323697

2. Responsible AI principles and approach. (n.d.). Retrieved July 16, 2024, from https://www.microsoft.com/en-us/ai/principles-and-approach

3. Judgment call. (n.d.). Retrieved July 16, 2024, from https://learn.microsoft.com/en-us/azure/architecture/guide/responsible-innovation/judgmentcall

Value Posture	Action Orientation	Ethical Framework
Eliciting values	Consensus building	Deontological
Critically engaging	Evaluating	Consequentialist
Defamiliarizing	Framing	Virtue
	Generating	Pragmatist

Method Input	Method Mechanic	Method Output
Concepts	Altering	Concepts
Stakeholder Info	Storytelling	Stakeholder Info
Constraints/Goals	Filtering	Constraints/Goals
Values	Creating	Values
Use Context	Mapping	Evaluation Outcomes

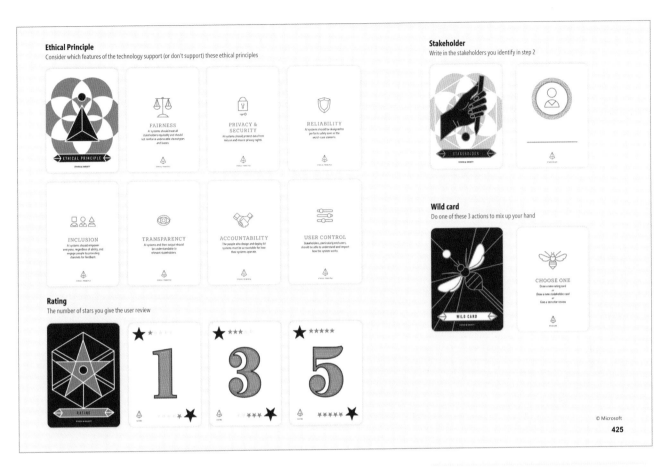

Ethical Principle
Consider which features of the technology support (or don't support) these ethical principles

FAIRNESS
AI systems should treat all stakeholders equitably and should not reinforce undesirable stereotypes and biases

PRIVACY & SECURITY
AI systems should protect data from misuse and ensure privacy rights.

RELIABILITY
AI systems should be designed to perform safely even in the worst-case scenario.

INCLUSION
AI systems should empower everyone, regardless of ability, and engage people by providing channels for feedback.

TRANSPARENCY
AI systems and their output should be understandable to relevant stakeholders.

ACCOUNTABILITY
The people who design and deploy AI systems must be accountable for how their systems operate.

USER CONTROL
Stakeholders, particularly end users, should be able to understand and impact how the system works

Stakeholder
Write in the stakeholders you identify in step 2

Wild card
Do one of these 3 actions to mix up your hand

CHOOSE ONE
Draw a new rating card
or
Draw a new stakeholder card
or
Give a zero star review

Rating
The number of stars you give the user review

© Microsoft

425

★☆☆☆☆   *Reliability*
ETHICAL PRINCIPLE

This system is even worse than the old body scanners! It constantly needs to be updated and each time we have to take it offline and re-certify it before we can start using it again. When it's running, it works well, we haven't had any security incidents. But each month it goes offline for about 3 days to update and re-certify.

Security Employee
STAKEHOLDER

A portion of the game cards, including Ethical Principle Cards that describe each Microsoft Responsible AI principle, Stakeholder Cards that indicate the stakeholders identified in a previous step of the game, and Rating Cards and Wild Cards to indicate what kind of review to write (top).

An example review and related cards from the game deck for a facial recognition scenario at the airport (bottom).

Top image courtesy of Stephanie Ballard and Microsoft, reproduced from Ballard et al. (2019). Bottom image courtesy of Microsoft.

See also TIMELINES • EMPATHIC WALK-THROUGH • STAKEHOLDER TOKENS

54 Kaleidoscope

Kaleidoscope supports you in applying an intersectional lens in your design work, helping you consider ways to make experiences more inclusive and equitable.[1]

#evaluateoutcomes #applyvalues #alignmyteam

People are multidimensional and complicated. Each person has many identities, encompassing race, gender, abilities, profession, and more. Each of these identities gives us more or less power, and the combination of these identities—described through the concept of intersectionality—can lead to inequitable or uninclusive experiences.

Kaleidoscope provides ways for you to use concepts from intersectionality throughout the design process, accounting for the role of social structures, policies, and political factors. Use these guiding questions and considerations to encourage reflection and equitable outcomes in areas such as:[2]

- **Planning:** Ensure that your budget, methods, and scope will enable you to bring an intersectional lens to your work. *Who will be impacted by this project, directly and indirectly? Which communities will we engage and why?*

- **Research:** Verify that you are still on the right track and reflect on whether your approach aligns with what you have learned. *How would we describe our relationships with community members we've engaged?*

- **Analysis:** Build insights about the forces and factors that impact stakeholders' experiences. *Have we listened deeply and fully to the community members we have engaged?*

- **Design:** Ensure that early design outcomes are aligned with the needs and contexts of the communities you are working with. *In what ways have community members shaped our designs?*

- **Evaluation:** Check if your methods of evaluation are inclusive for your stakeholders and are providing you with meaningful feedback. *Whom have we engaged for feedback and testing?*

- **Storytelling:** Craft narratives that highlight impacts and outcomes in dignified, human terms. *How are we illustrating the factors and forces that affect people differently in this context?*

1. Kaleidoscope. (n.d.). *Artefact Group*. Retrieved July 25, 2024, from https://kaleidoscope.artefactgroup.com/

2. Synthesized and quoted from the Kaleidoscope website.

Value Posture	Action Orientation	Ethical Framework
Eliciting values	Consensus building	Deontological
Critically engaging	Evaluating	Consequentialist
Defamiliarizing	Framing	Virtue
	Generating	Pragmatist

Method Input	Method Mechanic	Method Output
Concepts	Altering	Concepts
Stakeholder Info	Storytelling	Stakeholder Info
Constraints/Goals	Filtering	Constraints/Goals
Values	Creating	Values
Use Context	Mapping	Evaluation Outcomes

planning

You're putting your proposal or plan together for a project. You want to make sure you're baking equity and inclusion into the scope, methods, budget, and timeline.

kickoff

Your project is approved and you're just getting started! You want to align your team and stakeholders and start to develop a deeper understanding of the "problem," its context and implications, who you'll engage and how, and what success will look like.

research

You're about halfway through your initial research/exploration phase. You want to check if the path that you're on still makes the most sense, given what you set out to do and what you've been learning.

analysis

You're done with your initial research/exploration phase and faced with tons of information. You want to pull insights that describe the major factors and forces that impact experiences and figure out which perspectives to highlight.

design

You've got early iterations of a design solution. You want to make sure your designs are rooted in what you've learned and aligned to the needs and contexts of the communities that they will impact.

evaluation

You have design solutions that you want to test and get feedback on. You want to check if your testing methods are inclusive and are getting you feedback that is meaningful.

storytelling

You're ready to describe your process and tell a story about the intended impacts of your design. You want to craft compelling narratives that paint a dignified, human picture, and highlight the details that are relevant to your designs.

Examples of cards for different phases of the design process with prompts to get your team started (top).

Kaleidoscope allows your team to embrace the complexity of identities, examine the context more thoroughly, identify who holds power in a context, and reflect on how and whether a solution will serve a community appropriately (bottom).

Images courtesy of the Artefact Group.

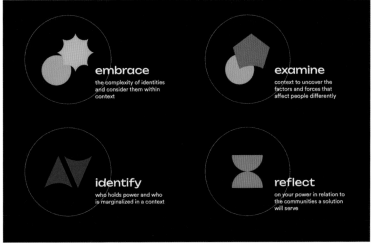

embrace
the complexity of identities and consider them within context

examine
context to uncover the factors and forces that affect people differently

identify
who holds power and who is marginalized in a context

reflect
on your power in relation to the communities a solution will serve

See also INTERSECTIONALITY • FEMINIST DESIGN PRINCIPLES • WORKERS TAROT DECK

55 Lake of Ethical Tensions

Lake of Ethical Tensions allows you to visualize how ethical tensions manifesting at different levels impact your ethical decision-making.[1]

#alignmyteam #designresponsibility

Ethical tensions exist as a "felt conflict between two or more differing perspectives related to individual practices, organizational practices, or applied ethical outcomes."[2] These ethical tensions often lead to value trade-offs or conflicts in cross-disciplinary teams.

Lake of Ethical Tensions[3] visualizes how ethical tensions create "ripples" in a designer's ethical decision-making, impacting users or product creation, and then propagating outward to impact a larger portion of the designer's ecosystem. Visualizing these tensions begins with identifying one or more ethical tensions you face in their everyday work. Placing an ethical tension at the center, map the types of ripples that are formed to help you identify the impact or influence of each ethical tension.[1] The ethical tensions can be described through different types of ripples:

- **Personal/individual** visualizes how the ethical tension is impacting one's own disciplinary and personal values, processes, and practices. For instance: *How is this ethical tension conflicting with my disciplinary values that I was taught to support?*

- **Organizational** visualizes the propagation of the ethical tension to members of one's team, organizations, and/or external clients' values, processes, and methods. For instance: *How is this ethical tension impacting the dynamics of product development between the UX designer's team and software engineering team? How is this ethical tension implying an institutional conflict or required change in practices?*

- **Societal** visualizes the propagation of the ethical tension to the larger ecosystem, including primary and secondary users, the environment, and society. For instance: *How does this ethical tension have long-term consequences on the community using the product or society at large?*

You can create one ripple structure for each ethical tension with ripples around it based on the intensity of the tension and involved actors, methods, values, and practices. Multiple ripple structures combine to create a "Lake" of Ethical Tensions that intersect and overlap. Visualize these overlaps to identify how the ripples impact your design features, product, and/or service.

1. Pillai, A. G., Sachathep, T., & Ahmadpour, N. (2022). Exploring the experience of ethical tensions and the role of community in UX practice. *Nordic Human-Computer Interaction Conference*, Article 60. https://doi.org/10.1145/3546155.3546683

2. Chivukula, S. S., Obi, I., Carlock, T. V., & Gray, C. M. (2023). Wrangling ethical design complexity: dilemmas, tensions, and situations. *Designing Interactive Systems Conference (DIS Companion '23)*. https://dl.acm.org/doi/abs/10.1145/3563703.3596632

3. Inspired by the Impact ripple canvas. (n.d.). *Design. Think. Make. Break. Repeat.* Retrieved July 9, 2024, from https://designthinkmakebreakrepeat.com/toolkit/impact-ripple/

Value Posture	Action Orientation	Ethical Framework
Eliciting values	Consensus building	Deontological
Critically engaging	Evaluating	Consequentialist
Defamiliarizing	Framing	Virtue
	Generating	Pragmatist

Method Input	Method Mechanic	Method Output
Concepts	Altering	Concepts
Stakeholder Info	Storytelling	Stakeholder Info
Constraints/Goals	Filtering	Constraints/Goals
Values	Creating	Values
Use Context	Mapping	Evaluation Outcomes

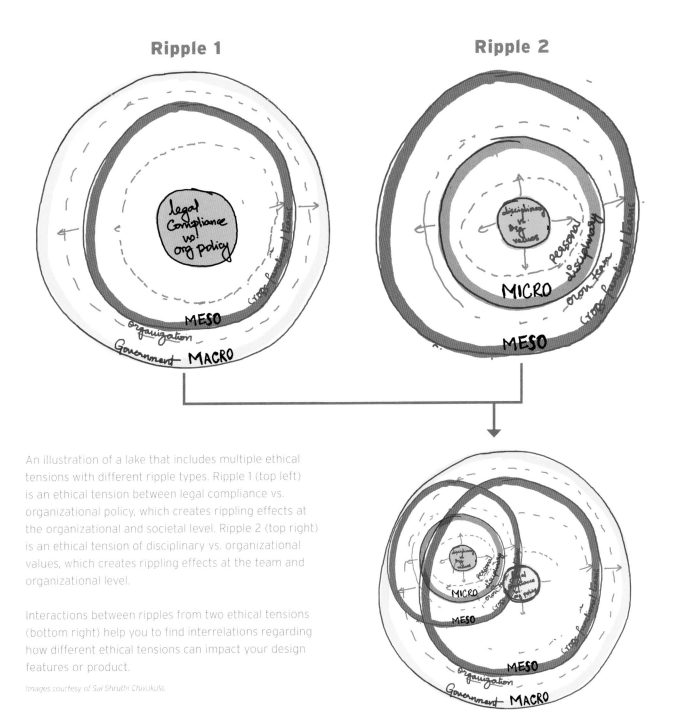

Ripple 1

Ripple 2

legal Compliance vs org policy

MESO
organization
Government MACRO

disciplinary vs. org. values

personal
org team
disciplinary
cross functional team
MICRO

MESO

An illustration of a lake that includes multiple ethical tensions with different ripple types. Ripple 1 (top left) is an ethical tension between legal compliance vs. organizational policy, which creates rippling effects at the organizational and societal level. Ripple 2 (top right) is an ethical tension of disciplinary vs. organizational values, which creates rippling effects at the team and organizational level.

Interactions between ripples from two ethical tensions (bottom right) help you to find interrelations regarding how different ethical tensions can impact your design features or product.

Images courtesy of Sai Shruthi Chivukula.

MICRO
MESO
MESO
organization
Government MACRO

See also ETHICAL TENSION CARDS • VALUES LEVERS • LAYERS OF EFFECT

56 Layers of Effect

Layers of Effect breaks down complex effects of your designs based on primary, secondary, and tertiary dimensions.[1]

#breakmydesign #evaluateoutcomes #identifyvalues

Designers build features into products using a prioritized list of values, visions, and operable factors that are relevant to their business or other stakeholder needs. The prioritization of these features is based on the design team's understanding of the user's needs, the shareholder's benefits or business needs, and the potential for future expansion of the product. Each of these priorities includes a set of layered ethical consequences or unintended harms that warrant further scrutiny.

Layers of Effect allows designers to break down aspects of the design product or service to forecast ways to achieve "no significant harm" across three dimensions:[2]

- **Primary effects** are intended at production of the design. These effects are known and intentional as relevant to the users, and can be placed at the innermost circle beside the product.

- **Secondary effects** are generative in nature and can evolve over time to grow the product. These effects are also known and intentional and are relevant to the company shareholders. These can be placed onto a second layer outward from the product.

- **Tertiary effects** are unforeseen and emerge only once the product or service is in use. These effects are unintended consequences that can be good or bad, and can be placed in an expandable outer layer from the product to indicate its unlimited and evolving nature.

1. Zhou, K. (2021). Layers of effect. *Design Ethically Toolkit.* https://www.designethically.com/layers

Further Reading

Zhou, K. (2023). *Design Ethically Toolkit.* https://www.designethically.com/toolkit

Value Posture	Action Orientation	Ethical Framework
Eliciting values	Consensus building	Deontological
Critically engaging	Evaluating	Consequentialist
Defamiliarizing	Framing	Virtue
	Generating	Pragmatist

Method Input	Method Mechanic	Method Output
Concepts	Altering	Concepts
Stakeholder Info	Storytelling	Stakeholder Info
Constraints/Goals	Filtering	Constraints/Goals
Values	Creating	Values
Use Context	Mapping	Evaluation Outcomes

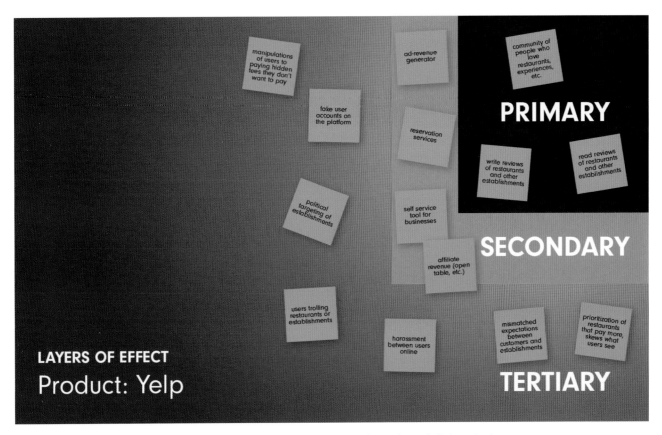

Example mapping of the three Layers of Effect (primary, secondary, tertiary) for a digital product.

Image courtesy of Kat Zhou.

See also *LAKE OF ETHICAL TENSIONS • JUDGMENT CALL • DICHOTOMY MAPPING*

METHOD

57 Make It (Critical)

Make It (Critical) encourages you to playfully interpret current realities and consider other realities based on a set of provocative statements.[1]

#breakmydesign #evaluateoutcomes #identifyvalues

Value-centered design work focuses on acknowledging and embedding core human values into design work. However, considering alternative values may result in identifying novel design approaches that might not be immediately intuitive or rational.

Make It (Critical) is a deck of cards that provides a pragmatic means for designers to activate conceptual or theoretical approaches such as critical design or speculative design. The deck includes a wide range of prompts that allow the designer to consider new critically focused and action-oriented directions for future ideation. In keeping with the goal of critical design, the outcomes are not meant to become real products or concepts in their own right, but rather serve as ways to explore the design space and better understand what values might be relevant and what kinds of futures are more or less desirable.

Examples of the prompts ask the designer "make this…":[1]

- …promote sustainability
- …slightly subversive
- …reveal a hidden truth
- …answer life's tough questions
- …self-protective
- …an outlet for frustration
- …comforting
- …rely on superstition
- …increase tranquility
- …improve empathy for others
- …open up new lines of communication
- …a spiritual activity
- …standoffish
- …show respect
- …an intimate experience
- …surprisingly productive
- …judgmental
- …cater to nostalgia
- …somewhat mystical

1. Stallings, M. (2013). *Make it (critical): an ideation tool based on critical and speculative design* [Masters Capstone]. Indiana University Bloomington.

Value Posture	Action Orientation	Ethical Framework	Method Input	Method Mechanic	Method Output
Eliciting values	Consensus building	Deontological	Concepts	Altering	Concepts
Critically engaging	Evaluating	Consequentialist	Stakeholder Info	Storytelling	Stakeholder Info
Defamiliarizing	Framing	Virtue	Constraints/Goals	Filtering	Constraints/Goals
	Generating	Pragmatist	Values	Creating	Values
			Use Context	Mapping	Evaluation Outcomes

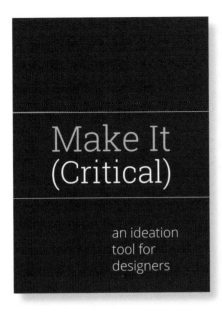

Make It (Critical)

Make this...
promote
sustainability

makeitcritical.com

Flower Lamp
Interactive Institute Swedish ICT, 2006

"If the household has a decreasing trend of electricity use, the Flower lamp rewards you by slowly opening up to "bloom". If, on the other hand, use is increasing, the lamp folds its petals together." *photo by Anette Andersson*

Make It
(Critical)

an ideation
tool for
designers

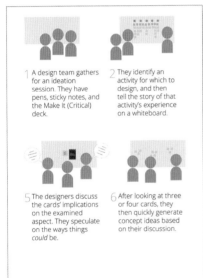

1 A design team gathers for an ideation session. They have pens, sticky notes, and the Make It (Critical) deck.

2 They identify an activity for which to design, and then tell the story of that activity's experience on a whiteboard.

5 The designers discuss the cards' implications on the examined aspect. They speculate on the ways things *could* be.

6 After looking at three or four cards, they then quickly generate concept ideas based on their discussion.

Make It (Critical)

Make this...
keep track of
something
mundane

makeitcritical.com

Candy Camera
Shad Gross, 2013

"A traditional-style gumball machine that has been retrofitted with a trigger, web camera, and LCD screen. Turning the machine's crank causes the camera to capture an image, which is then added to an automated slideshow."

Instructions to engage with the Make It Critical method and examples of two of the cards ("Make this promote sustainability"; "Make this keep track of something mundane") with corresponding photo examples on the card backs.

Image courtesy of Michael Stallings.

See also CRITICAL DESIGN • SPECULATIVE DESIGN • QUEERING

58 Maslow Mirrored

Maslow Mirrored enables you to identify positive and negative effects of your product on a particular type of user based on Abraham Maslow's needs hierarchy.[1]

#breakmydesign #evaluateoutcomes

Designers build features, products, and services based on human needs, requiring that we understand how humans view the world and what humans need to feel safe, secure, and actualized. Maslow has divided these needs into hierarchical categories, building from basic survival to transcendence:[2]

- **Physiological needs** relate to basic survival needs such as food, water, utilities, and shelter.

- **Safety needs** relate to emotional security, financial security, law and order, well-being, and protection from any harm.

- **Love needs** relate to emotional support, collective enterprise, belongingness, and connectedness to a group.

- **Esteem needs** relate to a sense of accomplishment, respect, and self-value.

- **Self-actualization needs** relate to personal growth, health, desires, and meaning of one's life.

- **Transcendence needs** relate to "beyond the self" outlook of growth, spiritual awakening, and altruism to serve.

Maslow Mirrored guides the designer to identify how each of the need categories could be satisfied by a product or service for a particular kind of user, and if so, what the positive or negative impact might be. Designers can brainstorm the positive aspects on the right and then write the negative aspects on the left creating a mirrored image of good and bad consequences of a product as it impacts a specific user.

1. Zhou, K. (2021). Maslow mirrored. *Design Ethically Toolkit*. https://www.designethically.com/maslow-mirrored

2. Quoted from Zhou, 2021.

Further Reading

Zhou, K. (2023). *Design Ethically Toolkit*. https://www.designethically.com/toolkit

Value Posture	Action Orientation	Ethical Framework
Eliciting values	Consensus building	Deontological
Critically engaging	Evaluating	Consequentialist
Defamiliarizing	Framing	Virtue
	Generating	Pragmatist

Method Input	Method Mechanic	Method Output
Concepts	Altering	Concepts
Stakeholder Info	Storytelling	Stakeholder Info
Constraints/Goals	Filtering	Constraints/Goals
Values	Creating	Values
Use Context	Mapping	Evaluation Outcomes

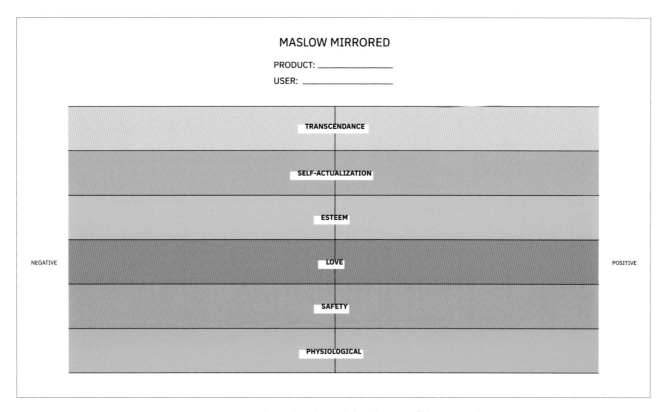

Worksheet with spaces for negative and positive characteristics relating to one of the six Maslow needs hierarchy elements: transcendence, self-actualization, esteem, love, safety, and physiological.

Image courtesy of Kat Zhou.

See also *INVERTED BEHAVIOR MODEL • HUMANE DESIGN GUIDE*

59 Method (Resonance) Heuristics

Method (Resonance) Heuristics guide you in evaluating and customizing methods for ethical decision-making based on your design goals, ecological factors, and visual aesthetics.[1]

#evaluateoutcomes #alignmyteam

Design methods have both a prescriptive and performative nature,[2] meaning that a method can be considered "useful" for practical application based on its prescriptive characteristics (e.g., how easy is it to use this method?), the performance of the method as part of a designer's normal "toolbox" (e.g., what purpose does this method serve to further my design activity?), and performance of the method in a specific work context (e.g., if applied, how does the method align with other practices in my team or organizational setting?).

Any resource (such as those listed in this book) can be used by designers in multiple ways based on different elements of the design situation. For instance, different use contexts, constraints, or scenarios may demand a customized approach. Similarly, different work situations such as internal team dynamics, interdisciplinary team explorations, and stakeholder alignment could shape the selection or use of a resource. And finally, a designer's perception of the ease of use of a resource, including the time needed to use or apply it, its perceived relevance, or the need to combine multiple resources, adds additional complexity.

Method (Resonance) Heuristics allows you to identify, evaluate, and iterate upon any resource you select to enhance your ethical decision-making by using heuristics in three main categories:

- **Design intentions and Phase heuristics** list a set of use cases for where and when a resource can be used or you want to tweak to be appropriated at any stage of a design process.

- **Ecology heuristics** list different ways part of a resource or a whole resource can align (or not) with the current practices in your team, organization, and ecological practices.

- **Artifact heuristics** list visual or content-based factors related to the method that makes it easy or difficult to use the method.

1. Chivukula, S. S. (2023). Method-resonance heuristics. *shruthichivukula*. https://shruthichivukula.com/aeiou-toolkit/methodresonance-heuristics-ethicstool

2. Gray, C. M. (2022). Languaging design methods. *Design Studies, 78*, 101076. https://doi.org/10.1016/j.destud.2021.101076

Value Posture	Action Orientation	Ethical Framework
Eliciting values	Consensus building	Deontological
Critically engaging	Evaluating	Consequentialist
Defamiliarizing	Framing	Virtue
	Generating	Pragmatist

Method Input	Method Mechanic	Method Output
Concepts	Altering	Concepts
Stakeholder Info	Storytelling	Stakeholder Info
Constraints/Goals	Filtering	Constraints/Goals
Values	Creating	Values
Use Context	Mapping	Evaluation Outcomes

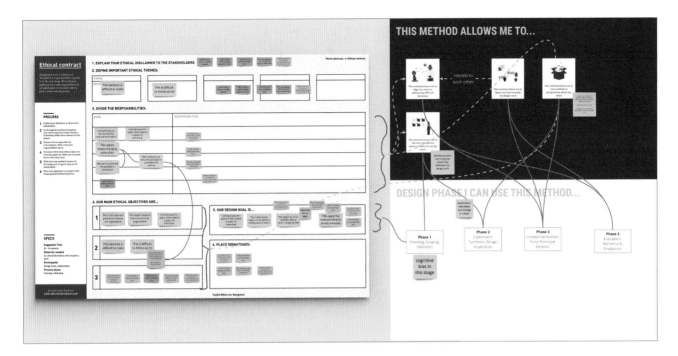

Method (Resonance) Heuristics are applied to "Ethical Contract," a method to align ethical responsibilities of a team of designers and developers through a sprint. Designer identified that the method could be used to align and remove cognitive bias across stakeholders when used in Phase 1: Planning and Scoping using Phase heuristics, and found it difficult to list "ethical themes" using Ecology heuristics, saying that it was not a part of their everyday practice at their work.

Image courtesy of Sai Shruthi Chivukula.

See also (TACTICS OF) SOFT RESISTANCE • VALUES LEVERS • A.E.I.O.YOU

60 Monitoring Checklist

Monitoring Checklist provides guidance for you to evaluate your product or service based on values of autonomy, transparency, and safety.[1]

#evaluateoutcomes #alignmyteam

Design features, products, and services are not static and don't always work as anticipated in the initial production cycle. Instead, design outcomes need constant monitoring to better understand their intended and unintended consequences on users, adversaries, and society, including how particular values might help a designer understand what future iteration is needed for product success.

Monitoring Checklist provides a systematic approach to assess the ethical qualities of a design product or service based on asking questions related to three key values:[2]

- **Autonomy** allows you to monitor if users are provided with features to share feedback, report negative behaviors, customize their experience, and balance user experience with shareholder demands.

- **Transparency** allows you to track if the features manipulate a user's sense of reality, spread misinformation, trick users to give personal data or privacy, and hide important information needed to make informed decisions.

- **Safety** allows you to identify if features cause indirect or direct harm, infringe on a user's privacy, exploit the user's agency without their awareness, or exclude any set of humans from accessing the product or service.

Using the concept of Monitoring Checklist, you can:

- Identify a set of values relevant for your design context and generate a checklist to evaluate your design product or service.

- Update your set of monitoring questions relevant to specific job functions during scrum meetings.

- Share and standardize the practice of creating, applying, and customizing monitoring checklists within your organization.

1. Zhou, K. (2021). Monitoring checklist. *Design Ethically Toolkit.* https://www.designethically.com/monitoring

2. Quoted from Zhou, 2021.

Further Reading

Zhou, K. (2023). *Design Ethically Toolkit.* https://www.designethically.com/toolkit

Value Posture	Action Orientation	Ethical Framework
Eliciting values	Consensus building	Deontological
Critically engaging	Evaluating	Consequentialist
Defamiliarizing	Framing	Virtue
	Generating	Pragmatist

Method Input	Method Mechanic	Method Output
Concepts	Altering	Concepts
Stakeholder Info	Storytelling	Stakeholder Info
Constraints/Goals	Filtering	Constraints/Goals
Values	Creating	Values
Use Context	Mapping	Evaluation Outcomes

At this point in time, is our product:

AUTONOMY

- Sacrificing enjoyable user experience for shareholder demands?
- Making it intentionally difficult for users to accomplish a task that benefits them (and does not harm others)?
- Not allowing users to share their feedback or easily ask for help?
- Making it hard for users to report negative behavior or outcomes?
- Not allowing users to customize their experience (notifications, accessibility, privacy, etc.)?

TRANSPARENCY

- Manipulating their sense of reality in an untruthful way?
- Spreading misinformation?
- Tricking people into paying money?
- Deliberately hiding information regarding the consequences of certain user actions?
- Tricking users into providing personal data that they don't intend on giving?

SAFETY

- Emotionally manipulating users in any capacity?
- Infringing on users' privacy in a way of which they are unaware?
- Excluding any users?
- Exploiting user data or giving it to any other entity that plans on exploiting the data?
- Inaccessible to any users?
- Vulnerable to any breaches from malicious third-party entities?
- Causing indirect or direct physical harm on users, nonusers, employees, etc.?

Checklist questions courtesy of Kat Zhou.

See also TAO FRAMEWORK • DIGITAL ETHICS COMPASS

61 Moral Agent

Moral Agent challenges your moral creativity, enabling you to translate values into design outcomes in a fun and engaging manner.[1]

#identifyvalues #applyvalues

Ideating to generate new ideas and perspectives on a project is central to design work. To generate new ideas, designers can draw on a range of sources of inspiration, including outputs from user research, knowledge of user needs, behaviors, and pain points, or by considering heuristics that help identify new potential design directions. Similarly, a designer can leverage moral values to brainstorm new ideas and thereby build more ethical design outcomes. Using this approach, values can be considered as practical and creative resources to consider different forms of ethical engagement.

Moral Agent is an ideation game based on a set of moral values that are activated by shuffling a deck of cards. A team of designers start with a specific design goal. Then, each designer is dealt a set of random moral value cards, which they then use to ideate features or products based on the team's chosen design goal. Each moral value card contains a value, its definition, and set of reflective prompts that guide to brainstorm ideas.[1] Using Moral Agent, you can:

- **Brainstorm** a set of ideas across multiple values and then combine to create features or products.

- **Shape** a particular idea based on a sequence of values by picking up cards one after the other.

- **Discuss** in your team to identify different ways one or more values can be translated into features or products.

- **Circulate** a particular idea you designed based on a value to another designer to build over it based on another value.

1. Gispen, J. (2017). Moral agent. *Ethics for Designers*. https://www.ethicsfordesigners.com/moral-agent

Further Reading

Gispen, J. (2017). Ethics for designers toolkit. *Ethics for Designers*. https://www.ethicsfordesigners.com/tools

Value Posture	Action Orientation	Ethical Framework
Eliciting values	Consensus building	Deontological
Critically engaging	Evaluating	Consequentialist
Defamiliarizing	Framing	Virtue
	Generating	Pragmatist

Method Input	Method Mechanic	Method Output
Concepts	Altering	Concepts
Stakeholder Info	Storytelling	Stakeholder Info
Constraints/Goals	Filtering	Constraints/Goals
Values	Creating	Values
Use Context	Mapping	Evaluation Outcomes

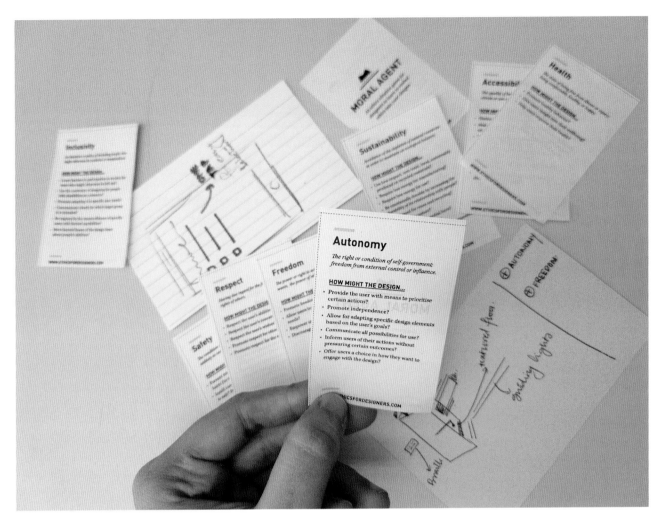

Using Autonomy and Freedom Moral Value Cards to guide design ideas to sketch for a technology-mediated doorway entrance.

Image courtesy of Sai Shruthi Chivukula with cards courtesy of Jet Gispen.

See also *TAROT CARDS OF TECH* • *MORAL VALUE MAP*

62 Moral and Legal Decks

Moral and Legal Decks enable you to engage in structured reflection on the ethical and legal implications of your design outcomes.[1]

#breakmydesign #evaluateoutcomes #applyvalues

Legal and governmental entities increasingly regulate which kinds of features and outcomes are lawful, providing guidance through regulation or legislation on what types of design decisions are deemed good for society and lawful. Thus, in addition to generating ethical design outcomes based on judgments about whether they are "good" or "bad," designers must also assess the intersection of "legal, ethical, technical and social implications of new information technologies" when determining what kinds of design decisions to make.[1]

Moral and Legal Decks provide designers with a holistic means to consider ethical implications and build legal compliance into technologies by design and default.[2]

- The **Moral Deck** is a collection of critical ethical questions designers need to ask of their new technology. These questions are grouped into four themes: privacy, ethics, law, and security. For each theme, further values and probes are presented for designer reflection. For instance, a card under the *Security* theme presents the value of *Obfuscation,* probing "How does your technology protect people's identities? Does it use anonymization or pseudonymization techniques?"

- The **Legal Deck** is a quick reference to rights, principles, definitions, and responsibilities from five European legal frameworks, including GDPR, the e-Privacy Regulation, and Budapest Convention on Cybercrime. Each card in the deck allows the designer to identify design outcomes that are prohibited, decisions that constitute illegal moves, and the responsibilities of a designer as they focus on generating solutions.

1. Urquhart, L., & Craigon, P. (2018, July 17). Moral and legal IT cards. *Lachlan's Research.* https://lachlansresearch.com/the-moral-it-legal-it-decks/

2. Urquhart, L., & J. Craigon, P. (2021). The moral-IT deck: a tool for ethics by design. *Journal of Responsible Innovation, 8*(1), 94-126. https://doi.org/10.1080/23299460.2021.1880112

Value Posture	Action Orientation	Ethical Framework
Eliciting values	Consensus building	Deontological
Critically engaging	Evaluating	Consequentialist
Defamiliarizing	Framing	Virtue
	Generating	Pragmatist

Method Input	Method Mechanic	Method Output
Concepts	Altering	Concepts
Stakeholder Info	Storytelling	Stakeholder Info
Constraints/Goals	Filtering	Constraints/Goals
Values	Creating	Values
Use Context	Mapping	Evaluation Outcomes

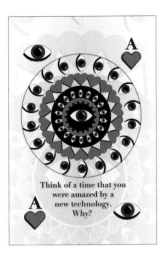

Examples of cards from the Moral (top left and bottom) and Legal decks (top right) that enable exploration of ethical issues and legal requirements.

See also MORAL VALUE MAP • MORAL AGENT

63 Moral Value Map

Moral Value Map helps you map concerns that might arise through your designs in a context of use based on relevant moral values.[1]

#breakmydesign #evaluateoutcomes #identifyvalues

Ethical theories draw heavily from moral philosophy to define values that humans can manifest and operationalize in their ways of thinking and doing right and wrong. Moral values embody aspects of a human's everyday being and self-awareness. On the other hand, in practice, designers constantly inscribe a range of values into the solutions they generate, and values are a manifestation of ethical decision-making.

Moral Value Map encourages designers to evaluate their designs and consider opportunities to embed moral values into their decision-making. This mapping exercise helps situate what specific moral values to work with in relation to generated designs and stakeholder-specific value priorities. Mapping based on moral values with your stakeholders or team members can help resolve any value conflicts and priorities. The mapping encourages a series of translations of these Values into Concerns in context of use (Value x Context of Use = Concern) and Concerns into Effects of your designs. "The design *inhibits/supports/limits/enhances/prevents/enables/reinforces/undermines/challenges* this concern." The Effects of your design could be used to iterate your existing designs.

Based on the type of design outcome, you can identify moral values related to human users that focus on experiential and embodied affects of a given product on a user, in a context, and on use practices. Examples of these values include:[1]

· **Entertainment:** Being excited or feeling heightened arousal.

· **Physical well-being:** Feeling healthy, energetic, or physically robust.

· **Exploration:** Satisfying one's curiosity about personally meaningful events.

· **Belonging:** Building/maintaining attachments, friendships, intimacy, or a sense of community.

· **Equity:** Promoting fairness, justice, reciprocity, or equality.

· **Giving:** Giving approval, support, assistance, advice, or validation to others.

1. Gispen, J. (2017). Moral value map. *Ethics for Designers.* https://www.ethicsfordesigners.com/moral-value-map

Further Reading

Gispen, J. (2017). Ethics for designers toolkit. *Ethics for Designers.* https://www.ethicsfordesigners.com/tools

Value Posture	Action Orientation	Ethical Framework
Eliciting values	Consensus building	Deontological
Critically engaging	Evaluating	Consequentialist
Defamiliarizing	Framing	Virtue
	Generating	Pragmatist

Method Input	Method Mechanic	Method Output
Concepts	Altering	Concepts
Stakeholder Info	Storytelling	Stakeholder Info
Constraints/Goals	Filtering	Constraints/Goals
Values	Creating	Values
Use Context	Mapping	Evaluation Outcomes

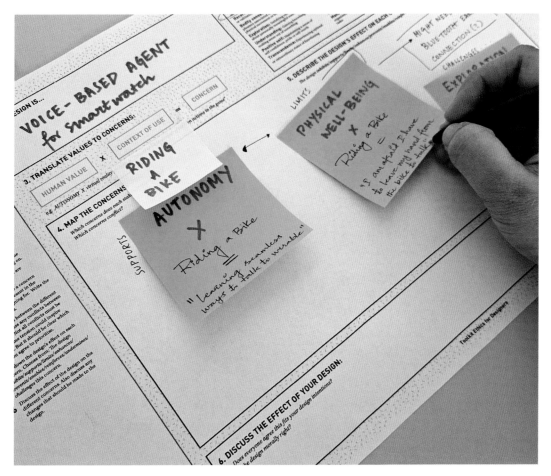

An example of the Moral Value Map template being used to evaluate a voice-based agent for a smart watch based on the moral values of autonomy, physical well-being, and exploration. Theme of Concerns revolves around interacting with the agent on the watch and balancing the act of biking.

Image courtesy of Sai Shruthi Chivukula based on worksheet from Jet Gispen.

VALUE
X
USE CONTEXT
=
CONCERN

See also HUVALUE • EMPATHIC WALK-THROUGH • WORRYSTORMING

64 More-Than-Human Design

More-Than-Human Design enables you to consider nonhuman actors, capabilities, and knowledge when considering the impacts and outcomes of your design work.[1,2]

#newperspectives #identifyvalues #applyvalues

Design approaches that put the focus on human needs instead of technological capabilities are well known to most designers, using titles such as "human-centered design" or "user-centered design." More-Than-Human Design, drawing on post-humanist perspectives, expands our understanding even further to consider the wide range of actors, dependencies, and relations that shape the world that we live in. This approach acknowledges that many more stakeholders than just humans are included in the design context and impacts of design. And in doing so, this framing of design work encourages critical reflection on humanity's role in environmental and socio-technical change, including the ways these changes can and do shape not only humans but also the world around us.

Key questions in More-Than-Human Design include:[3]

- **Who or what are the actors:** Identify the human and nonhuman actors involved and for whom the design should be desirable. Consider both more-than-human species (e.g., nature, the planet, and anything that goes beyond only human flourishing) and more-than-human things (e.g., robots, AI agents, sensors, devices, and digital platforms).

- **Distribution of capabilities and agency:** Examine how power is distributed across humans, machines, and natural systems. Consider new methodologies that acknowledge and incorporate broader forms of intelligence and life.

- **New knowledge and partnerships:** Identify new stakeholders and partnerships needed to design for complex, emergent problems. Consider the role of technologies and actors from other species as participants and partners in the design process.

1. Forlano, L. (2017). Posthumanism and design. *She Ji: The Journal of Design, Economics, and Innovation, 3*(1), 16-29. https://doi.org/10.1016/j.sheji.2017.08.001

2. Bekker, T., Eriksson, E., Fougt, S. S., Hansen, A.-M., Nilsson, E. M., & Yoo, D. (2023, April 28). Challenges in teaching more-than-human perspectives in human-computer interaction education. *Proceedings of the 5th Annual Symposium on HCI Education.* https://doi.org/10.1145/3587399.3587406

3. Quoted and synthesized from Forlano (2017) and Bekker et al. (2023).

Further Reading

Design and post-humanism network. (n.d.). https://designandposthumanism.org/

Forlano, L., & Sedini, C. (2021). More than human trading zones in design research and pedagogy. In *Routledge Handbook of Art, Science, and Technology Studies* (pp. 198-213). Routledge. https://doi.org/10.4324/9780429437069-15

Value Posture	Action Orientation	Ethical Framework		Method Input	Method Mechanic	Method Output
Eliciting values	Consensus building	Deontological		Concepts	Altering	Concepts
Critically engaging	Evaluating	Consequentialist		Stakeholder Info	Storytelling	Stakeholder Info
Defamiliarizing	Framing	Virtue		Constraints/Goals	Filtering	Constraints/Goals
	Generating	Pragmatist		Values	Creating	Values
				Use Context	Mapping	Evaluation Outcomes

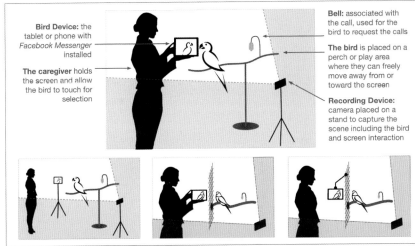

Bird Device: the tablet or phone with *Facebook Messenger* installed

The caregiver holds the screen and allow the bird to touch for selection

Bell: associated with the call, used for the bird to request the calls

The bird is placed on a perch or play area where they can freely move away from or toward the screen

Recording Device: camera placed on a stand to capture the scene including the bird and screen interaction

A Parrot-to-Parrot Video-Calling System (left) that allows birds to call other birds on mobile devices (bottom) in ways that value the animals' agency and goals as part of a broader enrichment strategy.

Images courtesy of Rebecca Kleinberger, Megha M. Vemuri, Jennifer Cunha, and Ilyena Hirskyj-Douglas. Reproduced with permission from Kleinberger, R., Cunha, J., Vemuri, M. M., & Hirskyj-Douglas, I. (2023, April 19). Birds of a feather video-flock together: design and evaluation of an agency-based parrot-to-parrot video-calling system for interspecies ethical enrichment. Proceedings of the 2023 CHI Conference on Human Factors in Computing Systems. CHI '23: CHI Conference on Human Factors in Computing Systems, Hamburg Germany. https://doi.org/10.1145/3544548.3581166.

Try Out a Multispecies Ethnography

Activity courtesy of Laura Forlano

Choose a specific plant, animal, or microorganism/microbe (bacteria, fungi, algae, protozoa, and viruses) to focus on. Draw on your own experience, read journal articles or newspaper/magazine articles, and/or listen to podcasts and watching videos about the topic in order to develop your understanding. For example, if you are interested in birds, consider going to the Cornell University Ornithology Lab to listen to/watch videos about a specific species of birds.

As part of your ethnographic work, consider documenting the following:

· Your own experience of coronavirus, awareness of microorganisms in everyday life

· A favorite plant, animal, microorganism, or physical landscape, i.e., a houseplant, a pet, an experience you had on vacation in nature

· A plant, animal, microorganism that you are curious to know more about and/or understand better

See also MULTISPECIES DESIGN DECK · CRITICAL DESIGN · SLOW DESIGN

65 Motivation Matrix

The Motivation Matrix prioritizes a user's motivating factors to interact with your existing or new product to evaluate or build user value-centered design outcomes.[1]

#breakmydesign #evaluateoutcomes

The value centeredness of design products and services can be characterized by how well the product intentions align with the user's needs, values, and motivations. There are six "core types" of motivation that frame how users interact with design products and services, including incentive, achievement, social acceptance, fear, power, and growth.[1] Motivation Matrix prioritizes a user's motivation, context, and actions at the core of creating design products, resulting in user value-centered products.

The Motivation Matrix can be built by listing the six motivating factors as rows and one or more users in a different context as multiple columns, resulting in a matrix. For instance, a column could indicate a skilled unemployed person (user) looking for a new job (context). Once the framework of the matrix is in place, designers can draft statements to fill the matrix with potential user actions with the existing or new product in a particular context based on the motivation type. This collection of statements can frame user values, contextual factors, and motivating factors that can define pragmatic design values for generating, evaluating, and/or refining product or service features. You can use this matrix to:

- Identify instances of unintended consequences or manipulative motivations of users with your product or service ahead of time.

- Consider different users and a range of contexts in which your product or service could be used to diversify interactions.

- Include secondary users of your product or service to project consequences of your product or service.

1. Zhou, K. (2021). Motivation matrix. *Design Ethically Toolkit.* https://www.designethically.com/motivation-matrix

Further Reading

Zhou, K. (2023). *Design Ethically Toolkit.* https://www.designethically.com/toolkit

Value Posture	Action Orientation	Ethical Framework
Eliciting values	Consensus building	Deontological
Critically engaging	Evaluating	Consequentialist
Defamiliarizing	Framing	Virtue
	Generating	Pragmatist

Method Input	Method Mechanic	Method Output
Concepts	Altering	Concepts
Stakeholder Info	Storytelling	Stakeholder Info
Constraints/Goals	Filtering	Constraints/Goals
Values	Creating	Values
Use Context	Mapping	Evaluation Outcomes

	USER A @ CONTEXT A	USER B @ CONTEXT B
Incentive	[Motivation] + [Action]	[Motivation] + [Action]
Achievement	[Motivation] + [Action]	[Motivation] + [Action]
Social Acceptance	[Motivation] + [Action]	[Motivation] + [Action]
Fear	[Motivation] + [Action]	[Motivation] + [Action]
Power	[Motivation] + [Action]	[Motivation] + [Action]
Incentive	[Motivation] + [Action]	[Motivation] + [Action]

Motivation Matrix worksheet with spaces to indicate how different motivations might be supported in different ways for particular contexts and users.

Adapted from worksheet by Kat Zhou.

MOTIVATION TYPE
X
USE @ CONTEXT
=
MOTIVATION MATRIX

See also MASLOW MIRRORED • ETHICAL BLUEPRINT • NODDER'S 7 DEADLY SINS

66 Multispecies Design Deck

Multispecies Design Deck supports you in centering nonhuman beings, species, and worlds in the design of your product or service.[1]

#breakmydesign #newperspectives

More-Than-Human Design approaches decenter humans and their needs in order to think in more ecologically sensitive ways about products or services and the impact they have on the environment and our possible futures.

The Multispecies Design Deck allows you to leverage the knowledge and experience of nonhuman beings as a part of your design process, considering the possibilities, consequences, and circumstances of these additional actors within an ecology. Through this process, you can engage with and evaluate the impacts of human-centered designs on "other than human" beings. Elements of the Multispecies Design Deck can guide you in addressing following dimensions or qualities of these worlds:[2]

- **Transformation:** Learn about the biological process of how plants or nonhuman animals transform, restore, contain memory, perform movement, survive through adaptation, decompose, and rebuild, e.g., *How would our product disrupt or use biological mechanisms in nonhumans?*

- **Power and autonomy:** Understand the power human beings have over other species in different contexts as it relates to liberation, control, resilience, agency, revolution, and mechanisms they use to defend themselves, e.g., *How do power structures work in nonhuman communities and how will our design disrupt or support them?*

- **Relationality:** Consider the evolutionary aspects of the species in these worlds in terms of time and rhythm, legacies, histories, traces, and relationality, e.g., *How will your design products implement or remove traces of nonhuman species?*

- **Kinship:** Contemplate the role of community-focused behaviors and generational concerns such as cohabitation, balance, entanglements, and coexistence, e.g., *How does our design product or service support or eradicate communities of nonhuman beings?*

- **Disturbance:** Map the behaviors of conflict in different ecosystems and contexts through warning, toxicity, and death, e.g., *How does our product or service disturb these species and to what extremes?*

1. Smith, N., & Hurst, A. (2023). Multispecies design cards. *Some Quiet Future.* http://somequietfuture.com/research#/multispecies-design/

2. Summarized and quoted from Smith & Hurst (2023).

Further Reading

Smith, N., Bardzell, S., & Bardzell, J. (2017, May 2). Designing for cohabitation: naturecultures, hybrids, and decentering the human in design. *Proceedings of the 2017 CHI Conference on Human Factors in Computing Systems.* https://doi.org/10.1145/3025453.3025948

Value Posture	Action Orientation	Ethical Framework		Method Input	Method Mechanic	Method Output
Eliciting values	Consensus building	Deontological		Concepts	Altering	Concepts
Critically engaging	Evaluating	Consequentialist		Stakeholder Info	Storytelling	Stakeholder Info
Defamiliarizing	Framing	Virtue		Constraints/Goals	Filtering	Constraints/Goals
	Generating	Pragmatist		Values	Creating	Values
				Use Context	Mapping	Evaluation Outcomes

Examples of the Multispecies Design Deck cards with evocative imagery and
qualities to help you consider more-than-human perspectives in your design work.

Image courtesy of Nancy Smith.

See also CRITICAL DESIGN • QUEERING • MORE-THAN-HUMAN DESIGN

67 Nodder's 7 Deadly Sins

Nodder's 7 Deadly Sins use satire to critically engage with artifacts crafted at the intersection of customer psychology, behavioral economics, and marketing to evaluate "good" and "evil" futures.[1]

#evaluateoutcomes #designresponsibility

Users can easily be manipulated through the use of techniques from customer psychology, behavioral economics, marketing, and design. These manipulative aims can leverage a range of different concepts such as dark patterns, persuasive design, nudge theory, or even "asshole design."[2] Nodder's "7 Deadly Sins," popularly known through the book *Evil By Design*,[1] illustrate a human weakness that businesses can carefully leverage to market their products and achieve their goals, often at the expense of the user.

- **Pride** changes beliefs of users through concepts of solving by using gamification techniques, providing social proof, and validating user choices through similarities.

- **Sloth** revolves around getting greater outcomes with less effort by implementing techniques of bundling interactions, following the "default" options, or obfuscating important information.

- **Envy** creates desirability, aspirations, and status differences to drive behavior by letting people feel important, advertising their status, and creating a sense of achievement over others.

- **Lust** intensifies desire for any item by using flattery, emotions, "free" value, reciprocity, groupism, and commitment.

- **Gluttony** regulates moments of failure of self-control by making people work for a reward, escalating commitment, lure for scarcity (loss aversion), and relying on people's emotional feeling of commitment.

- **Anger** understands what causes the fear and acts to remove it by implementing humor, metaphysical arguments and anonymity, making people morally disengage by making an authority figure tell them to do things, and showing solutions.

- **Greed** reinforces desires by framing task achievements as "wins," rewarding the skill, not luck, and making products expensive for a bloated sense of appreciation.

Using this humorous framing, you can evaluate concepts by asking "Who Benefits?" through such outcomes. Is it the business itself? Is it the user? Does it support an equitable society?

1. Nodder, C. (2013). *Evil by design: interaction design to lead us into temptation.* John Wiley & Sons.

2. Gray, C. M., Chivukula, S. S., & Lee, A. (2020). What kind of work do "asshole designers" create? Describing properties of ethical concern on Reddit. *Proceedings of the 2020 ACM Designing Interactive Systems Conference*, 61-73. https://doi.org/10.1145/3357236.3395486

Further Reading

Nodder, C. (n.d.). *Evil by Design.* https://evilbydesign.info/

Value Posture	Action Orientation	Ethical Framework
Eliciting values	Consensus building	Deontological
Critically engaging	Evaluating	Consequentialist
Defamiliarizing	Framing	Virtue
	Generating	Pragmatist

Method Input	Method Mechanic	Method Output
Concepts	Altering	Concepts
Stakeholder Info	Storytelling	Stakeholder Info
Constraints/Goals	Filtering	Constraints/Goals
Values	Creating	Values
Use Context	Mapping	Evaluation Outcomes

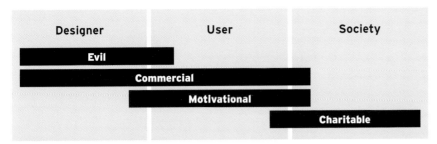

Designer	User	Society
Evil		
Commercial		
	Motivational	
		Charitable

Schema to identify the type of design (Evil, Commercial, Motivational, Charitable) based on whether a designer's decision is benefiting self (designer/developer/shareholder), users, and/or society.

Adapted from a schema by Chris Nodder.

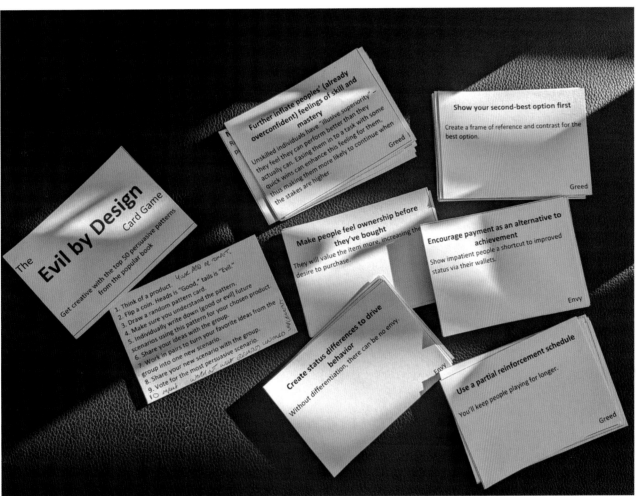

The 7 Deadly Sins and respective principles are used in a Persuasive Pattern Game where designers can draw a pattern card from the card deck to design for "good" or "evil" futures.

Image courtesy of Chris Nodder.

See also HUMANE BY DESIGN · FAIR PATTERNS · MASLOW MIRRORED

68 Normative Design Scheme

Normative Design Scheme allows you to assess your design goals and brainstorm ideas based on normative ethical theories.[1]

#evaluateoutcomes #applyvalues #designresponsibility

As designers set goals for the outputs of their design activity, they must make many choices about what methods to use, which values to inscribe, what users they will prioritize, the purpose of the product or service, and relevant ethical objectives.[2] However, these goals have many facets and components that can be complex to understand and evaluate.

Normative Design Scheme enables you to break down your design goals into components to better assess whether you are considering the "right" things and encouraging you to iterate on the goals using normative ethical theories. First, a design goal has to be formulated into three parts to clearly identify: the Intention (*We want to...*), the Design (*By doing...*), and the Effect (*In order to...*).[1] For each of these parts, you can then apply a normative ethical theory to assess and iterate (How can you change?) on the design goal in the following way:

· **Intention ← Virtue Ethics:** Assess the designer's intention for creating the product or service in relation to actions of a virtuous person. Designers can ask: "How could our design stimulate virtuous behavior?"

· **Design ← Deontology:** Assess the product or service to identify whether it abides by moral norms and the duty of a ethical designer. Designers can ask: "Which moral and social norms apply to our design?"

· **Effect ← Consequentialism:** Assess the effect of the design, including if it produces the best and actual purpose to most people who are expected to engage with the product or service. Designers can ask: "What are the consequences of our design on different stakeholders?"

Using the Normative Design Scheme, you can also use the same three-part structure to brainstorm ideas to build ethical design outcomes rooted from the normative ethical theories of deontology, consequentialism, and virtue.

1. Gispen, J. (2017). Normative design scheme. *Ethics for Designers*. https://www.ethicsfordesigners.com/normative-design-scheme

2. Gispen, J. (2017). Ethical contract. In *Ethics for Designers*. https://www.ethicsfordesigners.com/ethical-contract

Further Reading

Gispen, J. (2017). Ethics for designers toolkit. *Ethics for Designers*. https://www.ethicsfordesigners.com/tools

Value Posture	Action Orientation	Ethical Framework		Method Input	Method Mechanic	Method Output
Eliciting values	Consensus building	Deontological		Concepts	Altering	Concepts
Critically engaging	Evaluating	Consequentialist		Stakeholder Info	Storytelling	Stakeholder Info
Defamiliarizing	Framing	Virtue		Constraints/Goals	Filtering	Constraints/Goals
	Generating	Pragmatist		Values	Creating	Values
				Use Context	Mapping	Evaluation Outcomes

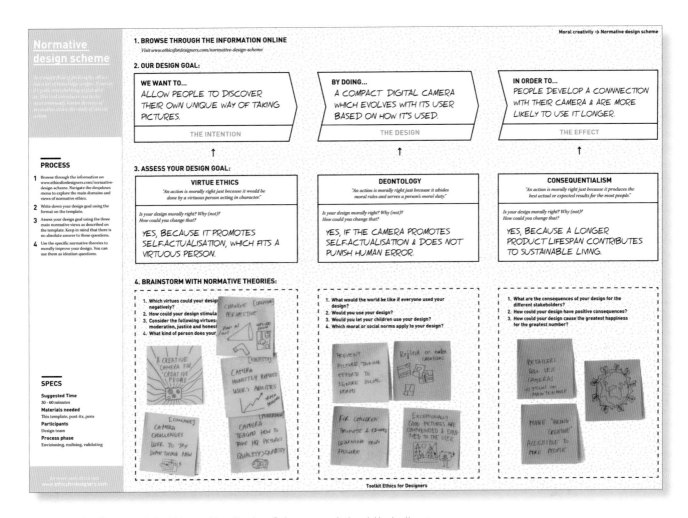

An example of a completed Normative Design Scheme worksheet that allows
the designer to consider different design outcomes for cameras based on
virtue, deontological, and consequentialist ethics considerations.

Image courtesy of Jet Gispen.

See also LAYERS OF EFFECT • ENVISIONING CARDS • VALUE VOTING

69 Oracle for Transfeminist Technologies

Oracle for Transfeminist Technologies helps you conceptualize transfeminist technological products and services, foreseeing and ideating more inclusive futures.[1]

#newperspectives #identifyvalues #applyvalues

To foresee or imagine a more inclusive design world, designers need to consider approaches that draw from intersectional ways of looking at the kinds of humans. Building on these approaches, designers can then identify what values should be embedded in products and services.

Oracle for Transfeminist Technologies builds upon transfeminist values, encompassing a set of cards that can help designers foresee and ideate transfeminist technologies from the future and reflect on how these futures might support or contest existing norms around ableist and noninclusive designs. Designers can randomly draw two Value cards, the Territories + Bodies card, one Object, and one Situation card from the Oracle related to transfeminist ideologies to design concepts:[2]

- **Values** include solidarity, socio-environmental justice, resilience, queerness, pleasure, open source, nonbinary, multispecies, intuition, intersectionality, interoperability, embodiedness, decoloniality, diversity, decentralization, consent, agency, and autonomy.

- **Territories + Bodies** is a reminder that "you carry stories of the body and the territories you inhabit."

- **Objects** include wine, umbrella, trash bin, spoon, skateboard, sandals, plant, mirror, lipstick, headphones, hat, envelope, and any other daily objects.

- **Situations** include guaranteed access to the internet and technology; defending the right to freedom of political, religious, and sexual expression; rethinking and reclaiming pornography; granting unrestricted access to information; and using technology as a tool for feminist resistance.

1. The oracle for transfeminist technologies. (n.d.). Retrieved December 28, 2022, from https://www.transfeministech.codingrights.org/

2. Quoted from The Oracle for Transfeminist Technologies cards.

Value Posture	Action Orientation	Ethical Framework
Eliciting values	Consensus building	Deontological
Critically engaging	Evaluating	Consequentialist
Defamiliarizing	Framing	Virtue
	Generating	Pragmatist

Method Input	Method Mechanic	Method Output
Concepts	Altering	Concepts
Stakeholder Info	Storytelling	Stakeholder Info
Constraints/Goals	Filtering	Constraints/Goals
Values	Creating	Values
Use Context	Mapping	Evaluation Outcomes

Examples of Value cards (top), Object cards (middle), and Situation cards (bottom) that you can use to divine potential futures.

Images courtesy of Coding Rights and the Design Justice Network, including concept and coordination by Joana Varon (Coding Rights) and Sasha Constanza-Chock (Design Justice Network), with design and illustration by Clarote (Coding Rights).

USE TECHNOLOGY AS A TOOL FOR ENVIRONMENTAL INTERSECTIONAL JUSTICE

RESILIENCE

See also TAROT CARDS OF TECH • FEMINIST INTERACTION PRINCIPLES • QUEERING

70 Participatory Design

Participatory Design enables you to ensure that "those who will use the technology have a voice in its design," supporting "mutual learning for designers and users."[1]

#applyvalues #newperspectives #designresponsibility

Participatory Design, often shortened simply to "PD," emerged as part of a Scandinavian tradition of design activism in the 1960s. Early PD efforts in Scandinavia were focused on interactions between designers, trade unions, and other stakeholders, with the goal of enhancing democracy by enabling workers to have a say in their own working conditions.[1] With overarching goals of empowerment and emancipation,[2] modern PD activity can be characterized as a research discipline, a type of design practice, and a conceptual vocabulary that prioritizes the needs and participation of multiple types of stakeholders in complex contexts and ecologies.

Common mechanisms of PD include concepts such as balancing power relations among differing stakeholders, using playful methods to explore design spaces, encouraging hands-on participation in considering the role of future technologies through prototyping, and engaging in "futuring."[2] While the landscape of PD is vast, Bannon and colleagues describe some considerations when contextualizing PD for our modern political and economic challenges:[3]

- **Consider what role democracy has in our current technology landscape.** While labor unions were the focus in the early history of PD, large "surveillance capitalism" platforms may be a more relevant contemporary threat to emancipation and the proper functioning of democracy.

- **Creatively explore the role of methods to enable PD activities.** How might design approaches be used to explore research spaces in new ways, or how can new methods (like those in this book) be used to democratize stakeholder relations in workshops or other research activities?

1. Simonsen, J., & Robertson, T. (2012). *Routledge international handbook of participatory design.* Routledge

2. Hansen, N. B., Dindler, C., Halskov, K., Iversen, O. S., Bossen, C., Basballe, D. A., & Schouten, B. (2020). How participatory design works: mechanisms and effects. *Proceedings of the 31st Australian Conference on Human-Computer-Interaction*, 30–41. https://doi.org/10.1145/3369457.3369460

3. Bannon, L., Bardzell, J., & Bødker, S. (2018). Reimagining participatory design. *Interactions, 26*(1), 26-32. https://doi.org/10.1145/3292015

Value Posture	Action Orientation	Ethical Framework
Eliciting values	Consensus building	Deontological
Critically engaging	Evaluating	Consequentialist
Defamiliarizing	Framing	Virtue
	Generating	Pragmatist

Method Input	Method Mechanic	Method Output
Concepts	Altering	Concepts
Stakeholder Info	Storytelling	Stakeholder Info
Constraints/Goals	Filtering	Constraints/Goals
Values	Creating	Values
Use Context	Mapping	Evaluation Outcomes

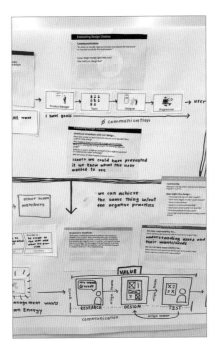

Designers completing activities as part of a Participatory Design workshop. The activities are generatively and physically focused, allowing the participants to cocreate materials together by incorporating their own perspectives.

Images courtesy of Colin M. Gray and UXP² lab members.

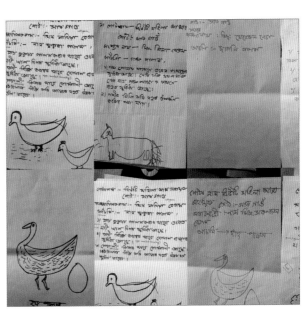

An example of participatory design with women in Sathgaon, a northeastern Indian village. Through sketching, they shared their microfinancing techniques and identified potential improvements for building revenue in their village.

Images courtesy of Sai Shruthi Chivukula.

See also FUTURES CONE • WORKERS TAROT DECK • DESIGN JUSTICE PRINCIPLES

71 Pledge Works

Pledge Works invites you to support responsible design by writing pledges that link your design work to specific goals.[1]

#alignmyteam #designresponsibility

Many professions have codes of ethics or other tools to guide responsible and ethical behavior. However, these types of resources can be abstract and difficult to put into practice in the context of everyday design activity.

Pledge Works "bridge[s] the gap between good intentions and everyday product decisions."[1] Pledges can be made at every step of the design process in different levels of specificity, resulting in a flexible mechanism to articulate goals for yourself and your design team. You can write context-based pledges for specific types of work or contexts, or role-based pledges that are written with a specific employee's professional role in mind. Each pledge also includes indications of a specific value and context. Consider using one of these types of pledges:[2]

- **Simple Pledges** are promises that indicate how you want to act. They can be company level (e.g., *"We pledge to respect people we build products for and treat them as friends, not users."*) or project level (e.g., *"We will ensure people's anonymity on votes both in the UI and on the API."*).

- **Responsible Stories** incorporate the person making the pledge, the pledge itself, and the reason the person is making the pledge. Consider a project-level responsibility story like this one: *"As a responsible team, we pledge to use simple and inclusive language in the UI because we want to make our tool accessible to non-native English speakers and easy to adopt in diverse teams."*

- **To Whom Pledges** extend the responsible story format, incorporating the intended audience for the pledge. For instance: *"As a responsible UX professional, I pledge to the planet: I will minimize digital waste and use tools that aim to reduce our environmental impact because I want to do my part in keeping the climate livable for future generations."*

1. Pledge works. (2022, March 1). *Responsible Tech. Work.* https://responsibletech.work/tools/development/pledge-works/

2. Synthesized and quoted from the Pledge Works website.

Value Posture	Action Orientation	Ethical Framework
Eliciting values	Consensus building	Deontological
Critically engaging	Evaluating	Consequentialist
Defamiliarizing	Framing	Virtue
	Generating	Pragmatist

Method Input	Method Mechanic	Method Output
Concepts	Altering	Concepts
Stakeholder Info	Storytelling	Stakeholder Info
Constraints/Goals	Filtering	Constraints/Goals
Values	Creating	Values
Use Context	Mapping	Evaluation Outcomes

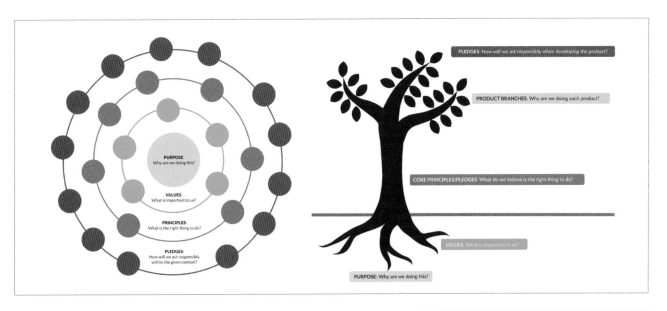

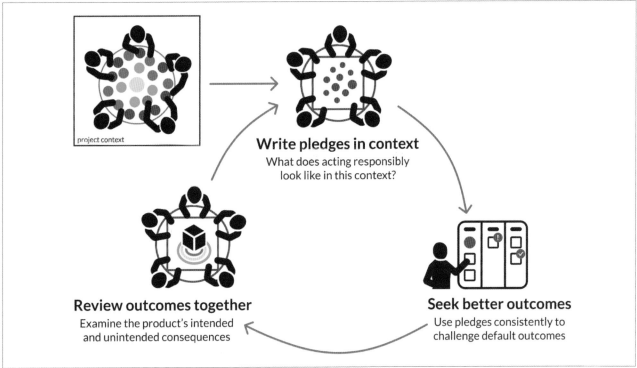

(top) A diagram that identifies how pledges can support purposes, values, and principles.
(bottom) Examples of how pledges can be written and used by teams in project contexts to support better outcomes over time.

See also HIPPOCRATIC OATH • ETHICAL CONTRACT

72 Privacy by Design

Privacy by Design prepares you to proactively embed privacy into systems, supporting users' privacy through transparent, visible, and respectful solutions.[1]

#evaluateoutcomes #applyvalues

Our modern world is surrounded by systems that capture and use data to provide services. However, data can contribute to systems that surveil, control, and manipulate users. Data practices increasingly must abide by regulatory standards to protect users' interests at every stage of the product life cycle, but there are also opportunities to raise privacy protections even further.

Privacy by Design is a proactive approach that ensures privacy is considered and embedded into systems and processes from the beginning, rather than as an afterthought. Using this approach, anticipate and prevent events that threaten user privacy, building trust and protecting user data across the entire technology life cycle. Integrate these seven principles into your work practices:[2]

- **Proactive, not reactive; preventive, not remedial:** Anticipate and prevent privacy issues before they occur, and correct negative impacts that do occur in systematic and creative ways.

- **Privacy as the default:** Automatically protect personal data in any system or business practice by default, requiring no action from the individual to maintain their privacy.

- **Privacy embedded into design:** Ensure privacy as an integral part of the system's design and architecture, not as an add-on. Embed privacy into both technologies and business processes.

- **Full functionality—positive-sum, not zero-sum:** Aim for a win-win situation where all legitimate interests and objectives are accommodated without unnecessary trade-offs.

- **End-to-end security—life cycle protection:** Protect users' privacy across the entire life cycle of the data, from collection to secure destruction, ensuring comprehensive security.

- **Visibility and transparency:** Ensure that all systems operate according to promised privacy standards, with all components visible and able to be independently verified.

- **Respect for user privacy:** Champion the interests of users through strong privacy defaults, appropriate notice, and user-friendly options that empower them to manage their data.

1. Cavoukian, A. (2009). *Privacy by design: the 7 foundational principles.* Information & Privacy Commissioner of Canada.

2. Quoted and synthesized from Cavoukian (2009).

Further Reading

Agencia Española Protección Datos. (2019). A guide to privacy by design. https://www.aepd.es/guides/guide-to-privacy-by-design.pdf

Value Posture	Action Orientation	Ethical Framework
Eliciting values	Consensus building	Deontological
Critically engaging	Evaluating	Consequentialist
Defamiliarizing	Framing	Virtue
	Generating	Pragmatist

Method Input	Method Mechanic	Method Output
Concepts	Altering	Concepts
Stakeholder Info	Storytelling	Stakeholder Info
Constraints/Goals	Filtering	Constraints/Goals
Values	Creating	Values
Use Context	Mapping	Evaluation Outcomes

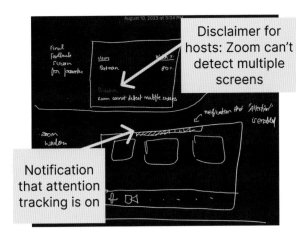

Disclaimer for hosts: Zoom can't detect multiple screens

Notification that attention tracking is on

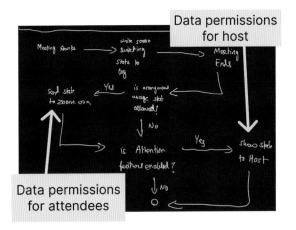

Data permissions for host

Data permissions for attendees

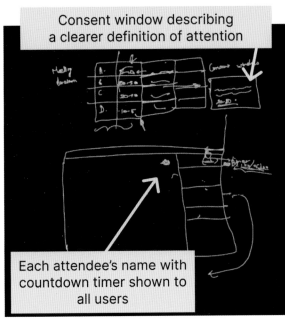

Consent window describing a clearer definition of attention

Each attendee's name with countdown timer shown to all users

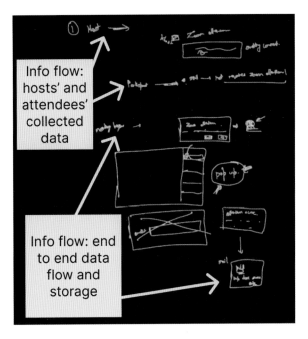

Info flow: hosts' and attendees' collected data

Info flow: end to end data flow and storage

Sketches of the Zoom interface created by software engineers to envision how privacy could be more successfully embedded into the system, building on a deprecated feature in Zoom for "attendee attention tracking." The resulting sketches included features to ensure informed consent, an indication of how data would be collected and stored, and important notifications about attention tracking.

Images courtesy of Tony Li, Arshia Arya, and Haojian Jin. Reproduced with permission from Li, T. W., Arya, A., & Jin, H. (2024, May 11). Redesigning privacy with user feedback: the case of Zoom attendee attention tracking. Proceedings of the CHI Conference on Human Factors in Computing Systems. CHI '24: CHI Conference on Human Factors in Computing Systems. Honolulu, Hawaii. https://doi.org/10.1145/3613904.3642594.

73 Privacy Entanglements

Privacy Entanglements help you identify and reimagine privacy harms and violations by positioning fictional technology in real-world contexts.[1]

#breakmydesign #newperspectives #evaluateoutcomes

Privacy and surveillance products and services are increasingly under scrutiny for their exploitation of user information. While there are many methods and approaches to evaluate privacy issues, it is sometimes helpful to pair current realities with potential futures to identify potential consequences of products.

Privacy Entanglements combine the worlds of as is (real) and alternate, imaginary, or speculative (fictional) to allow designers to investigate, reflect upon, and identify privacy and surveillance issues with digital products and services. This approach allows designers to activate privacy principles and anti-privacy concerns in the real world, drawing from a fictional scenario to evaluate design products or services. To engage with Privacy Entanglements:[2]

1. Select a fictional technological product or service leveraging existing speculative examples.[3]

2. Position and reimagine these fictional products in new realities where the same technologies can be used with new sets of users and contexts.

3. List ways to promote privacy-ensuring interactions and scenarios for your product.

4. Identify potential privacy violations, issues, or harms caused through privacy surveillance, profiling, and harmful impacts.

5. List design objectives that your team can apply to your privacy product or service.

1. Wong, R. Y., Van Wyk, E., & Pierce, J. (2017). Real-fictional entanglements: using science fiction and design fiction to interrogate sensing technologies. *Proceedings of the 2017 Conference on Designing Interactive Systems.* https://doi.org/10.1145/3064663.3064682

2. Adapted and synthesized from Wong et al. (2017).

3. Fictional technological product examples: https://richmondywong.com/docs/circleWorkbookSupplementalMaterials.pdf

Further Reading

Merrill, N. (2020). Security fictions: bridging speculative design and computer security. *Proceedings of the 2020 ACM Designing Interactive Systems Conference,* 1727–1735. https://doi.org/10.1145/3357236.3395451

Value Posture	Action Orientation	Ethical Framework
Eliciting values	Consensus building	Deontological
Critically engaging	Evaluating	Consequentialist
Defamiliarizing	Framing	Virtue
	Generating	Pragmatist

Method Input	Method Mechanic	Method Output
Concepts	Altering	Concepts
Stakeholder Info	Storytelling	Stakeholder Info
Constraints/Goals	Filtering	Constraints/Goals
Values	Creating	Values
Use Context	Mapping	Evaluation Outcomes

An example of a Privacy Entanglement called SeeChange.

SeeChange is described as "a small camera, about the size of a lollipop, which wirelessly records and broadcasts live high-definition video. Its battery lasts for 2 years without recharging. It can be used indoors or outdoors and can be mounted discreetly."[1,3]

Images courtesy of Richmond Wong, Ellen Van Wyk, and James Pierce. Text courtesy of Richmond Wong.

POSITIONING FICTIONAL TECHNOLOGY IN TWO REAL-WORLD CONTEXTS AND USERS

Real-World New Context
Using airport security as a context for SeeChange, an airport surveillance system automatically assigns threat statuses to people by color-coding them.[3]

Privacy harms: Racial profiling through surveillance systems.

Real-World New Context
Using police enforcement as a context for SeeChange, the License Plate Tracker allows a government official to find a person's location history and traffic camera images without restriction.[1]

Privacy support: Easy identification of criminals drawn from multiple cameras and real-time data processing.

See also DESIGN FICTION MEMOS • FUTURES CONE • JUDGMENT CALL

74 Provocatyping

Provocatyping is a critical approach to prototyping that intentionally provokes, defamiliarizes, and allows you to inspect ethical concerns in your product.[1]

#newperspectives #identifyvalues #breakmydesign

Human-centered designers often focus their work on creating design outcomes that are "market-ready." However, some ethical considerations can only be realized by testing the boundaries of social acceptability through creative prototyping.

Provocatyping focuses on making prototypes that are intrusive or provocative in order to highlight what kinds of futures designers do and do not want, similar to the goals of Provotyping.[2] The goal of this method is to provoke thought and generate discussions about ethical concerns, allowing designers to reflect on the consequences of their design choices.

Provocatyping focuses on identifying ethical concerns through ideation and reflection:[3]

1. Begin by designing a version of a specific product or service that is as unethical and irresponsible as possible, while still including some functionality that would be desirable for users.

2. Exaggerate aspects of the product functionality to be as absurd as possible through sketches or descriptions. The intention is not for you to actually launch the product, but rather as a generatively oriented thought experiment.

3. Reflect on why the solution is unethical. Who is it harming, and why? Could an existing solution develop into the more extreme provocatype, and what conditions would be necessary for this to occur?

1. Bowles, C. (2018). *Future ethics.* Nownext Press.

2. Boer, L., & Donovan, J. (2012). Prototypes for participatory innovation. *Proceedings of the Designing Interactive Systems Conference,* 388-397. https://doi.org/10.1145/2317956.2318014

3. Adapted from The Digital Ethics Compass: https://ddc.dk/tools/toolkit-the-digital-ethics-compass/.

Value Posture	Action Orientation	Ethical Framework
Eliciting values	Consensus building	Deontological
Critically engaging	Evaluating	Consequentialist
Defamiliarizing	Framing	Virtue
	Generating	Pragmatist

Method Input	Method Mechanic	Method Output
Concepts	Altering	Concepts
Stakeholder Info	Storytelling	Stakeholder Info
Constraints/Goals	Filtering	Constraints/Goals
Value Context	Creating	Values
Use Context	Mapping	Evaluation Outcomes

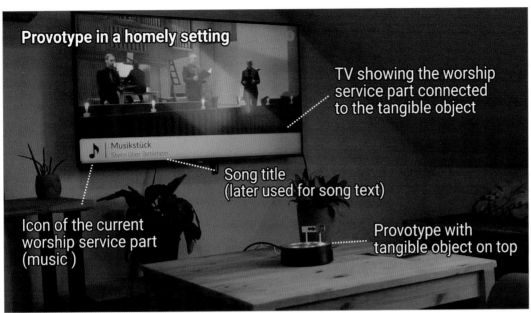

Provotype in a homely setting

TV showing the worship service part connected to the tangible object

Musikstück
Stern über Betlehem

Song title (later used for song text)

Icon of the current worship service part (music)

Provotype with tangible object on top

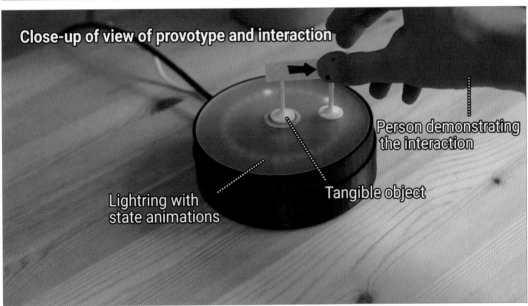

Close-up of view of provotype and interaction

Person demonstrating the interaction

Lightring with state animations

Tangible object

Examples of the "God-I-Box" provotype that enabled the design team to question the interplay of religion and technology. This provotype was used to consider the role of technology in supporting a user's experience in an online worship service.

Image courtesy of Sara Wolf. Reproduced with permission from Wolf, S. Steinmüller B., Mörike, F. Luthe, S., & Hurtienne, J. (2023). The God-I-Box: iteratively provotyping technology-mediated worship services. Proceedings of the 2023 ACM Designing Interactive Systems Conference. DIS '23. Designing Interactive Systems Conference, Pittsburgh, Pennsylvania. https://doi.org/10.1145/3563657.3596029.

See also *CRITICAL DESIGN • SPECULATIVE ENACTMENTS*

75 Queering

Queering encourages you to intentionally disrupt, question, or mock dominant discourses, promoting resistance through design action.[1]

#breakmydesign #applyvalues #newperspectives

Not all approaches to design fit within the mainstream of society. Instead, some critical approaches resist existing norms and structures and celebrate what alternate realities could exist. Queering, building on a legacy of queer theory, "involves disruption or breaking down categories; it is a form of creative subversion that troubles the status quo."[2] Using queering as a design approach involves creating artifacts and systems that question, mock, or subvert societal and technological norms.

Incorporating Queering into your design work involves thinking obliquely, making trouble, and being contrary to mainstream approaches—resisting the creation of efficient, effective, and usable systems and instead celebrating flexibility, appropriation, and pluralism.[1] Queering encourages designing for nonintended uses, allowing users to redefine and repurpose technologies in ways that resist rigid expectations regarding gender, identity, and roles.

To implement Queering in your design practice, consider these strategies that defy straightforward, normative design approaches and are instead focused on "contrariness."[3]

- **Forget:** Consider and redefine what information is forgotten and which information is remembered in the first place. This strategy can help you resist the surveilling properties of technology.

- **Obscure:** Consider what functionality should be opt-in rather than opt-out by default, complicating notions of what information should be public and what information might be problematic if revealed to the outside world.

- **Cheat:** Consider opportunities to operate outside of the normal way of doing things, operating as a hacker or tinkerer that tests the limits of systems.

- **Elude:** Consider ways to resist unified systems of control and instead contemplate how infusing these systems with inaccurate or incomplete information might celebrate pluralism and alternate readings of reality.

1. Light, A. (2011). HCI as heterodoxy: technologies of identity and the queering of interaction with computers. *Interacting with Computers, 23*(5), 430-438. https://doi.org/10.1016/j.intcom.2011.02.002

2. Tran, A.-T., Rothschild, A., Kender, K., Osipova, E., Kinnee, B., Taylor, J., Meyer, L. S., Haimson, O. L., Light, A., & Disalvo, C. (2024). Making trouble: techniques for queering data and AI systems. *Designing Interactive Systems Conference*, 381-384. https://doi.org/10.1145/3656156.3658393

3. Adapted from Light (2011).

Value Posture	Action Orientation	Ethical Framework	Method Input	Method Mechanic	Method Output
Eliciting values	Consensus building	Deontological	Concepts	Altering	Concepts
Critically engaging	Evaluating	Consequentialist	Stakeholder Info	Storytelling	Stakeholder Info
Defamiliarizing	Framing	Virtue	Constraints/Goals	Filtering	Constraints/Goals
	Generating	Pragmatist	Values	Creating	Values
			Use Context	Mapping	Evaluation Outcomes

Button Portraits, a tangible design centered on NFC-enabled buttons and leveraging queer HCI scholarship, encourages participants to engage with queer history in an embodied way. The top images show a participant fastening a button onto their bag while reflecting on how they valued queer history, while the bottom image shows the technology used to drive the interactions.

Photos courtesy of Alexandra Teixeira Riggs and detailed in Riggs, A. T., Janicki, S., Howell, N., & Sullivan, A. (2024, May 11). Designing an archive of feelings: queering tangible interaction with button portraits. Proceedings of the CHI Conference on Human Factors in Computing Systems. CHI '24: CHI Conference on Human Factors in Computing Systems. Honolulu, Hawaii. https://doi.org/10.1145/3613904.3642312.

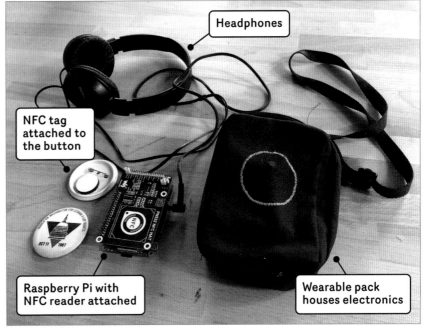

See also CRITICAL DESIGN • ORACLE FOR TRANSFEMINIST TECHNOLOGIES

76 Reflective Design

Reflective Design focuses your attention on critical reflection as a means of identifying new design spaces, engaging both designers and end users in critical reflective practices.[1]

#identifyvalues #evaluateoutcomes #newperspectives

Designers regularly confront design spaces that are shaped by hidden forces that can only be identified through critical reflection. Reflective design is an approach to design that "support[s] both designers and users in ongoing critical reflection about technology and its relationship to human life."[1] Using this approach, a designer can "bring[] unconscious aspects of experience to conscious awareness" and use this knowledge to engage in new ways with technology users. You can implement reflective design through six strategies:[2]

- **Provide for interpretive flexibility.** Introduce and encourage ambiguity as a resource and not as a factor to be eliminated; build open-ended systems where the reflection itself is an irreducible part of the final experience.

- **Give users license to participate.** Present the "strange" in a way that gives footholds for interpretation and bridges from the familiar to the unfamiliar.

- **Provide dynamic feedback to users.** Collect information from users that can be used as a stimulus for reflection. Presenting information back to a user is a way to both stimulate their reflection and give them license to participate.

- **Inspire rich feedback from users.** Evaluation and reflection become an inherent part of the design, inspiring user reflection, which can provide additional value.

- **Build technology as a probe.** Design systems can be used as a stimulus to understand larger social practices, thereby understanding users and their behaviors and as a way of reflecting back on the practices of technology design and evaluation.

- **Invert metaphors and cross boundaries.** Metaphors can help the designer invert traditional assumptions and identify practices that are currently not designed for.

1. Sengers, P., Boehner, K., David, S., & Kaye, J. "Jofish." (2005). Reflective design. *Proceedings of the 4th Decennial Conference on Critical Computing: Between Sense and Sensibility*, 49–58. https://doi.org/10.1145/1094562.1094569

2. Quoted and synthesized from Sengers et al. (2005).

Further Reading

Bentvelzen, M., Wozniak, P. W., Herbes, P. S. F., Stefanidi, E., & Niess, J. (2022). Revisiting reflection in HCI: four design resources for technologies that support reflection. *Proceedings of the ACM on Interactive, Mobile, Wearable and Ubiquitous Technologies, 6*(1), 1–27. https://doi.org/10.1145/3517233

Value Posture	Action Orientation	Ethical Framework
Eliciting values	Consensus building	Deontological
Critically engaging	Evaluating	Consequentialist
Defamiliarizing	Framing	Virtue
	Generating	Pragmatist

Method Input	Method Mechanic	Method Output
Concepts	Altering	Concepts
Stakeholder Info	Storytelling	Stakeholder Info
Constraints/Goals	Filtering	Constraints/Goals
Values	Creating	Values
Use Context	Mapping	Evaluation Outcomes

Photobox, a technology probe that uses reflective design principles to encourage users to reflect on anticipation and slowness. "The behavior Photobox enacts is to search its owner's Flickr collection, randomly select a single image, and then print this image within the box where it will wait to be discovered."

Photos courtesy of William Odom and detailed in Odom, W., Selby, M., Sellen, A., Kirk, D., Banks, R., & Regan, T. (2012, June 11). Photobox: on the design of a slow technology. Proceedings of the Designing Interactive Systems Conference. DIS '12: Designing Interactive Systems Conference 2012, Newcastle Upon Tyne, United Kingdom. https://doi.org/10.1145/2317956.2318055.

77 Refusal

Refusal offers a way for you to push back against and reject technology hegemony and power, either as an individual or in your job role.[1]

#applyvalues #designresponsibility

Refusal is a powerful act of resistance, allowing designers to reject unethical practices, harmful technologies, or projects that perpetuate injustice. Rather than only doing what you are asked, refusal emphasizes the importance of standing up for ethical principles, even when it means refusing to participate in or endorse certain technologies or projects.

The impact of refusal goes beyond simply saying "no." Refusal is a "generative and strategic act … that opens up space to renegotiate the assumptions underlying sociotechnical endeavors."[1] By refusing to comply with unethical demands, designers can challenge the status quo and advocate for more just and equitable technological practices. This practice can manifest in various forms, such as declining to work on projects that violate ethical standards. The #TechWontBuildIt movement resisted Google's involvement in Department of Defense projects,[2] while Microsoft employees protested against a company contract with US Immigration and Customs Enforcement that was likely to harm marginalized individuals.[3]

To implement Refusal in your design practice:

- **Reject harmful projects.** Assess the ethical implications of your projects. If a project violates your ethical principles, refuse to participate and explain your reasoning to stakeholders.

- **Advocate for ethical practices.** Use your influence to promote ethical design practices in your organization. Encourage colleagues to refuse working on projects that harm society.

- **Engage in collective action.** Join or form collectives of like-minded professionals who are committed to ethical design. Collective refusal[4] can amplify your impact and create a stronger push against unethical practices.

- **Re-center marginalized voices.** Use refusal as a means to bring attention to marginalized communities and their perspectives. Challenge projects that perpetuate inequalities and advocate for more inclusive design approaches.

1. Barabas, C. (2022). Refusal in data ethics: reimagining the code beneath the code of computation in the carceral state. *Engaging Science, Technology, and Society, 8*(2), 35–57. https://doi.org/10.17351/ests2022.1233

2. #TechWontBuildIt: the new tech resistance. (n.d.). Retrieved July 22, 2024, from https://radius.mit.edu/programs/techwontbuildit-new-tech-resistance

3. Paulas, R. (2018, September 4). A new kind of labor movement in silicon valley. *The Atlantic.* https://www.theatlantic.com/technology/archive/2018/09/tech-labor-movement/567808/

4. Zong, J., & Nathan Matias, J. (2020, August 12). Building collective power to refuse harmful data systems. *Citizens and Technology Lab.* https://citizensandtech.org/2020/08/collective-refusal/

Value Posture	Action Orientation	Ethical Framework
Eliciting values	Consensus building	Deontological
Critically engaging	Evaluating	Consequentialist
Defamiliarizing	Framing	Virtue
	Generating	Pragmatist

Method Input	Method Mechanic	Method Output
Concepts	Altering	Concepts
Stakeholder Info	Storytelling	Stakeholder Info
Constraints/Goals	Filtering	Constraints/Goals
Values	Creating	Values
Use Context	Mapping	Evaluation Outcomes

A picket line outside of a Microsoft office building, with protesting workers who hold signs with the slogans "Tech Won't Build It" and "#CancelTheContract" in the wake of the company's contract with US Immigration and Customs Enforcement in 2018.

Photo courtesy of Science for the People.

Buttons created and worn by Amazon workers in 2019 articulating a message of solidarity and refusal: "We won't build it."

Public post from the @WeWontBuildIt Twitter/X account.

See also (TACTICS OF) SOFT RESISTANCE • PLEDGE WORKS

78 Responsible AI Practices

Responsible AI Practices support you in integrating ethical considerations into your product, ensuring that these systems are fair, accountable, transparent, and aligned with societal values.[1]

#evaluateoutcomes #applyvalues #alignmyteam

AI is rapidly being integrated into products and services; however, this functionality brings with it a range of ethical issues that designers need to address. Responsible AI focuses on understanding and mitigating risks posed by AI technologies on society, addressing issues such as fairness, accountability, and transparency.

Responsible AI Practices provide examples of how teams of designers and developers can work together to create AI applications that are ethically sound and socially beneficial. Consider these opportunities to implement responsible AI practices in your work:[2]

- **Building and reinforcing an RAI lens:** Cultivate a mindset within your organization that consistently considers the ethical implications of AI systems. This involves sensitizing yourself and your team to potential risks and biases inherent in AI technologies and regularly engaging in self-education and discussions about responsible AI with your team members to keep these issues at the forefront of your design process.

- **Responsible prototyping:** When designing AI applications, create prototypes that reflect responsible AI principles, surfacing potential ethical issues early in the design process. This includes considering the user's mental model of AI, ensuring that the AI's capabilities are clearly communicated, and using prompt programming to test the AI's responses in realistic scenarios.

- **Responsible evaluation:** Conduct a thorough and ongoing evaluation of your AI applications with diverse user groups, seeking to prevent harmful model output before engaging users. By using feedback loops and a diverse range of participants, you can help ensure that the AI system is inclusive and does not perpetuate biases.

1. Wang, Q., Madaio, M., Kane, S., Kapania, S., Terry, M., & Wilcox, L. (2023, April 19). Designing responsible AI: adaptations of UX practice to meet responsible AI challenges. *Proceedings of the 2023 CHI Conference on Human Factors in Computing Systems*. https://doi.org/10.1145/3544548.3581278

2. Synthesized and quoted from Wang et al. (2023).

3. Responsible AI principles and approach. (n.d.). Retrieved July 16, 2024, from https://www.microsoft.com/en-us/ai/principles-and-approach

Further Reading

Amershi, S., Weld, D., Vorvoreanu, M., Fourney, A., Nushi, B., Collisson, P., Suh, J., Iqbal, S., Bennett, P. N., Inkpen, K., Teevan, J., Kikin-Gil, R., & Horvitz, E. (2019). Guidelines for human-AI interaction. *Proceedings of the 2019 CHI Conference on Human Factors in Computing Systems*, 1-13. https://doi.org/10.1145/3290605.3300233

Value Posture	Action Orientation	Ethical Framework
Eliciting values	Consensus building	Deontological
Critically engaging	Evaluating	Consequentialist
Defamiliarizing	Framing	Virtue
	Generating	Pragmatist

Method Input	Method Mechanic	Method Output
Concepts	Altering	Concepts
Stakeholder Info	Storytelling	Stakeholder Info
Constraints/Goals	Filtering	Constraints/Goals
Values	Creating	Values
Use Context	Mapping	Evaluation Outcomes

Fairness

How might an AI system allocate opportunities, resources, or information in ways that are fair to the humans who use it?

Reliability and Safety

How might the system function well for people across different use conditions and contexts, including ones it was not originally intended for?

Privacy and Security

How might the system be designed to support privacy and security?

Inclusiveness

How might the system be designed to be inclusive of people of all abilities?

Transparency

How might people misunderstand, misuse, or incorrectly estimate the capabilities of the system?

Accountability

How can we create oversight so that humans can be accountable and in control?

Responsible AI principles and guiding questions quoted from the Microsoft website.[5]

See also VALUES LEVERS • DATA FEMINISM • WHITE HAT DESIGN PATTERNS

79 Responsible Design Prism

Responsible Design Prism enables you to consider a spectrum of irresponsible to responsible design practices that are mediated by the design artifact, the user, and relevant guidelines.[1]

#designresponsibility

Responsible design practices are those that enable a designer's ethical action, awareness, and advocacy. These practices include the tools and considerations that the designer uses to craft design outcomes that celebrate user agency and value. These practices can be seen as in opposition to manipulative or deceptive alternatives (e.g., "dark patterns") that represent irresponsible design practices.

The Responsible Design Prism includes three primary facets or sides for you to evaluate your design practices: the user, the guidelines and incentives that are being followed, and the design artifact and its purpose. These elements are connected in three-dimensional space as a prism, contrasting the user as a means to an end (irresponsible design) on one end versus the user as themselves (responsible design) on the other end. To use this prism as a source of reflection:

- **Self-reflection:** Where do you stand within the prism and what values do you seek to embed in your work? What forces are acting upon you that shape your behavior and goals?

- **Organization and work ecology:** Where does your organization push you to be and where do you want to be? How do you work with others in your team that are on different points within the prism?

- **Translation:** How can you translate dark patterns into guidelines that can help you build responsible designs? How can you seek to change or better align values with business incentives without using dark patterns?

- **Recovery:** How do you find your way back to the "right side" of the prism?

1. Mildner, T. (2024). *Mitigating dark patterns through responsible design-ethical design considerations for user-centred technologies.* [Doctoral Dissertation], Universität Bremen. https://doi.org/10.26092/elib/3095

Further Reading

Gray, C. M., & Chivukula, S. S. (2019). Ethical mediation in UX practice. *Proceedings of the 2019 CHI Conference on Human Factors in Computing Systems.* https://doi.org/10.1145/3290605.3300408

Value Posture	Action Orientation	Ethical Framework
Eliciting values	Consensus building	Deontological
Critically engaging	Evaluating	Consequentialist
Defamiliarizing	Framing	Virtue
	Generating	Pragmatist

Method Input	Method Mechanic	Method Output
Concepts	Altering	Concepts
Stakeholder Info	Storytelling	Stakeholder Info
Constraints/Goals	Filtering	Constraints/Goals
Values	Creating	Values
Use Context	Mapping	Evaluation Outcomes

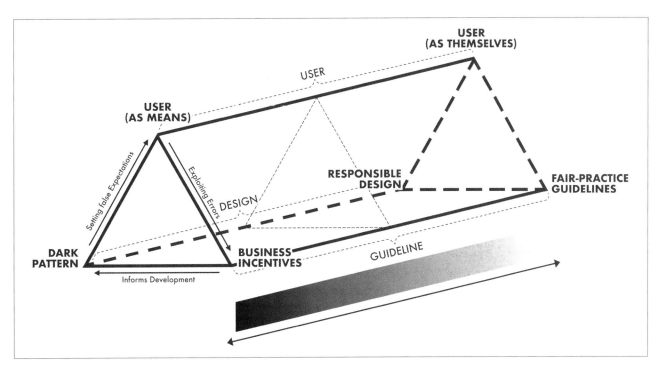

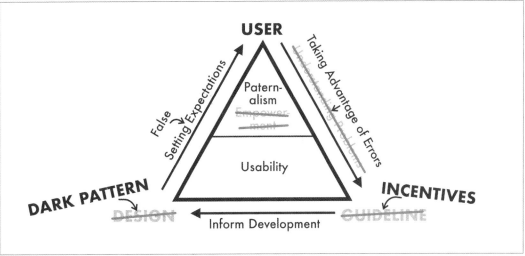

(top) This diagram visualizes the Responsible Design Prism within a three-dimensional space, including axes for design, user, and guidelines.[1] This prism extends from the brighter and responsible side on the right to darker or irresponsible alternatives on the left.

(bottom) An example of the irresponsible end of the prism that "takes advantage of errors" and incorporates dark patterns, focusing on paternalism instead of empowerment.

Images courtesy of Thomas Milaner.

See also FAIR PATTERNS • WHITE HAT DESIGN PATTERNS • ANOTHER LENS

80 Security Cards

Security Cards help you become more aware of the security threats, adversaries, and human impacts your product inadvertently contains.[1]

#breakmydesign #evaluateoutcomes #applyvalues

Digital products and services include embedded forms of security controls that can cause a range of breaches, compromises, and threats to occur. Security Cards provide a range of factors to help you take on the role of an adversary who might seek to compromise these security systems and users who might be impacted by heightened or diminished security.

Security cards provide four ways to consider the security of your product or service:[2]

- **Human impacts** may lead to compromised security, due to factors such as emotional well-being, financial well-being, physical well-being, societal well-being, personal data, or relationships.

- **Adversary's motivations** include potential motivations to attack security systems, such as desire or obsession, curiosity or boredom, diplomacy or warfare, access or convenience, malice or revenge, or politics.

- **Adversary's resources** include the range of technical and social tools needed to attack systems, such as expertise, impunity, inside capabilities or knowledge, money, or influence.

- **Adversary's methods** include potential approaches to attacking a system, such as attack cover-up, indirect attack, manipulation or coercion, multiphase attack, or technological attack.

By using Security Cards, you can:

- Build stronger security in your product or service by envisioning different adversary strengths.

- Evaluate and refine current security solutions based on the Security Cards.

- Craft adversary personas to ideate using anti-personas to consider how users are protected (or not) through existing security systems.

1. Denning, T., Friedman, B., & and Kohno, T. (2013). *The security cards: a security threat brainstorming toolkit.* http://securitycards.cs.washington.edu/

2. Categories summarized from Denning et al. (2013).

Further Reading

VSD Lab. https://vsdesign.org/toolkits/

Value Posture	Action Orientation	Ethical Framework
Eliciting values	Consensus building	Deontological
Critically engaging	Evaluating	Consequentialist
Defamiliarizing	Framing	Virtue
	Generating	Pragmatist

Method Input	Method Mechanic	Method Output
Concepts	Altering	Concepts
Stakeholder Info	Storytelling	Stakeholder Info
Constraints/Goals	Filtering	Constraints/Goals
Values	Creating	Values
Use Context	Mapping	Evaluation Outcomes

Security
and
Privacy
Threat
Discovery
Cards

Examples of cards from the Human
Impacts, Adversary's Motivations,
Resources, and Methods portions of
the card deck.

*Developed by Tamara Denning, Batya Friedman, and
Tadayoshi Kohno. Photography by Nell C. Grey, Daisy Yoo,
and J. P. Arsenault. Graphic Design by Daisy Fry ©2013
University of Washington. This work is made available
under the terms of the Creative Commons Attribution-
NonCommercial-NoDerivs 3.0 License.*

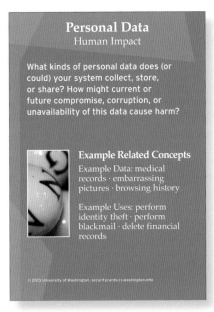

Personal Data
Human Impact

What kinds of personal data does (or
could) your system collect, store,
or share? How might current or
future compromise, corruption, or
unavailability of this data cause harm?

Example Related Concepts

Example Data: medical
records · embarrassing
pictures · browsing history

Example Uses: perform
identity theft · perform
blackmail · delete financial
records

© 2013 University of Washington, securitycards.cs.washington.edu

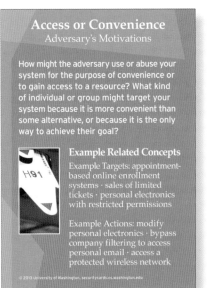

Access or Convenience
Adversary's Motivations

How might the adversary use or abuse your
system for the purpose of convenience or
to gain access to a resource? What kind
of individual or group might target your
system because it is more convenient than
some alternative, or because it is the only
way to achieve their goal?

Example Related Concepts

Example Targets: appointment-
based online enrollment
systems · sales of limited
tickets · personal electronics
with restricted permissions

Example Actions: modify
personal electronics · bypass
company filtering to access
personal email · access a
protected wireless network

© 2013 University of Washington, securitycards.cs.washington.edu

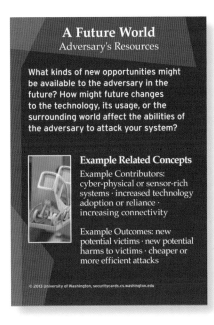

A Future World
Adversary's Resources

What kinds of new opportunities might
be available to the adversary in the
future? How might future changes
to the technology, its usage, or the
surrounding world affect the abilities of
the adversary to attack your system?

Example Related Concepts

Example Contributors:
cyber-physical or sensor-rich
systems · increased technology
adoption or reliance ·
increasing connectivity

Example Outcomes: new
potential victims · new potential
harms to victims · cheaper or
more efficient attacks

© 2013 University of Washington, securitycards.cs.washington.edu

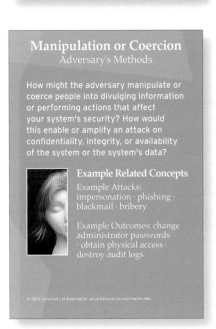

Manipulation or Coercion
Adversary's Methods

How might the adversary manipulate or
coerce people into divulging information
or performing actions that affect
your system's security? How would
this enable or amplify an attack on
confidentiality, integrity, or availability
of the system or the system's data?

Example Related Concepts

Example Attacks:
impersonation · phishing ·
blackmail · bribery

Example Outcomes: change
administrator passwords
· obtain physical access ·
destroy audit logs

© 2013 University of Washington, securitycards.cs.washington.edu

See also ADVERSARY PERSONAS · MORAL AND LEGAL DECKS

81 Slow Design

Slow Design helps you support long-term, human-technology relationships that are reflective, indeterminate, and value-laden.[1]

#evaluateoutcomes #newperspectives #applyvalues

The design of new technologies is often focused on the ideals of efficiency and speed of delivery, often neglecting other important aspects of human flourishing or alternate values that could be embedded into digital systems. With the broad adoption of digital systems in many areas of our lives, concerns are being raised over the ubiquity, place, and pace of new technologies and how they mediate people's experiences in their everyday lives. Slow design (originally referred to as slow technology) seeks to subvert this assumption, instead focusing on "creating technology that surrounds us and therefore is part of our lives over long periods of time."[2]

Slow design argues that designers should expand their focus beyond using technology to make people's lives more efficient toward creating technology that can persist with our lives over longer time periods and support ongoing experiences of interpretation, contemplation, and reflection. By doing so, slow design outcomes help challenge values of optimization, instead focusing on using moments of self-reflection to critically reflect on technology itself. As shown in the example of Olo Radio,[3] a research product created with slow design in mind, a person might be able to actively reflect and reminisce on a complex history of past experiences listening to particular pieces of music. Similarly, Memory Tracer[4] provides a means of investigating and exploring one's location history through spatial and tangible engagement.

Slow design helps you question what qualities a technology ought to have if it were to coexist with us over a wider temporal trajectory:

- Slow design isn't just about a "slow/fast" dichotomy, and slowness is not solely a matter of "speed."

- Slow design should actively facilitate longer-term human-technology relations.

- Slow design requires working with temporal pacing, presence, and expression.

1. Odom, W., Stolterman, E., & Chen, A. Y. S. (2021). Extending a theory of slow technology for design through artifact analysis. *Human-Computer Interaction*, 1-30. https://doi.org/10.1080/07370024.2021.1913416

2. Hallnäs, L., & Redström, J. (2001). Slow technology – designing for reflection. *Personal and Ubiquitous Computing*, 5(3), 201-212. https://doi.org/10.1007/PL00000019

3. Odom, W., & Duel, T. (2018). On the design of OLO Radio: investigating metadata as a design material. *Proceedings of the 2018 CHI Conference on Human Factors in Computing Systems*. https://doi.org/10.1145/3173574.3173678

4. White, J., Odom, W., Brand, N., & Zhong, C. (2023, April 19). Memory tracer & memory compass: investigating personal location histories as a design material for everyday reminiscence. *Proceedings of the 2023 CHI Conference on Human Factors in Computing Systems*. https://doi.org/10.1145/3544548.3581426

Value Posture	Action Orientation	Ethical Framework
Eliciting values	Consensus building	Deontological
Critically engaging	Evaluating	Consequentialist
Defamiliarizing	Framing	Virtue
	Generating	Pragmatist

Method Input	Method Mechanic	Method Output
Concepts	Altering	Concepts
Stakeholder Info	Storytelling	Stakeholder Info
Constraints/Goals	Filtering	Constraints/Goals
Values	Creating	Values
Use Context	Mapping	Evaluation Outcomes

The Memory Tracer[4] research product uses ambient cues to engage with a user's location history.

Image courtesy of William Odom.

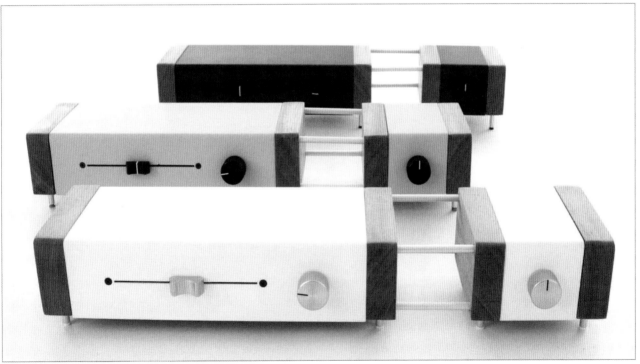

Prototypes of OLO Radio,[3] a research product that allows a user to engage and reminisce with their music listening history (and underlying metadata) in alternative ways.

Image courtesy of William Odom.

See also *REFLECTIVE DESIGN • MORE-THAN-HUMAN DESIGN*

82 Social Accessibility Cards

Social Accessibility Cards prompt you to incorporate social factors when making your work accessible for multiple populations.[1]

#breakmydesign #newperspectives #applyvalues

Designers have to consider human, situational, functional, technical, and social factors in order to successfully conduct research with users, identify solutions, and evaluate final solutions. However, these factors do not always result in inclusive design outcomes. By adding accessibility as a primary factor to consider throughout your work practices, you can better "incorporate[] social situations of use and functional usability"[1] into your design work.

Social Accessibility Cards provide an overarching support structure to "discuss scenarios with users with and without disabilities,"[1] thereby better understanding social situations, factors, and awareness in relation to accessibility at any stage of the design process. Using these cards, you can build your sensitivity toward conducting research and evaluating technology with and for people with disabilities across a range of moments:[2]

- **Getting to know users:** Include users with disabilities early in your research to ask questions not only about disability and accessibility risks but also to learn about their technology interaction in general in a range of different social situations.

- **Nonuse:** Consider social situations where technology use is unappealing or inappropriate for particular types of users.

- **That "awkward moment":** Identify social situations and technological interventions that could contribute to or alleviate awkward interactions.

- **Perceptions of "special" technology:** Explore the reactions of users without disabilities toward unfamiliar technologies designed for users with disabilities.

- **My professional life:** Consider the desires and priorities of users with disabilities to present themselves professionally in the workplace or in other contexts outside of the home.

- **Just like every one else:** Compare and contrast alternative modes and accommodations and their impacts on accessibility.

1. Shinohara, K., Jacobo, N., Pratt, W., & Wobbrock, J. O. (2020). Design for social accessibility method cards: engaging users and reflecting on social scenarios for accessible design. *ACM Transactions on Accessible Computing, 12*(4), 1-33. https://doi.org/10.1145/3369903

2. Quoted or synthesized from the Social Accessibility Cards, available at https://cair.rit.edu/share/Tabloid_DSAMethodCards.pdf.

Value Posture	Action Orientation	Ethical Framework
Eliciting values	Consensus building	Deontological
Critically engaging	Evaluating	Consequentialist
Defamiliarizing	Framing	Virtue
	Generating	Pragmatist

Method Input	Method Mechanic	Method Output
Concepts	Altering	Concepts
Stakeholder Info	Storytelling	Stakeholder Info
Constraints/Goals	Filtering	Constraints/Goals
Values	Creating	Values
Use Context	Mapping	Evaluation Outcomes

Non-Use

Consider
What are social situations (i.e., a party, at work) where technology use is unappealing or inappropriate?

To what extent does comfort or discomfort depend on the way technology functions? For example, text-to-speech may be an unappealing functional solution if the social situation calls for a quiet environment.

Design + Reflect
How might your design incorporate functions that are inappropriate or unappealing to use around others?

Ask Users
• When do you feel un/comfortable using technology?
• When do you choose not to use technology?

Non-Use

People may choose not to use technology in some social situations if they feel uncomfortable, such as when worrying that others will notice hearing aids, or when feeling rude that a talking watch announces every hour.

Just Like Every One Else

Consider
Different modes are often used to provide access, such as text-to-speech. How might modes impact how users:

• Find directions using Google Maps?
• Browse an "accessible" version of a webpage versus "the original"?

Design + Reflect
How do alternative modes and accommodations (e.g., voice vs. touch input) result in differences in access? How might the use of modes create different user experiences?

Ask Users
• When have different modes not provided equal access?
• Describe a time when an accommodation required more work for you to do the same thing as others.

Just Like Every One Else

Alternative accommodation does not always mean access is the same for disabled people. For example, sometimes there is only one accessible entrance to a building and it is in the back.

Examples of the Social Accessibility Cards, which contain elements to consider, design, and reflect upon and questions to ask users.

See also KALEIDOSCOPE • INCLUSIVE ACTIVITY CARDS • ACCESSIBILITY

83 Social Justice Strategies

Social Justice Strategies encourage you to address systemic social issues in a justice-oriented way, focusing on equity, participation, and the impacts of design decisions on marginalized communities.[1]

#evaluateoutcomes #newperspectives #applyvalues

Complex design challenges involve the needs of many stakeholder groups, but not all groups or individuals have the same levels of power or capacity to enact change. The concept of social justice explores how these inequities can be corrected, "explicitly tak[ing] into account how historicity, identity, and social and political context (e.g., class, race, gender, ability, health and wellness, and so on) impact people's lived experiences."[1]

Social Justice Strategies emphasize a commitment to ethical and political responsibility when designers address large-scale social issues. This approach is rooted in understanding and mitigating the power imbalances and inequities that exist within society. Consider implementing these design strategies to increase your awareness of justice-related impacts of your work:[2]

- **Transformation:** Focus on long-term, structural changes that combat systemic inequalities. Design interventions that transform power relations, creating equitable social structures.

- **Recognition:** Identify and articulate unjust practices, policies, and laws. Frame problems in a way that highlights the experiences of marginalized groups and legitimizes their concerns.

- **Reciprocity:** Develop equitable relationships between designers and stakeholders. Design interventions that seek to change inequitable relations and create opportunities for more balanced engagements.

- **Enablement:** Facilitate opportunities for people to develop and fulfill their potential as humans. Design systems that allow for participation and self-determination.

- **Distribution:** Ensure the equitable distribution of the benefits and burdens of social systems. Design for the redistribution of resources in a way that promotes social equity.

- **Accountability:** Hold those who benefit from or perpetuate oppression responsible. Create systems that enable marginalized groups to destabilize dominant power structures.

1. Dombrowski, L., Harmon, E., & Fox, S. (2016). Social justice-oriented interaction design: outlining key design strategies and commitments. *Proceedings of the 2016 ACM Conference on Designing Interactive Systems*, 656–671. https://doi.org/10.1145/2901790.2901861

2. Quoted and synthesized from Dombrowski et al. (2016).

3. Gray, C. M., Williams, R. M., Parsons, P. C., Toombs, A. L., & Westbrook, A. (2023). Trajectories of student engagement with social justice-informed design work. In B. Hokanson, M. Exter, M. M. Schmidt, & A. A. Tawfik (Eds.), *Toward Inclusive Learning Design: Social Justice, Equity, and Community* (pp. 289–301). Springer Nature Switzerland. https://doi.org/10.1007/978-3-031-37697-9_22

Further Reading

Chordia, I., Baltaxe-Admony, L. B., Boone, A., Sheehan, A., Dombrowski, L., Le Dantec, C. A., Ringland, K. E., & Smith, A. D. R. (2024, May 11). Social justice in HCI: a systematic literature review. *Proceedings of the CHI Conference on Human Factors in Computing Systems*. https://doi.org/10.1145/3613904.3642704

Value Posture	Action Orientation	Ethical Framework
Eliciting values	Consensus building	Deontological
Critically engaging	Evaluating	Consequentialist
Defamiliarizing	Framing	Virtue
	Generating	Pragmatist

Method Input	Method Mechanic	Method Output
Concepts	Altering	Concepts
Stakeholder Info	Storytelling	Stakeholder Info
Constraints/Goals	Filtering	Constraints/Goals
Values	Creating	Values
Use Context	Mapping	Evaluation Outcomes

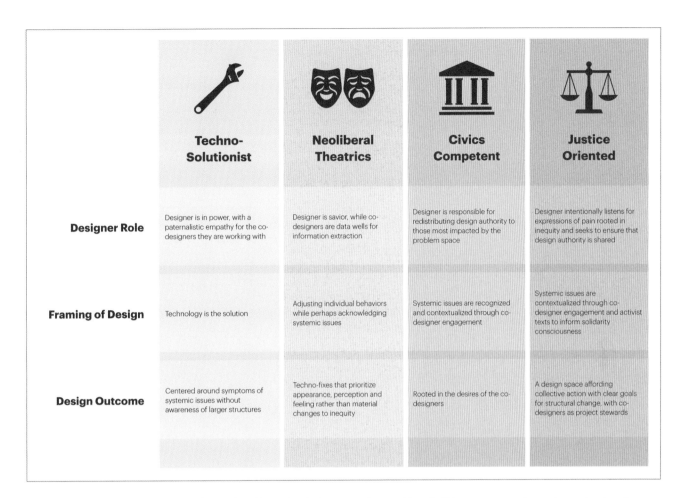

	Techno-Solutionist	Neoliberal Theatrics	Civics Competent	Justice Oriented
Designer Role	Designer is in power, with a paternalistic empathy for the co-designers they are working with	Designer is savior, while co-designers are data wells for information extraction	Designer is responsible for redistributing design authority to those most impacted by the problem space	Designer intentionally listens for expressions of pain rooted in inequity and seeks to ensure that design authority is shared
Framing of Design	Technology is the solution	Adjusting individual behaviors while perhaps acknowledging systemic issues	Systemic issues are recognized and contextualized through co-designer engagement	Systemic issues are contextualized through co-designer engagement and activist texts to inform solidarity consciousness
Design Outcome	Centered around symptoms of systemic issues without awareness of larger structures	Techno-fixes that prioritize appearance, perception and feeling rather than material changes to inequity	Rooted in the desires of the co-designers	A design space affording collective action with clear goals for structural change, with co-designers as project stewards

Different attitudes designers use toward justice-oriented approaches as they build more competence in understanding and applying social justice in their work.

Image courtesy of Colin M. Gray, reproduced with permission from Gray et al. (2023).[3]

See also DESIGN JUSTICE PRINCIPLES • TAROT CARDS OF TECH • FEMINIST INTERACTION QUALITIES

84 Speculative Design

Speculative Design pushes you to consider alternative realities, raising questions and challenging assumptions about the present and future of technology and society.[1]

#breakmydesign #newperspectives #identifyvalues

Design work is often grounded in current market realities and business needs, but sometimes engagement with potential futures or alternative realities can lead to new insights regarding what kinds of design outcomes or impacts should be further investigated.

Speculative Design encourages designers to think beyond the constraints of current reality and explore what could be. By creating hypothetical scenarios and prototypes that exist in alternate worlds, designers can investigate potential futures and their ethical implications. In doing so, you can uncover hidden assumptions and stimulate discussion about desirable and undesirable futures. To use a Speculative Design approach, consider starting with one of these "bridging techniques" that brings together the audience's version of reality and salient elements of the fictional concept:[2]

- **Design for context:** Consider the space or environment in which a future product might exist, grounding a concept in a reality that is familiar (at least in some respects) and logical.

- **The uncanny:** Identify ways to provoke, creating a space where a concept tests conceptual or practical boundaries while still appearing familiar to the reader.

- **Verisimilitude:** Create an environment where disbelief can successfully be suspended and any fictional elements feel as if they could exist in that version of reality.

- **Alternative presents:** Present a counterfactual or alternate history that allows reinterpretation of the present and reflection on the embedded logic that makes this alternate history function.

1. Auger, J. (2013). Speculative design: crafting the speculation. *Digital Creativity, 24*(1), 11-35. https://doi.org/10.1080/14626268.2013.767276

2. Synthesized and quoted from Auger (2013).

3. Smith, N. (2024). Present/future objects: creating material knowledge in speculative design. *EduCHI '24: 6th Annual Symposium on HCI Education.* https://doi.org/10.1145/3658619.3658629

Further Reading

Dunne, A., & Raby, F. (2013). *Speculative everything: design, fiction, and social dreaming.* MIT Press.

Pierce, J. (2021). In tension with progression: grasping the frictional tendencies of speculative, critical, and other alternative designs. *Proceedings of the 2021 CHI Conference on Human Factors in Computing Systems.* https://doi.org/10.1145/3411764.3445406

Value Posture	Action Orientation	Ethical Framework
Eliciting values	Consensus building	Deontological
Critically engaging	Evaluating	Consequentialist
Defamiliarizing	Framing	Virtue
	Generating	Pragmatist

Method Input	Method Mechanic	Method Output
Concepts	Altering	Concepts
Stakeholder Info	Storytelling	Stakeholder Info
Constraints/Goals	Filtering	Constraints/Goals
Values	Creating	Values
Use Context	Mapping	Evaluation Outcomes

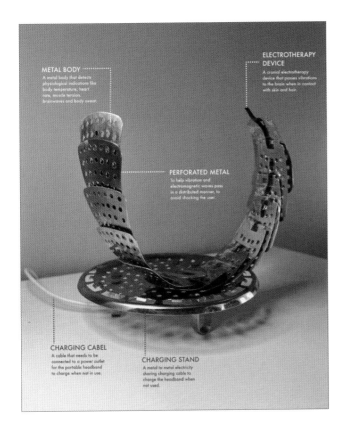

METAL BODY
A metal body that detects physiological indications like body temperature, heart rate, muscle tension, brainwaves and body sweat.

ELECTROTHERAPY DEVICE
A cranial electrotherapy device that passes vibrations to the brain when in contact with skin and hair.

PERFORATED METAL
To help vibration and electromagnetic waves pass in a distributed manner, to avoid shocking the user.

CHARGING CABEL
A cable that needs to be connected to a power outlet for the portable headband to charge when not in use.

CHARGING STAND
A metal to metal electricity sharing charging cable to charge the headband when not used.

"The Intelliband imagines a future world where AI has had a negative effect on people—influencing their cognitive abilities, memory, attention span, and their overall health and well-being. The Intelliband offers personalized experiences that help people push back against this decline with biofeedback, memory retention, and emotional regulation."[3]

Images courtesy of Akshata Karekar. Text quoted from Smith (2024).[3]

PRESENT OBJECT

"Transtemporal Travel Binoculars [are] a binocular-like device that allows a user to see the world from any moment in time. The device plays with reality by suggesting that we can 'create small wormholes in the barrels of the binoculars' in order to seamlessly move from place to place. One of the especially playful elements of this piece is the movement of the grinding arm, which spins round and round as one holds the binoculars up."

Images courtesy of Sagarika Konanuru. Text quoted from Smith (2024).[2]

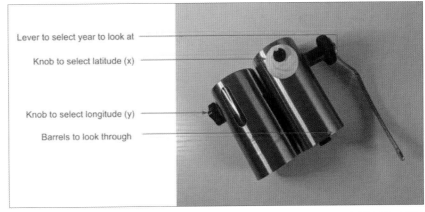

Lever to select year to look at

Knob to select latitude (x)

Knob to select longitude (y)

Barrels to look through

Present Object: Coffee Grinder

GIF

See also REFLECTIVE DESIGN • PRIVACY ENTANGLEMENTS

85 Speculative Enactments

Speculative Enactments encourage you to engage speculatively in real contexts with real participants, "bringing plausible futures briefly to life."[1]

#breakmydesign #newperspectives #identifyvalues

There are many ways for designers to speculate on the future and use these speculations to inform design work. However, many of these methods produce concepts disconnected from our current reality and can sometimes lack a sense of consequence for those participating.

Speculative Enactments invite participants to actively engage with speculative scenarios, fostering a deeper understanding of potential future technologies and social dynamics in a grounded way. By designing scenarios that are immersive and impactful, participants can reflect on these futures in a tangible way. To create a Speculative Enactment:[2]

1. **Define the speculative scenario.** Choose a future-oriented theme or technology and develop a framing narrative for this context that considers potential social, ethical, and technological implications.

2. **Design the experience.** Create immersive and diegetic elements that bring the speculative scenario to life, ensuring that participants can engage meaningfully.

3. **Recruit participants.** Identify participants who can benefit from and contribute to the enactment. Prepare them by providing context and background information.

4. **Facilitate the enactment.** Guide participants through the scenario, maximizing opportunities to build realism and immersion into their interactions.

5. **Collect data and reflections.** Gather qualitative data and encourage participants to reflect on their experiences and the broader implications of the speculative scenario.

6. **Analyze and synthesize insights.** Identify key themes, insights, and potential implications of the enactment outcomes on your design work.

1. Elsden, C., Chatting, D., Durrant, A. C., Garbett, A., Nissen, B., Vines, J., & Kirk, D. S. (2017). On speculative enactments. *Proceedings of the 2017 CHI Conference on Human Factors in Computing Systems,* 5386-5399. https://doi.org/10.1145/3025453.3025503

2. Synthesized and quoted from Elsden et al. (2017).

3. Nelissen, L., & Funk, M. (2022). Rationalizing dark patterns: examining the process of designing privacy UX through speculative enactments. *International Journal of Design,* 16(1), 77-94. http://ijdesign.org/index.php/IJDesign/article/view/4117

Value Posture	Action Orientation	Ethical Framework
Eliciting values	Consensus building	Deontological
Critically engaging	Evaluating	Consequentialist
Defamiliarizing	Framing	Virtue
	Generating	Pragmatist

Method Input	Method Mechanic	Method Output
Concepts	Altering	Concepts
Stakeholder Info	Storytelling	Stakeholder Info
Constraints/Goals	Filtering	Constraints/Goals
Values	Creating	Values
Use Context	Mapping	Evaluation Outcomes

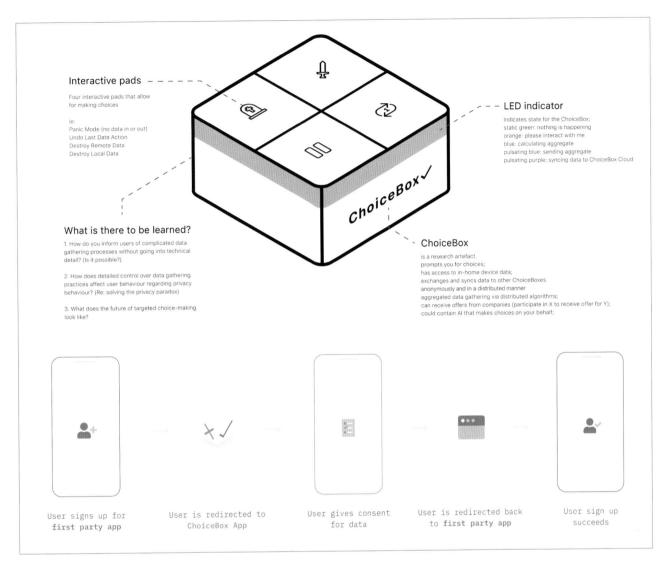

Interactive pads – – – – – –

Four interactive pads that allow
for making choices

ie:
Panic Mode (no data in or out)
Undo Last Data Action
Destroy Remote Data
Destroy Local Data

LED indicator

Indicates state for the ChoiceBox;
static green: nothing is happening
orange: please interact with me
blue: calculating aggregate
pulsating blue: sending aggregate
pulsating purple: syncing data to ChoiceBox Cloud

What is there to be learned?

1. How do you inform users of complicated data
gathering processes without going into technical
detail? (Is it possible?)

2. How does detailed control over data gathering
practices affect user behaviour regarding privacy
behaviour? (Re: solving the privacy paradox)

3. What does the future of targeted choice-making
look like?

ChoiceBox✓

ChoiceBox

is a research artefact.
prompts you for choices;
has access to in-home device data;
exchanges and syncs data to other ChoiceBoxes
anonymously and in a distributed manner
aggregated data gathering via distributed algorithms;
can receive offers from companies (participate in X to receive offer for Y);
could contain AI that makes choices on your behalf;

User signs up for
first party app

User is redirected to
ChoiceBox App

User gives consent
for data

User is redirected back
to **first party app**

User sign up
succeeds

An example of Speculative Enactments where designers
created the ChoiceBox research artifact[3] that could then
be interacted with by users to consider, reflect upon, and
make privacy-related choices.

Image and text courtesy of Lei Nelissen and Mathias Funk.

*"...the speculative approach comes to life through
three elements: (1) a roleplay in which participants
assume a Junior UX Designer position in the
fictional WOWH Design Agency; (2) a set of clients
for this agency, each requiring a GDPR Consent
Notice to be designed by the participant; (3) the
ChoiceBox device, a data management device that
acts as a canvas for GDPR Consent Notices."[3]*

See also SPECULATIVE DESIGN • TIMELINES • FUTURES CONE

86 Stakeholder Tokens

Stakeholder Tokens support you in identifying a more inclusive set of stakeholders and understanding their interrelationships and dynamics in the use of your product or service.[1]

#breakmydesign #newperspectives

Designers often want to understand who uses a product or what type(s) of stakeholders are impacted by the use or nonuse of a product over time. A range of ethics-focused resources enable the identification of direct, indirect, and adversary users intended for products and services.

Stakeholder Tokens help you generate an inclusive set of stakeholders, surfacing hidden or neglected groups, articulating complex stakeholder relationships, and distinguishing core from peripheral stakeholders.[1] This approach supports your analysis of stakeholders by building a physical representation to identify different stakeholders, and relations among them, by performing the following steps:[2]

1. Derive an initial list of direct and indirect individual and group stakeholders, casting a wide net with a diverse and inclusive approach, ensuring that underrepresented groups are included.

2. Use any tangible and easily movable object, with one color or shape for each identified type of stakeholder operating as a "Stakeholder Token."

3. Place these tokens on a large piece of paper, drawing interrelationships among them to represent information flow, communication medium, value conflicts, and interactions between any two or more stakeholders that might result in (un)ethical impacts.

4. Implement your findings to refine features, products, or services.

1. Yoo, D. (2021). Stakeholder tokens: a constructive method for value sensitive design stakeholder analysis. *Ethics and Information Technology, 23*, 63-67. https://doi.org/10.1007/s10676-018-9474-4

2. Adapted and synthesized from Yoo (2021).

3. Stake Holder Analysis with Lovely Links (SHALL): https://fredvanamstel.com/tools/shall

Value Posture	Action Orientation	Ethical Framework
Eliciting values	Consensus building	Deontological
Critically engaging	Evaluating	Consequentialist
Defamiliarizing	Framing	Virtue
	Generating	Pragmatist

Method Input	Method Mechanic	Method Output
Concepts	Altering	Concepts
Stakeholder Info	Storytelling	Stakeholder Info
Constraints/Goals	Filtering	Constraints/Goals
Values	Creating	Values
Use Context	Mapping	Evaluation Outcomes

Stake Holder Analysis with Lovely Links
(SHALL)[3] is a method that depicts a
team of designers using threads to
identity connections across different
stakeholders using Lego figures.

Images courtesy of Frederick van Amstel.

See also ADVERSARY PERSONAS • DIVERSE VOICES • ETHICS PATHWAYS

87 TAO Framework

TAO Framework supports you in building nonmanipulative and trustworthy digital solutions by safeguarding a user's trust in your design products.[1]

#breakmydesign #applyvalues

Deceptive design practices, also known as "dark patterns," impair consumer autonomy and undermine users' privacy and trust in a service or product. Users worldwide have increasingly reported feeling tricked while using digital products, sometimes leading to lower conversion rates due to the manipulation they experience. In response, researchers at the Pranava Institute believe "it becomes imperative for designers to build digital experiences which safeguard consumers and prioritize user trust."[1] Trust is often built through small changes throughout a product or service that prioritize user value.

The TAO Framework—encompassing transparency, agency, and ownership—provides a checklist to ensure trust in design outcomes by anchoring three core values:[1]

- **Transparency** values information and data being presented and used in accessible and clear ways, reliable sources and saving of information and data, consistency in language and messaging throughout the product, and pricing that is inclusive, selective, optional, and rewarding.

- **Agency** values meaningful consent with easy language and flexibility in preferences and permissions, and choice for users to personalize, alter, and retract sharing their personal data.

- **Ownership** values designs that activate user's ownership rights, security measures that safeguard digital assets owned by users, and protective steps to empower users about their personal and financial data in accordance with legal requirements.

1. Vashist, T., Krishnakumar, S. and Kamalakannan, D. (2023, October). Design beyond deception: a practitioner's manual to tackle deceptive design. *The Pranava Institute*. https://www.design.pranavainstitute.com/manual

Value Posture	Action Orientation	Ethical Framework
Eliciting values	Consensus building	Deontological
Critically engaging	Evaluating	Consequentialist
Defamiliarizing	Framing	Virtue
	Generating	Pragmatist

Method Input	Method Mechanic	Method Output
Concepts	Altering	Concepts
Stakeholder Info	Storytelling	Stakeholder Info
Constraints/Goals	Filtering	Constraints/Goals
Values	Creating	Values
Use Context	Mapping	Evaluation Outcomes

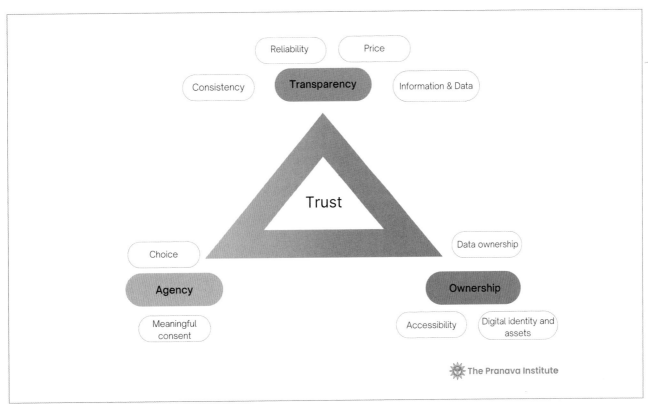

A diagram indicating sample components of each element of the TAO Framework.

Image courtesy of the Pranava Institute.

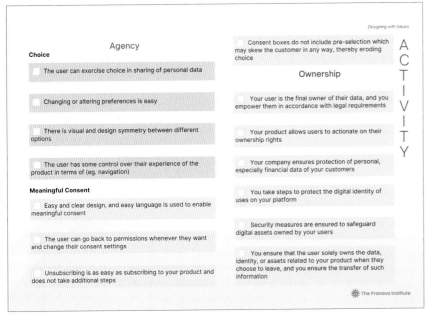

Designing with Values

Agency

Choice

☐ The user can exercise choice in sharing of personal data

☐ Changing or altering preferences is easy

☐ There is visual and design symmetry between different options

☐ The user has some control over their experience of the product in terms of (eg. navigation)

Meaningful Consent

☐ Easy and clear design, and easy language is used to enable meaningful consent

☐ The user can go back to permissions whenever they want and change their consent settings

☐ Unsubscribing is as easy as subscribing to your product and does not take additional steps

☐ Consent boxes do not include pre-selection which may skew the customer in any way, thereby eroding choice

Ownership

☐ Your user is the final owner of their data, and you empower them in accordance with legal requirements

☐ Your product allows users to actionate on their ownership rights

☐ Your company ensures protection of personal, especially financial data of your customers

☐ You take steps to protect the digital identity of uses on your platform

☐ Security measures are ensured to safeguard digital assets owned by your users

☐ You ensure that the user solely owns the data, identity, or assets related to your product when they choose to leave, and you ensure the transfer of such information

A C T I V I T Y

The Pranava Institute

A portion of the checklist allowing a designer to assess the degree to which their design work supports users' agency and ownership.

Image courtesy of the Pranava Institute.

See also MONITORING CHECKLIST · NORMATIVE DESIGN SCHEME

88 (Tactics of) Soft Resistance

Soft Resistance empowers you to subtly contest, subvert, and reshape the values and practices as an "insider" in your organization.[1]

#applyvalues #designresponsibility

In large technology companies, designers often find themselves navigating complex organizational structures that may not always prioritize ethical considerations, or find themselves in situations where they are not welcomed into such decisions. This is often experienced as a conflict between a designer's personal values and the values they are able to embed or enact in their professional work.

(Tactics of) Soft Resistance offers a way for designers to create incremental changes that may lead to more significant shifts over time, even within environments dominated by powerful corporate incentives. Through these tactics, you can enact change from within their company, leveraging existing systems and practices to promote more value-conscious design decisions. Some sample tactics include:[2]

- **Broadening who the "user" is in user research:** Tactically expanding the definition of the "user" to include diverse and marginalized groups, ensuring that their perspectives and needs are considered in the design process.

- **Designing affordances subversively:** Using goals contrary to business interests in products or systems, such as pitching functionality to support unionization but calling it "team collaboration."

- **Expanding on and subverting design resources for others:** Creating design resources to share perspectives with others in the organization, such as using existing tools like personas with new dimensions to think about specific values.

- **Using organizational values to create spaces for new forms of values work:** Aligning ethical initiatives with the company's existing goals, such as framing inclusive design as a way to reach broader markets.

1. Wong, R. Y. (2021). Tactics of soft resistance in user experience professionals' values work tactics of soft resistance in user experience professionals' values work. *Proceedings of the ACM on Human-Computer Interaction, 5*(CSCW2), Article 355. https://doi.org/10.1145/3479499

2. Synthesized from Wong (2021).

Value Posture	Action Orientation	Ethical Framework
Eliciting values	Consensus building	Deontological
Critically engaging	Evaluating	Consequentialist
Defamiliarizing	Framing	Virtue
	Generating	Pragmatist

Method Input	Method Mechanic	Method Output
Concepts	Altering	Concepts
Stakeholder Info	Storytelling	Stakeholder Info
Constraints/Goals	Filtering	Constraints/Goals
Values	Creating	Values
Use Context	Mapping	Evaluation Outcomes

A FICTIONAL SCENARIO:

Sam (a UX designer) and Taylor (a manager) are in a meeting room discussing the design of a new product feature.

Sam: Hi Taylor, thanks for meeting with me. I wanted to discuss some ideas for our new feature.

Taylor: Sure, Sam. What's on your mind?

Sam: Well, I've been thinking about how we define our user base. Typically, we focus on our primary user demographic, but I believe we should broaden our research to include more diverse groups, especially marginalized communities. It will give us a fuller picture of how different users might interact with our product.

> Sam broadens who the user is to include diverse or marginalized groups.

Taylor: Interesting point. But why do you think that's necessary?

Sam: Including a wider range of users can uncover unique needs and potential issues we might overlook otherwise. For instance, considering users with disabilities can help us design more accessible features, which aligns with our company's value of inclusivity.

> Sam connects this initiative to organizational values, justifying this form of values work.

Taylor: That makes sense. But how do we balance that with our current project timelines and resources?

Sam: One way is to integrate values-oriented metrics into our existing performance indicators. By tracking inclusivity and accessibility as key metrics, we can justify the resources and ensure that these considerations are seen as integral to our approach.

> Sam shows how making a plan to track values can make it relevant to the use of organizational resources.

Taylor: It sounds promising but challenging. Do you have any examples of how we might do that practically?

Sam: Sure. We could start small by adding inclusivity checkpoints in our design reviews. Also, framing these inclusivity enhancements in terms of potential market expansion can make it more appealing from a business perspective. For instance, highlighting how improving accessibility could open up our product to a larger customer base.

> Sam creates a new type of values work that embeds values into the design process.

Taylor: That's a smart approach. I like the idea of framing it in business terms.

Adapted from examples in Wong (2021).

89 Tarot Cards of Tech

Tarot Cards of Tech encourage you to provocatively engage with the impact of your work, understanding and seeking to prevent unintended negative impacts by asking the "right" questions.[1]

#breakmydesign #evaluateoutcomes #designresponsibility

Many ethical impacts of technologies can be better understood through creative and imaginative methods. Tarot decks have long been used by designers and creative professionals because they "invite multifaceted and personal reflection, drawing from a mix of past, present, and future fears, desires, and experiences."[2]

Tarot Cards of Tech include twelve cards divided into three dimensions that invite considerations about the impacts of technology on society: Scale and Disruption, Usage, and Equity and Access. The card deck invites you to "ditch the Silicon Valley mantra, 'Move fast and break things' for a new approach: Slow down and ask the right questions."[1]

For your product or situation:

- **Draw** a Tarot Card from the deck and identify how the dimension(s) and card might be useful/relevant to your product or situation.

- **Use** the sample questions on each card as a provocative invitation for you and your team members to evaluate the potential effects and consequences of your product. Consider not only the "obvious" consequences but also those that might lurk underneath the surface.

- **Implement** your findings into your product design approach, not just seeking to fix bugs but also to "reveal opportunities for creating positive change."[1]

1. The tarot cards of tech. (n.d.). *Artefact Group*. Retrieved July 16, 2024, from https://tarotcardsoftech.artefactgroup.com/

2. Michelson, R., Lustig, C., Rosner, D., Hoy, J., & Santos, D. R. (2024, July). Worlding with tarot: design, divination, and the technological imagination. *DIS '24: Proceedings of the 2024 ACM Designing Interactive Systems Conference*. https://doi.org/10.1145/3643834.3660735

Value Posture	Action Orientation	Ethical Framework
Eliciting values	Consensus building	Deontological
Critically engaging	Evaluating	Consequentialist
Defamiliarizing	Framing	Virtue
	Generating	Pragmatist

Method Input	Method Mechanic	Method Output
Concepts	Altering	Concepts
Stakeholder Info	Storytelling	Stakeholder Info
Constraints/Goals	Filtering	Constraints/Goals
Values	Creating	Values
Use Context	Mapping	Evaluation Outcomes

A set of the Tarot Cards of Tech being used by a team of designers to consider and iterate on their design outcomes.

Image courtesy of the Artefact Group.

THE
SCANDAL

◆

What's the worst headline about your product you can imagine?

What about your business model would concern users most?

In what scenarios could your product cause harm or endanger people?

If your product was used entirely opposite of how it's intended, what does that look like?

MOTHER NATURE

An example of one of the Tarot Cards in the Scale and Disruption set labeled "The Scandal." This card includes questions you can use to consider how your design solution or business model could produce harm by considering the "worst headline about your product you can imagine."

Image courtesy of the Artefact Group.

See also BLACK MIRROR BRAINSTORMING • DILEMMA POSTCARDS • ANTI-HEROES

90 Timelines

Timelines allow you to visually map new perspectives on a technology that you want to explore, indicating how values and ethical considerations intertwine with politics.[1]

#identifyvalues #designresponsibility #breakmydesign

The impacts of technologies on society are often difficult to explore in the abstract. However, one way of mapping these consequences based on different perspectives on existing technologies or systems is by considering what potential future timelines could exist, and use that knowledge to discuss the values, ethics, and politics implicit in all design work on a more regular basis.

Timelines is a design activity to engage in perspective-taking scenarios that form discussions about ethics and values in technology. Building on other methods such as the Futures Cone and Value-Sensitive Design, this method "creat[es] a space for participants to propose and surface discussion of values, ethics, and politics related to technology."[1] To use this mapping method, follow the steps below:[2]

1. Choose a technology, system, or feature that you want to explore.

2. Brainstorm a range of potential stakeholders on index cards, including people or entities that might be indirectly or directly related to the artifact.

3. Using sticky notes, brainstorm potential news headlines related to the technology or system.

4. Place the headlines on a large shared timeline triangle to create stories of events related to the technology or system.

5. Return to the stakeholder index cards from step 2. Brainstorm possible social media posts from situated points of view of different stakeholders.

6. Share your social media posts, and shift into a broader discussion to reflect on insights from the activity.

1. Wong, R. Y., & Nguyen, T. (2021, May 8). Timelines: a world-building activity for values advocacy. *Proceedings of the 2021 CHI Conference on Human Factors in Computing Systems.* https://doi.org/10.1145/3411764.3445447

2. Quoted from Wong et al. (2021).

Further Reading

Wong, R. Y., & Nguyen, T. (2021, May 7). *Timelines: a world-building activity for values advocacy* [Video]. Youtube. https://www.youtube.com/watch?v=gx1Zwqq7p_U

Value Posture	Action Orientation	Ethical Framework
Eliciting values	Consensus building	Deontological
Critically engaging	Evaluating	Consequentialist
Defamiliarizing	Framing	Virtue
	Generating	Pragmatist

Method Input	Method Mechanic	Method Output
Concepts	Altering	Concepts
Stakeholder Info	Storytelling	Stakeholder Info
Constraints/Goals	Filtering	Constraints/Goals
Values	Creating	Values
Use Context	Mapping	Evaluation Outcomes

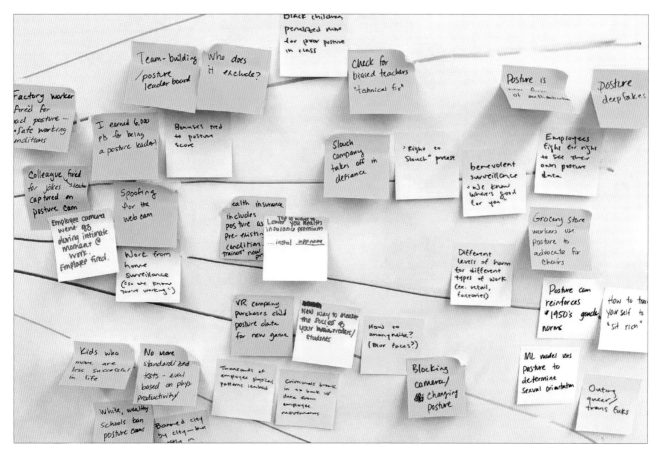

Example of a Timeline mapping activity, visualizing different ways that "posture cameras" could be used in the future to surveil workers for using bad posture in the workplace.

Image courtesy of Richmond Wong.

Posture is a new form of authentication.

How to train yourself to "sit rich."

White, wealthy schools ban posture cams.

Employee camera went off during intimate moment at work: employee fired.

Example headlines related to posture-monitoring technologies.

Headlines quoted from Wong et al. (2021).[1]

See also FUTURES CONE • BLACK MIRROR BRAINSTORMING • EMPATHIC WALK-THROUGH

91 Tracing (Ethical) Complexity

Tracing (Ethical) Complexity allows you to map your ethical responsibility in relation to a range of individual, organizational, and societal factors.[1]

#identifyvalues #designresponsibility

A designer's ethical decision-making occurs within a complex and situated environment. This ethical design complexity, which Gray and Chivukula define as a "complex and choreographed arrangements of ethical considerations that are continuously mediated by the designer through the lens of their organization, individual practices, and ethical frameworks,"[2] brings with it many different components, actors, and types of knowledge. Thus, a designer's responsibility is not just defined by their design activity as they create or shape a digital product or service, but also in relation to their personal, disciplinary, organizational, ecological, and societal commitments.

Tracing (Ethical) Complexity allows you to map relational aspects of acquiring new ethical knowledge, creating spaces for ethical awareness, interactions that cause ethical tensions, and opportunities for new or refined ethical supports. The tracing process can be visualized using a range of *actors or roles* involved in the interactions of ethical decision-making; *aspects and processes* of education, mindsets, policies, revenue, product, and tools; and *bodies* including society, other organizations, and government roles. Ethical complexity can be mapped across three key areas:[1]

- **Individual:** Values, practices, and beliefs that describe a designer's personal ethical responsibility as an individual without a focus on their organization or societal role.

- **Within organization:** Values, practices, and policies that comprise a designer's role within their organization that shape, confine, or expand their ethical decision-making or ethical responsibility.

- **Beyond organization:** Values, requirements, and policies that constantly shape, constrain, or expand a designer's ethical responsibility beyond their organizational role.

1. Chivukula, S. S. (2023). Trace the (ethical) complexity toolkit. *shruthichivukula*. https://shruthichivukula.com/aeiou-toolkit/tracethecomplexity-ethicstool

2. Gray, C. M., & Chivukula, S. S. (2019). Ethical mediation in UX practice. *Proceedings of the 2019 CHI Conference on Human Factors in Computing Systems*, Article No. 178. https://doi.org/10.1145/3290605.3300408

Value Posture	Action Orientation	Ethical Framework
Eliciting values	Consensus building	Deontological
Critically engaging	**Evaluating**	Consequentialist
Defamiliarizing	Framing	Virtue
	Generating	**Pragmatist**

Method Input	Method Mechanic	Method Output
Concepts	Altering	Concepts
Stakeholder Info	Storytelling	**Stakeholder Info**
Constraints/Goals	Filtering	**Constraints/Goals**
Values	Creating	Values
Use Context	**Mapping**	**Evaluation Outcomes**

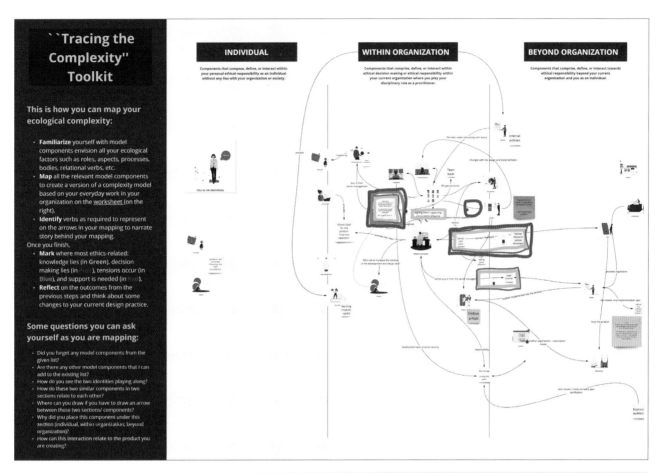

``Tracing the Complexity'' Toolkit

This is how you can map your ecological complexity:

- **Familiarize** yourself with model components envision all your ecological factors such as roles, aspects, processes, bodies, relational verbs, etc.
- **Map** all the relevant model components to create a version of a complexity model based on your everyday work in your organization on the worksheet (on the right).
- **Identify** verbs as required to represent on the arrows in your mapping to narrate story behind your mapping.

Once you finish,

- **Mark** where most ethics-related: knowledge lies (in Green), decision making lies (in Pink), tensions occur (in Blue), and support is needed (in Red).
- **Reflect** on the outcomes from the previous steps and think about some changes to your current design practice.

Some questions you can ask yourself as you are mapping:

- Did you forget any model components from the given list?
- Are there any other model components that I can add to the existing list?
- How do you see the two identities playing along?
- How do these two similar components in two sections relate to each other?
- Where can you draw if you have to draw an arrow between those two sections/ components?
- Why did you place this component under this section (individual, within organization, beyond organization)?
- How can this interaction relate to the product you are creating?

INDIVIDUAL
Components that compose, define, or interact within your personal ethical responsibility as an individual without any ties with your organization or society.

WITHIN ORGANIZATION
Components that comprise, define, or interact within ethical decision making or ethical responsibility within your current organization where you play your disciplinary role as a practitioner.

BEYOND ORGANIZATION
Components that comprise, define, or interact towards ethical responsibility beyond your current organization and you as an individual.

Mapped complexity of a software engineer's everyday decision-making individually, within the organization, and beyond using the Tracing (Ethical) Complexity worksheet.

Image courtesy of Sai Shruthi Chivukula.

Sample model components to envision different ecological factors such as people and aspects of complexity.

Image courtesy of Sai Shruthi Chivukula.

See also LAKE OF ETHICAL TENSIONS • STAKEHOLDER TOKENS • ETHICS PATHWAYS

METHOD

92 Value Dams and Flows

Value Dams and Flows help you generate features that are strongly opposed and advocated for as a way to navigate and balance values-oriented design trade-offs.[1]

#breakmydesign #identifyvalues #alignmyteam

Design trade-offs are inevitable, as teams work to balance disciplinary, human, and business values. These trade-offs require attention to potentially problematic and desired outcomes of products or services, and sensitization toward how to balance these outcomes in a value-driven way.

Value Dams and Value Flows enable designers to understand and regulate this balancing of value considerations. Value Dams are "technical features or organizational policies that are strongly opposed by even a small set of stakeholders," while Value Flows are "technical features or organizational policies that, for value reasons, a large percentage of stakeholders would like to see included in the overall system, even if the features or policies are not absolutely necessary for successful appropriation."[1]

To activate Value Dams and Value Flows:[2]

1. Identify stakeholders involved in setting design goals, engaging in decision-making, and interacting with your design outcomes within or outside your organization.

2. List potential and current Value Dams that even a minority of your stakeholders find problematic within your design space.

3. List potential and current Value Flows that a majority of your stakeholders wish to be embodied within your design space.

4. Discuss how your team can balance the identified Value Dams and Value Flows to systematically address values-oriented design trade-offs.

1. Miller, J. K., Friedman, B., Jancke, G., & Gill, B. (2007). Value tensions in design: the value sensitive design, development, and appropriation of a corporation's groupware system. *Proceedings of the 2007 International ACM Conference on Supporting Group Work*, 281-290. https://doi.org/10.1145/1316624.1316668

2. Adapted from Miller et al. (2007).

Further Reading

VSD Lab. https://vsdesign.org/toolkits/

Understanding value tensions. (2024). *Value Sensitive Design in Higher Education (VASE)*. https://teachingforvaluesindesign.eu/20_understandingvaluetensions.html

Value Posture	Action Orientation	Ethical Framework
Eliciting values	Consensus building	Deontological
Critically engaging	Evaluating	Consequentialist
Defamiliarizing	Framing	Virtue
	Generating	Pragmatist

Method Input	Method Mechanic	Method Output
Concepts	Altering	Concepts
Stakeholder Info	Storytelling	Stakeholder Info
Constraints/Goals	Filtering	Constraints/Goals
Values	Creating	Values
Use Context	Mapping	Evaluation Outcomes

DAMS

FLOWS

leadership advocating
for a system element or
organizational policy

the majority of stakeholders in
favor of implementing a system
element or policy

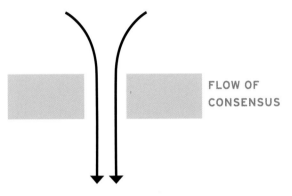

**DAM OF
DISAGREEMENT**

**FLOW OF
CONSENSUS**

stakeholders opposed
to a system element or
organizational policy

successful implementation
of the system element or
organizational policy

*"Consider the rights
and harms of persons
in the minority"[1] when
considering changes in
the workplace.*

*"[D]raw stakeholders
to the system or [...]
make systems with
uneven benefits more
attractive to those who
contribute."[1]*

See also VALUES LEVERS • MASLOW MIRRORED • DICHOTOMY MAPPING

93 Value-Sensitive Design

Value-Sensitive Design provides a structured approach for you to integrate human values into your design process, ensuring that your work supports and reflects the values of all stakeholders.[1]

#identifyvalues #applyvalues #evaluateoutcomes

Value-Sensitive Design (VSD) is an approach to design that considers human values throughout the design process. VSD incorporates conceptual, empirical, and technical investigations as part of its overarching methodological focus. **Conceptual** investigations allow the designer to consider the stakeholders that are impacted and how values are implicated in the design situation. **Empirical** investigations can then measure salient aspects of human activity, for instance, describing how stakeholders actually engage with values in specific situations. **Technical** investigations can be used to embed certain types of values into systems or technologies that can then be deployed and studied.

Using a VSD approach rejects the notion that technology is value-neutral, demonstrating how designed outcomes can have profound ethical implications. By making values explicit and integrating them into the design process, VSD aims to create technology that is ethical, fair, and aligned with societal values. You can apply aspects of Value-Sensitive Design using three key types of activities:[2]

- **Identify stakeholder values.** Engage with a diverse group of stakeholders to identify the values that are important to them. Use methods such as interviews, surveys, and focus groups to gather insights.

- **Incorporate values into design.** Translate stakeholder values into design requirements and criteria. Ensure that these values are reflected in the design choices and trade-offs.

- **Evaluate ethical implications.** Continuously assess the ethical implications of design decisions. Use tools such as ethical impact assessments to evaluate how well the design aligns with stakeholder values.

1. Friedman, B., Kahn, P. H., & Borning, A. (2020). Value sensitive design and information systems. In *The Ethics of Information Technologies* (pp. 289–313). Routledge. https://doi.org/10.4324/9781003075011-21

2. Friedman, B., & Hendry, D. G. (2019). *Value sensitive design: shaping technology with moral imagination.* MIT Press.

Value Posture	Action Orientation	Ethical Framework
Eliciting values	Consensus building	Deontological
Critically engaging	Evaluating	Consequentialist
Defamiliarizing	Framing	Virtue
	Generating	Pragmatist

Method Input	Method Mechanic	Method Output
Concepts	Altering	Concepts
Stakeholder Info	Storytelling	Stakeholder Info
Constraints/Goals	Filtering	Constraints/Goals
Values	Creating	Values
Use Context	Mapping	Evaluation Outcomes

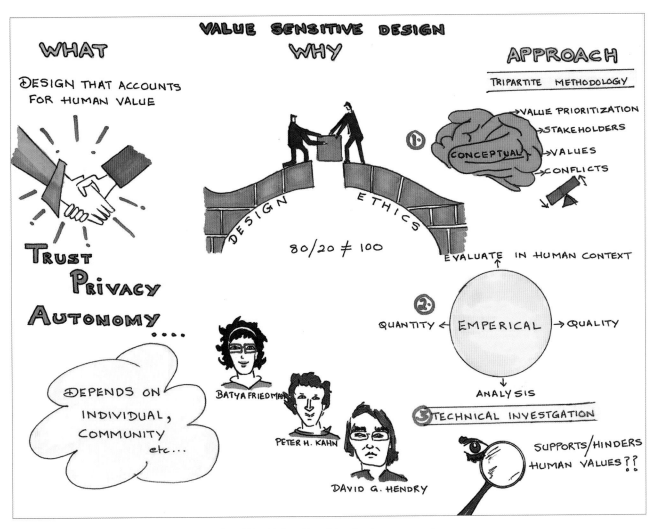

A sketch note visualizing key components of the Value-Sensitive Design approach.

Image courtesy of Ritesh Tiwari.

See also VALUES AT PLAY • HUVALUE

94 Value Voting

Value Voting encourages your team to identify values that you want to follow and embed within your design process.[1]

#identifyvalues #alignmyteam

Each team member has their own set of personal values and values that their profession focuses on. However, if these values are not discussed, it can lead to tensions or differences of opinion regarding which values best support the team's design goal and/or the company's vision or mission.

Value Voting is a team-building and alignment exercise that allows your team to identify and vote on a set of values that will be communicated within your team or embedded into your design process.

To build value-centered design outcomes through this method, follow these steps:[2]

1. Choose any set of values from HuValue, Moral Agent, Moral Value Map, Oracle for Transfeminist Technologies, or other sources.

2. Create physical cards or sticky notes with one value per card and arrange them in a large space.

3. Based on a design goal or team mission, each team member places a physical token on any values that they feel are important to achieving that mission.

4. Identify which values received the most and least votes across the team.

5. Discuss and draft definitions that operationalize the chosen values, including how the team pledges to abide by the values when building products or services.

1. Value voting. (2020, June 10). *Frederick van Amstel.* https://fredvanamstel.com/tools/value-voting

2. Adapted from https://fredvanamstel.com/tools/value-voting.

Further Reading

Find set of values at: https://studiocarreras.com/values.

Value Posture	Action Orientation	Ethical Framework	Method Input	Method Mechanic	Method Output
Eliciting values	Consensus building	Deontological	Concepts	Altering	Concepts
Critically engaging	Evaluating	Consequentialist	Stakeholder Info	Storytelling	Stakeholder Info
Defamiliarizing	Framing	Virtue	Constraints/Goals	Filtering	Constraints/Goals
	Generating	Pragmatist	Values	Creating	Values
			Use Context	Mapping	Evaluation Outcomes

A team of designers voting for different values by adding
Lego pieces to value cards.

Image courtesy of Frederick van Amstel. Value cards designed by Studio Carreras.

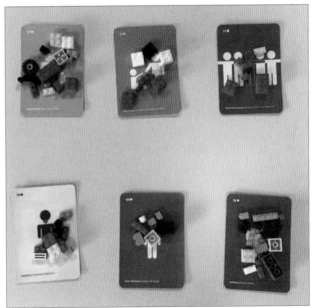

See also PLEDGE WORKS • ETHICAL CONTRACT

95 Values at Play

Values at Play provides you with strategies to systematically implement values throughout the design of digital games.[1]

#identifyvalues #applyvalues #alignmyteam

Designers embed a range of values through their design work that produce real impacts on people and society. These values can include human, technical, disciplinary, organizational, user, business, cultural, socio-economical, and spiritual perspectives, but given this range of values, alignment on which values or whose values can result in misaligned teams or products.

Values at Play is a "theoretically grounded approach that allow[] the team to consider human values in a rigorous and iterative manner throughout the design cycle,"[2] drawing on a range of value-oriented approaches in reflective practice and participatory design. Values at Play provides a range of strategies for designers to systematically implement values throughout their design process:[3]

- **Values discovery:** Create a working list of relevant values for our project from a range of sources (e.g., project goals, hypotheses, prior work, designer values, user or other stakeholder values).

- **Values-based conflict identification:** Identify and list values that are in conflict with functional and technical components of your design or factors that promote conflicts across two categories of values.

- **Value implementation and integration:** Prototype design concepts that are shaped by the identified values, working in iterative cycles with reflective review and participant feedback to identify where your designs do not uphold certain values.

- **Value verification:** Continuously verify if the identified and emerging set of values are being consistently used and continue to align with your updated project goals.

1. Flanagan, M., & Nissenbaum, H. (2014). *Values at play in digital games.* MIT Press. https://doi.org/10.1177/1461444816631742

2. Flanagan, M., Howe, D. C., & Nissenbaum, H. (2005). Values at play: design tradeoffs in socially-oriented game design. *Proceedings of the SIGCHI Conference on Human Factors in Computing Systems*, 751–760. https://doi.org/10.1145/1054972.1055076

3. Adapted from Flanagan et al. (2005).

Value Posture	Action Orientation	Ethical Framework
Eliciting values	Consensus building	Deontological
Critically engaging	Evaluating	Consequentialist
Defamiliarizing	Framing	Virtue
	Generating	Pragmatist

Method Input	Method Mechanic	Method Output
Concepts	Altering	Concepts
Stakeholder Info	Storytelling	Stakeholder Info
Constraints/Goals	Filtering	Constraints/Goals
Values	Creating	Values
Use Context	Mapping	Evaluation Outcomes

Play Style
Game for Good
3-8 players
20-40 minutes

1. Separately shuffle the blue values set and the pink games set.
2. Each player or team draws one card from each of these sets.
3. Brainstorm for 10 minutes. Each team develops a game idea that changes the game on the pink card so that it expresses the value on the blue card.
4. When time's up, each player or group pitches the game idea. Vote on 'em!

Play Style
Values Hunt
1+ players
10-30 minutes

1. Shuffle the blue values set. Each player chooses one of the cards.
2. Think of existing games that communicate that word, and how the game expresses it-- tell the group how it works.

Example: If you drew the cooperation card, you could talk about how Halo and World of Warcraft are games that require cooperation.

Grow-a-Game is a card deck designed to engage groups of designers to brainstorm novel game ideas that prioritize human values by activating the Values at Play framework.[3]

Image courtesy of Mary Flanagan.

See also DESIGN ETHIQUETTE TOOLKIT • HUVALUE

96 Values Levers

Values Levers enable you to leverage practices that help you and your team discuss and build consensus around values during the design process.[1]

#identifyvalues #designresponsibility

There are many ethical tools (like the ones in this book), but it is not always obvious where these tools can be implemented into organizational or team practices. In addition, there is a complicated interplay between one's personal values or concerns, those of a design team or profession, and those shared by an organization or its underlying culture.

Values Levers are "practices that open new conversations about social values and encourage consensus around those values as design criteria."[1] These practices are embedded in the work environment, leveraging communication that can open up or close down opportunities for discussion or consideration of values.[2] Types of Values Levers include:[3]

· **Working on interdisciplinary teams:** Technologists are more likely to need to engage with value considerations as a primary topic of conversation when they work with others from different disciplinary perspectives.

· **Designing around constraints:** Imposing constraints can lead to new forms of creativity to confront value conflicts or challenges.

· **Internalizing leader and team member advocacy:** Team members can raise value-related issues, making consideration of values culturally normative within the organization.

· **Experiencing self-testing:** Technologists can uncover value-related issues firsthand when they test systems rather than only experiencing them from a developer's perspective.

· **Gaining funding:** More resources can lead to more interdisciplinary team members and promote more regular discussions about values.

1. Shilton, K. (2013). Values levers: building ethics into design. *Science, Technology & Human Values, 38*(3), 374-397. https://doi.org/10.1177/0162243912436985

2. Shilton, K., & Koepfler, J. A. (2013). Making space for values: communication & values levers in a virtual team. *Proceedings of the 6th International Conference on Communities and Technologies,* 110-119. https://doi.org/10.1145/2482991.2482993

3. Quoted and synthesized from Shilton (2013).

Value Posture	Action Orientation	Ethical Framework
Eliciting values	Consensus building	Deontological
Critically engaging	Evaluating	Consequentialist
Defamiliarizing	Framing	Virtue
	Generating	Pragmatist

Method Input	Method Mechanic	Method Output
Concepts	Altering	Concepts
Stakeholder Info	Storytelling	Stakeholder Info
Constraints/Goals	Filtering	Constraints/Goals
Values	Creating	Values
Use Context	Mapping	Evaluation Outcomes

Communication Modes and Systems

How do members of an organization communicate? Consider face-to-face modes (breaks, meetings), mediated modes (code repositories, presentation decks, Zoom calls), and spanning modes (demos, scenarios, design artifacts).

ENABLE

Values Levers

How can new or adapted work practices leverage modes of communication to lead to more value sensitive and values-based outcomes?

ENABLE

Values-Based Design Decisions

What value orientations and outcomes do the Values Levers enable? Whose values are reflected and what role do the levers have in changing work practices or outcomes?

Diagram adapted from Shilton and Koepfler (2013).

See also (TACTICS OF) SOFT RESISTANCE • PLEDGE WORKS

97 Well-Being Design Cards

Well-Being Design Cards support you in designing mental health products or services that promote psychological well-being.[1]

#evaluateoutcomes #applyvalues #designresponsibility

The ubiquity of digital products and services has led to increased attention regarding how the use of these systems can impact our well-being. While other methods and approaches have been used to focus on vulnerability, accessibility, and disability, few resources allow designers to focus specifically on psychological well-being and mental health.

Well-Being Design Cards aid you in considering how to support not only physical needs but also cognitive and mental vulnerabilities and the well-being of users. The following principles help you consider aspects of your product or service that relate to mental health:[2]

- **Listen and respond.** Design features that provide a range of ways to express oneself, enable peer support, and allow users to tell their story.

- **Make it human.** Build features into your product that focus on building a positive self-image, show how to connect and provide assistance, and signpost availability of local services.

- **Give control.** Enable features that provide a visible record of progress, define personal milestones, and encourage self-care.

- **Be clear.** Use text and services to clearly lead with what is offered, managing expectations about what is and is not being offered by the product.

- **Adapt to changing needs.** Design for flexibility in needs, including prioritizing a user's feeling of safety and considering limitations due to a poor internet connection.

- **Create a safe space.** Provide a mechanism to exit or delete any shared information, offer a route to anonymity, and ensure transparency regarding how a user's information will be used.

- **Be reliable and consistent.** Design a mechanism that indicates clear signs of progress and easy task flows to access any information.

1. Design patterns for mental health. (n.d.). Retrieved July 23, 2024, from https://designpatternsformentalhealth.org/

2. Quoted and synthesized from the Design Patterns for Mental Health website.

3. Quoted from https://www.positivecomputing.org/blog/wellbeing-supportive-design-toolkit.

Further Reading

Well-being design cards (n.d.). https://www.positivecomputing.org/blog/wellbeing-supportive-design-toolkit

Value Posture	Action Orientation	Ethical Framework
Eliciting values	Consensus building	Deontological
Critically engaging	Evaluating	Consequentialist
Defamiliarizing	Framing	Virtue
	Generating	Pragmatist

Method Input	Method Mechanic	Method Output
Concepts	Altering	Concepts
Stakeholder Info	Storytelling	Stakeholder Info
Constraints/Goals	Filtering	Constraints/Goals
Values	Creating	Values
Use Context	Mapping	Evaluation Outcomes

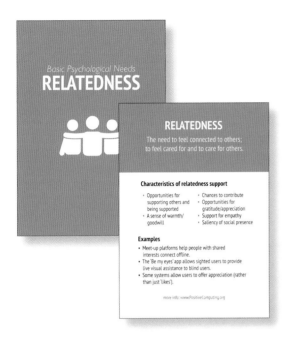

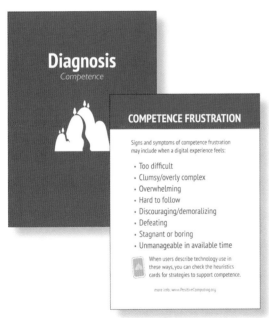

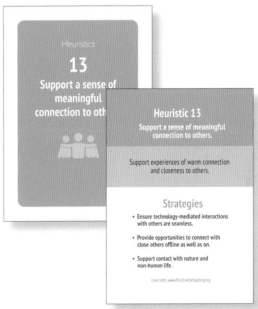

Examples from the deck of cards that provide insights and prompts for ideation, collaboration, and design. In four suits (psychological needs, spheres of experience, diagnosis, and heuristics) these cards give quick and easy access to the core concepts of well-being psychology as applied to technology with real-world examples and strategies.[3]

Images courtesy of Dorian Peters and licensed under the Creative Commons CC BY-NC license.

See also HUMANE BY DESIGN • FEMINIST INTERACTION PRINCIPLES

98 White Hat Design Patterns

White Hat Design Patterns provide ethical, human-centered alternatives to deceptive or manipulative practices such as dark patterns.[1]

#applyvalues #newperspectives #designresponsibility

Designers are increasingly influenced to use deceptive or manipulative design practices such as dark patterns in order to meet business objectives. To counter these tactics, often known as "black hat" techniques, White Hat Design Patterns offer a set of principles that can help industry individuals and teams generate designs using a philosophy centered on ethical design principles and practices. Use "white hat" patterns to "take the lead ... showing the rest of the organization how things can be done in a more ethical way, all of which will add to the incremental meaning change."[2]

Engage in these ethical White Hat best practices:[3]

- **Use data to improve the human experience.** Consider using product customization to make the user's experience better rather than changing the user's behaviors or subverting the user's goals through nudges.

- **Advertising without tracking.** Consider using open-source alternatives to tools such as Google Analytics and disable ad tracking on your product or service to protect users' privacy.

- **Always, always prioritize usability.** Ensure that your product follows basic usability expectations. If it's not usable, and it brings outsized value to the company instead of the user, it might include dark patterns!

- **Don't ask for more than you need.** Consider using data minimization practices to only ask for what you absolutely need to accomplish the user's goal.

- **Be transparent.** Ensure that all details that are relevant to a user's choice are easily available and not hidden away.

1. Falbe, T., Andersen, K., & Frederiksen, M. M. (2017). *White hat UX*. Smashing Media AG.

2. Falbe, T. (2018, March 16). Ethical design: the practical getting-started guide. *Smashing Magazine*. https://www.smashingmagazine.com/2018/03/ethical-design-practical-getting-started-guide/

3. Summarized from Falbe (2018).

Value Posture	Action Orientation	Ethical Framework
Eliciting values	Consensus building	Deontological
Critically engaging	Evaluating	Consequentialist
Defamiliarizing	Framing	Virtue
	Generating	Pragmatist

Method Input	Method Mechanic	Method Output
Concepts	Altering	Concepts
Stakeholder Info	Storytelling	Stakeholder Info
Constraints/Goals	Filtering	Constraints/Goals
Values	Creating	Values
Use Context	Mapping	Evaluation Outcomes

White Hat Practice:
Don't force the most expensive product onto a user. Ensure they can make up their own mind.

Black Hat Practice:
Use preselection of a larger product option in hopes that the user won't notice.

An example of a website that shows the contrasts between White Hat and Black Hat patterns. In the Black Hat example, a user is tricked into buying a specific product by preselecting it and hoping the user will not notice. Instead, use White Hat techniques to let the user make up their own mind.

Image and annotations courtesy of Trine Falbe and reproduced with permission.'

99 Workers Tarot Deck

Workers Tarot Deck encourages you to consider the impacts of design outcomes on workers, fostering empathy and solidarity between designers and workers.[1]

#breakmydesign #evaluateoutcomes #newperspectives

The condition of workers has become increasingly precarious in the modern era, impacted by changes in technological capacity alongside long-standing inequalities in which communities and groups are most commonly engaged in service work. As designers create and refine systems that involve service workers, they must confront evolving expectations of who a worker is and how these workers are impacted by designers' decisions.

The Workers Tarot Deck allows designers to question and more deeply understand the transformation of worker roles, using these realizations to identify "design levers, decisions and actions and objects of design that may affect workers and their work conditions."[1] By interacting with this deck, designers can build an understanding of the ethical and political implications of their designs on workers. The deck contains *archetype* cards, which tell the stories of different kinds of service workers (e.g., the gig courier, the wellness worker, the street vendor). The prompts to play come from the minor arcana cards, which include:[2]

- **Things:** Artifacts used by service workers, including visible aspects of the design situation that impact worker conditions (e.g., delivery apps, uniforms and dress codes).

- **Theories:** Theories and concepts by philosophers, sociologists, and design theorists that allow the designer to consider different framings of work (e.g., aesthetic labor, Hannah Arendt).

- **History:** Historical facts and movements that relate to workers or worker movements, including successful and unsuccessful efforts for workers (e.g., #RedforEd, the EEOC).

- **Trends:** Trends that impact the present and future of work as either threats or potential sources of empowerment (e.g., surveillance capitalism, the working poor).

1. Workers tarot. (n.d.). Retrieved July 21, 2024, from http://workerstarot.com/

2. Synthesized and quoted from Workers Tarot.

Further Reading

Michelson, R., Lustig, C., Rosner, D., Hoy, J., & Santos, D. R. (2024, July). Worlding with tarot: design, divination, and the technological imagination. *DIS '24: Designing Interactive Systems Conference.* https://doi.org/10.1145/3643834.3660735

Value Posture	Action Orientation	Ethical Framework
Eliciting values	Consensus building	Deontological
Critically engaging	Evaluating	Consequentialist
Defamiliarizing	Framing	Virtue
	Generating	Pragmatist

Method Input	Method Mechanic	Method Output
Concepts	Altering	Concepts
Stakeholder Info	Storytelling	Stakeholder Info
Constraints/Goals	Filtering	Constraints/Goals
Values	Creating	Values
Use Context	Mapping	Evaluation Outcomes

VII♠. EMOTIONAL LABOR

Smile, embodiment, commodity

Arlie Hochschild defines Emotional Labor as "commercial uses of feeling", "when emotional labor is put into the public marketplace, it behaves like a commodity." Hochschild talks about Emotional Labor affecting social classes and gender differently, "thus, there are both gender patterns and class patterns to the civic and commercial use of human feeling." While crucial to front line services jobs, it is largely unaccounted for in terms of compensation. Emotional labor affects both front office and back office service jobs.

References: Hochschild, A.R. (2003). The Managed Heart: Commercialization Of Human Feeling. Berkeley: University of California Press

HOURLY WORKER·

THE IMMIGRANT WORKER·

XIX. THE WAREHOUSE WORKER

The Big Eye, Omnipresence, Efficiency, Apollo, Drones

A former employee charged Amazon alleging it treats workers as if they were something less than people — in order to make it an ultra efficient system of one day delivery, the company imposes taxing routines, rules and metrics on workers, who "feel patronized and spied on" and stripped from their "personal initiative". During the COVID pandemic, workers in some facilities were feeling on the edge, like they were "risking their life for a dollar". While the company has publicly pledged to protect their workers, a growing number of protests and public petitions have arisen from corporate and warehouse employees.

Examples of cards in the Workers Tarot Deck, including theories such as Emotional Labor (top left), archetype cards that represent different kinds of workers (top right), and trends (bottom right).

Images courtesy of the Parsons DESiS Lab at The New School.

PLATFORM COOPS·

MANAGEMENT WATCH·

See also TAROT CARDS OF TECH · SOCIAL JUSTICE STRATEGIES

100 Worrystorming

Worrystorming encourages you to ideate in order to address concerns with your design solutions, and in doing so, build more value-centered design outcomes.[1]

#breakmydesign #evaluateoutcomes #identifyvalues

Brainstorming is a common approach for individuals or groups of designers to quickly generate ideas, concepts, and prototypes to address or better understand a design problem. The focus of brainstorming is on developing the highest quantity and quality of ideas possible in order to fully explore the design space and consider alternatives.

Worrystorming modifies the traditional brainstorming focus on idea generation, focusing on ideation as a means of identifying ethical dilemmas and future consequences relating to your work in order to proactively identify large small concerns with design ideas.[1] Worrystorming frames idea generation as a form of ethical evaluation, helping you consider your design responsibility in relation to existing products, generated solutions, and potential unethical dimensions of a design space. You can use the Worrystorming approach to consider and generate ideas relating to various stakeholders, use contexts, adversaries, potential pitfalls, human values, ethical paradigms, and design failures. To use this method, choose a design goal or existing product or service and do the following:

- **Generate ideas based on "worries."** Identify as many concerns, potential downsides, or value failures and write each one of them on a different sticky note.

- **Generate and refine "worry" clusters.** Collect all the concerns on the sticky notes in one place and construct affinities to generate themes of "worries" or concerns. Generate or refine concepts based on the themes of concerns identified to build more ethical design outcomes.

- **Frame "worry" clusters as values.** Derive ethical objectives or values from themes of concerns to frame a design space and avoid unintended consequences or concerns.

1. Worrystorming. (2021, October 5). The digital ethics compass-ethical workshop playbook. *DDC – Danish Design Center.* https://ddc.dk/tools/toolkit-the-digital-ethics-compass/

Value Posture	Action Orientation	Ethical Framework
Eliciting values	Consensus building	Deontological
Critically engaging	Evaluating	Consequentialist
Defamiliarizing	Framing	Virtue
	Generating	Pragmatist

Method Input	Method Mechanic	Method Output
Concepts	Altering	Concepts
Stakeholder Info	Storytelling	Stakeholder Info
Constraints/Goals	Filtering	Constraints/Goals
Values	Creating	Values
Use Context	Mapping	Evaluation Outcomes

An illustration of a designer in the process of Worrystorming as she ideates on clusters of concern related to communal values, negative environmental impacts, data breaches, and monetary loss.

Image courtesy of Sai Shruthi Chivukula.

See also EMPATHIC WALK-THROUGH • MORAL AGENT

Acknowledgments

The creation of *Universal Methods of Ethical Design* was made possible through the support of many individuals and organizations, to whom we owe a deep debt of gratitude. First, we extend our sincere thanks to the National Science Foundation, whose support through Award #1909714 was instrumental in bringing this work to life, enabling the Everyday Ethics project, which laid the groundwork for this collection.

The UXP² Lab was central to the empirical and collection-related work that made this book possible. We especially want to highlight undergraduate and graduate researchers who contributed in various capacities throughout this project from 2019 to 2024. Jingning Chen, Anne Pivonka, and Ziqing Li were invaluable in producing the collection of methods, which was later published online at everydayethics.uxp2.com, in the paper that documented our process, and in the initial collection of methods we used as a point of departure for this book. Thomas Carlock and Ja-Nae Duane also played pivotal roles in the evaluation process as we tried out different approaches to communicating the content of methods to practitioners. We also thank Shikha Mehta for her work in meticulously indexing the resources presented in the book. Our thanks also to Austin Toombs for being a sounding board and source of support throughout this journey.

We also want to express our sincere thanks to the researchers and design practitioners who generously contributed their resources and insights, which were essential to mapping this landscape of ethics-focused resources. Throughout the Everyday Ethics project, we learned from our many dedicated research participants through interviews, evaluation sessions, and co-design sessions, and their insights provided the foundation for much of the work presented in this book.

The team at Rockport Publishers provided guidance and support that made this journey smoother than we could have imagined. Their professionalism and dedication helped transform a vision into the tangible work you now hold in your hands.

This book is a testament to the collaborative spirit of the design and research communities as we jointly pursue social justice and responsible design outcomes, and we are deeply grateful to everyone who helped make it a reality.

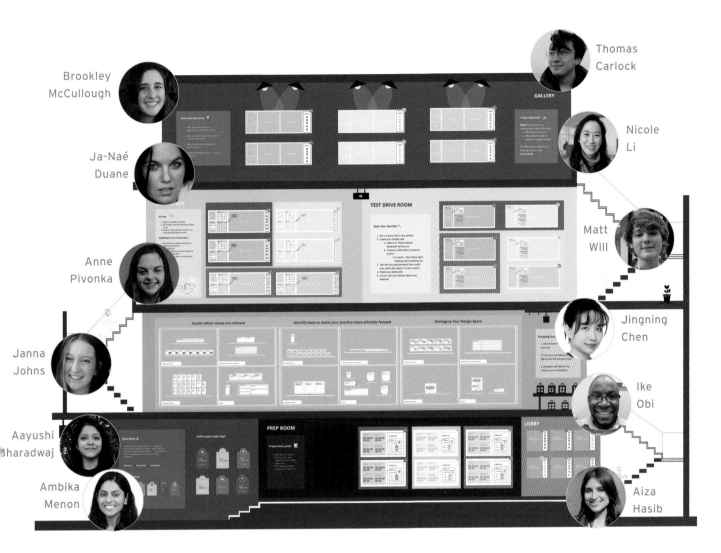

The co-design "house" pictured above was created by UXP² members as part of a series of workshops we ran from 2022 to 2023. This virtual space was designed to enable practitioners to use a range of resources now included in this book to make their own ethics-focused action plans. We use this house, annotated with the images of lab members who contributed to the Everyday Ethics project, as a memory to acknowledge and celebrate the work of all the researchers in our group and their commitment to empowering technology and design practitioners. They inspire us as teachers and designers every day.

Image courtesy of Sai Shruthi Chivukula, Colin M. Gray, and the UXP² Lab, based on the co-design house from https://everydayethics.uxp2.com/codesignworkshop/.

Related Readings

ACADEMICALLY-FOCUSED READINGS

Chivukula, S. S., Gray, C., Li, Z., Pivonka, A. C., & Chen, J. (2024). Surveying a landscape of ethics-focused design methods. *ACM Journal on Responsible Computing, 1*(3), Article No. 22. https://doi.org/10.1145/3678988

Chivukula, S. S., & Gray, C. M. (2024). Envisioning transformation structures to support ethical mediation practices. In C. M. Gray, E. Ciliotta Chehade, P. Hekkert, L. Forlano, P. Ciuccarelli, & P. Lloyd (Eds.), *DRS Biennial Conference Series.* Design Research Society. https://doi.org/10.21606/drs.2024.178

Chivukula, S. S., Gray, C. M., & Brier, J. (2019). Analyzing value discovery in design decisions through ethicography. *Proceedings of the 2019 CHI Conference on Human Factors in Computing Systems.* https://doi.org/10.1145/3290605.3300307

Chivukula, S. S., Hasib, A., Li, Z., Chen, J., & Gray, C. M. (2021). Identity claims that underlie ethical awareness and action. *Proceedings of the 2021 CHI Conference on Human Factors in Computing Systems.* https://doi.org/10.1145/3411764.3445375

Chivukula, S. S., Obi, I., Carlock, T. V., & Gray, C. M. (2023). Wrangling ethical design complexity: dilemmas, tensions, and situations. *Companion Publication of the 2023 ACM Designing Interactive Systems Conference,* 179-183. https://doi.org/10.1145/3563703.3596632

Chivukula, S. S., Watkins, C. R., Manocha, R., Chen, J., & Gray, C. M. (2020). Dimensions of UX practice that shape ethical awareness. *Proceedings of the 2020 CHI Conference on Human Factors in Computing Systems,* 1-13. https://doi.org/10.1145/3313831.3376459

Gray, C. M., & Chivukula, S. S. (2021). "That's dastardly ingenious": Ethical argumentation strategies on Reddit. *Proceedings of the ACM on Human-Computer Interaction, 5*(CSCW1), 1-25. https://doi.org/10.1145/3449144

Gray, C. M., & Chivukula, S. S. (2019). Ethical mediation in UX practice. *Proceedings of the 2019 CHI Conference on Human Factors in Computing Systems.* https://doi.org/10.1145/3290605.3300408

Gray, C. M., Chivukula, S. S., Carlock, T. V., Li, Z., & Duane, J.-N. (2023). Scaffolding ethics-focused methods for practice resonance. *Proceedings of the 2023 ACM Designing Interactive Systems Conference,* 2375-2391. https://doi.org/10.1145/3563657.3596111

Gray, C. M., Chivukula, S. S., Johns, J., Will, M., Obi, I., & Li, Z. (2024). Languaging ethics in technology practice. *ACM Journal on Responsible Computing, 1*(2), Article No. 15. https://doi.org/10.1145/3656468

Gray, C. M., Obi, I., Chivukula, S. S., Li, Z., Carlock, T. V., Will, M. S., Pivonka, A. C., Johns, J., Rigsbee, B., Menon, A. R., & Bharadwaj, A. (2024). Building an ethics-focused action plan: roles, process moves, and trajectories. *Proceedings of the CHI Conference on Human Factors in Computing Systems.* https://doi.org/10.1145/3613904.3642302

Lindberg, S., Karlström, P., & Männikkö Barbutiu, S. (2021). Design ethics in practice - points of departure. *Proceedings of the ACM on Human-Computer Interaction, 5*(CSCW1), 1-19. https://doi.org/10.1145/3449204

Lindberg, S., Karlström, P., & Männikkö Barbutiu, S. (2020). Cultivating ethics – a perspective from practice. *Proceedings of the 11th Nordic Conference on Human-Computer Interaction: Shaping Experiences, Shaping Society.* https://doi.org/10.1145/3419249.3420064

Lindberg, S., Rossitto, C., Knutsson, O., Karlström, P., & Männikkö Barbutiu, S. (2024). Doing good business? Design leaders' perspectives on ethics in design. *Proceedings of the ACM on Human-Computer Interaction, 8*(GROUP), 1-22. https://doi.org/10.1145/3633067

Shilton, K. (2018). Values and ethics in human-computer interaction. *Foundations and Trends® Human-Computer Interaction, 12*(2), 107-171. https://doi.org/10.1561/1100000073

Friedman, B., & Hendry, D. G. (2019). *Value sensitive design: shaping technology with moral imagination.* MIT Press.

Friedman, B., & Kahn, P. H., Jr. (2003). Human values, ethics, and design. In J. A. Jacko & A. Sears (Eds.), *The human-computer interaction handbook* (pp. 1223-1248). Lawrence Erlbaum Associates.

Friedman, B., Kahn, P., & Borning, A. (2002). *Value sensitive design: Theory and methods.* University of Washington Technical Report, 02-12.

Wong, R. Y., Madaio, M. A., & Merrill, N. (2023). Seeing like a toolkit: How toolkits envision the work of AI ethics. *Proceedings of the ACM on Human-Computer Interaction, 7*(CSCW1), 1-27. https://doi.org/10.1145/3579621

PRACTITIONER-FOCUSED BOOKS

Bowles, C. (2018). *Future ethics*. NowNext Press.

Falbe, T., Andersen, K., & Frederiksen, M. M. (2017). *White hat UX*. Smashing Media AG.

Monteiro, M. (2019). *Ruined by design: how designers destroyed the world, and what we can do to fix it*. Mule Design.

Nodder, C. (2013). *Evil by design: interaction design to lead us into temptation*. John Wiley & Sons, Inc.

Falbe, T., Frederiksen, M. M., & Andersen, K. (2020). *The ethical design handbook*. Smashing Media.

ETHICS- AND VALUES-FOCUSED TOOLKITS

Gispen, J. (2017). Ethical tools for designers. https://www.ethicsfordesigners.com/tools

VSD Lab. (n.d.). Value-sensitive design lab. https://vsdesign.org/toolkits/

UXP[2] Lab (n.d.). Ethics-focused methods. https://everydayethics.uxp2.com/methods/

Zhou, K. (2023). Design ethically toolkit. https://www.designethically.com/toolkit

Index

Other Books in the Rockport Universal Series

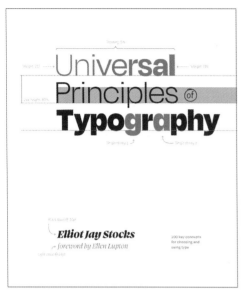

Universal Principles of Typography
978-0-7603-8338-4

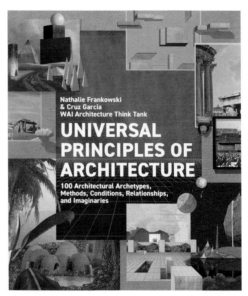

Universal Principles of Architecture
978-0-7603-8061-1

Universal Principles of Branding
978-0-7603-7820-5

**Universal Principles of Design,
Updated and Expanded Third Edition**
978-0-7603-7516-7

Universal Principles of UX

978-0-7603-7804-5

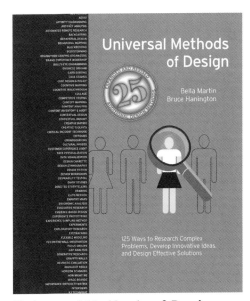

Universal Methods of Design, Expanded and Revised

978-1-63159-748-0

About the Authors

Sai Shruthi Chivukula is a design researcher with her research and teaching interests at the intersection of design, human-computer interaction (HCI), design practice, and ethics and values. She is an Assistant Professor of Information Experience at the School of Information, Pratt Institute, New York. Shruthi has more than ten years of experience in the UX design industry and academia. She takes a pragmatist ethics lens to describe and translate ethics and tech regulation in HCI and design practice and education. Through her work, she seeks to enable the ethical awareness of technology practitioners, describe impacts on users and society, and design supports for ethical action for designers and educators.

Photo courtesy of Sai Shruthi Chivukula.

Colin M. Gray is a researcher and designer focusing on HCI, design theory, and education. They are an Associate Professor and Director of Human-Computer Interaction Design in the Luddy School of Informatics, Computing, and Engineering at Indiana University Bloomington and are appointed as Guest Professor at Beijing Normal University, China, and Visiting Scholar at Northumbria University, United Kingdom. They have consulted on multiple legal cases relating to dark patterns and data protection and work with regulatory bodies and nonprofit organizations to increase awareness and action relating to deceptive and manipulative design practices. Colin's research and engagement activities cross multiple disciplines, including HCI, instructional design and technology, law and policy, design theory and education, and engineering and technology education.

Photo courtesy of Austin Toombs.